Jim Haynes is a first-generation Aussie whose mother migrated from the UK as a child during the Depression. His father arrived on a British warship at the end of WWII, met his mother and stayed. 'My parents always insisted we were Australian, not British,' says Jim.

Educated at Sydney Boys High and Sydney Teachers College, he taught for six years at Menindee, on the Darling River, and later at high schools in Northern New South Wales and in London. He has also worked in radio and as a nurse, cleaner and sapphire salesman, and has two degrees in literature from the University of New England and a master's degree from the University of Wales in the UK.

Jim formed the Bandy Bill & Co Bush Band in Inverell in 1978. He also worked in commercial radio and on the popular ABC *Australia All Over* program. In 1988 he signed as a solo recording artist with Festival Records, began touring and had a minor hit with 'Mow Ya Lawn'. Other record deals followed, along with hits like 'Since Cheryl Went Feral' and 'Don't Call Wagga Wagga Wagga'.

Having written and compiled 24 books, released many albums of songs, verse and humour and broadcast his weekly Australiana segment on Radio 2UE for fifteen years, Jim was awarded the Order of Australia Medal in 2016 'for service to the performing arts as an entertainer, author, broadcaster and historian'. He lives at Moore Park in Sydney with his wife, Robyn.

GREAT
AUSTRALIAN
SCAMS,
CONS &
RORTS

ALSO BY JIM HAYNES

The Big Book of Verse for Aussie Kids
Best Australian Racing Stories
The Great Australian Book of Limericks (2nd ed.)
The Best Australian Trucking Stories
The Best Australian Sea Stories
The Best Australian Bush Stories
The Best Australian Yarns
Australia's Best Unknown Stories
The Best Gallipoli Yarns and Forgotten Stories
The Big Book of Australian Racing Stories
Australia's Most Unbelievable True Stories

GREAT
AUSTRALIAN
SCAMS,
CONS &
RORTS

JIM HAYNES

ALLEN&UNWIN
SYDNEY・MELBOURNE・AUCKLAND・LONDON

First published in 2017

Allen & Unwin
83 Alexander Street
Crows Nest NSW 2065
Australia
Phone: (61 2) 8425 0100
Email: info@allenandunwin.com
Web: www.allenandunwin.com

Cataloguing-in-Publication details are available
from the National Library of Australia
www.trove.nla.gov.au

ISBN 978 1 76029 650 6

Set in 12/15 pt Minion Pro by Midland Typesetters, Australia
Printed and bound in Australia by Griffin Press

10 9 8 7 6 5

MIX
Paper from
responsible sources
FSC® C009448

The paper in this book is FSC® certified.
FSC® promotes environmentally responsible,
socially beneficial and economically viable
management of the world's forests.

This book is for my niece, Alison Dellit, and all her colleagues at the National Library of Australia, who, by their persistent commitment to Trove, make books like this one possible.

CONTENTS

SECTION THREE: The Sport of Kings and Con Men

INTRODUCTION

'Australian history is almost always pictur-
esque; indeed, it is so curious and strange, that
it is itself the chiefest novelty the country has
to offer, and so it pushes the other novelties
into second and third place. It does not read
like history, but like the most beautiful lies.
And all of a fresh new sort, no mouldy old stale
ones. It is full of surprises, and adventures, and
incongruities, and contradictions, and incredi-
bilities; but they are all true, they all happened.'

Mark Twain—*Following the Equator*

Whenever I told anyone I was writing about Australian scams,
cons and rorts during the time that I was researching and
writing this collection, the most common comment was something
along the lines of, 'Well, there's no shortage of material there' or
'You'll have plenty to choose from'.

It seems that many Australians are of the opinion that our
nation has a particularly rich history of deceitful behaviour,
cunning plans to relieve the gullible of their hard-earned cash,
and imaginative and risky schemes designed and carried out with
a certain, particularly Australian, panache and daring.

Perhaps it is so, although I am quite sure every nation has its
fair share of risk-taking, daring and imaginative scammers and
con men.

When our 'national character' is discussed, much is often made of our convict beginnings, and it is true that European settlement in Australia began with Sydney Cove being used as a dumping ground for the unwanted criminal elements of British society. This undeniable historic fact has been used to explain many elements of our national character, including our tolerance of alcohol, a tendency to bend the rules here and there, and the belief that everyone deserves a 'fair go'.

Whether these traits are part of any real national character or not is a very moot point. Perhaps this mythical 'Australian character' is something we'd like to believe. Perhaps it is merely part of the romance of the past.

Still, it is fascinating to read Mark Twain's assessment of Australia at the end of the 19th century—and I suspect he was on to something.

When Twain visited and made his observations, the European history of Australia was just a century old, the unmistakable influences of transportation, exploration and the discovery of gold were still very much a part of the society he experienced, analysed and enjoyed.

There are themes that run through the stories in this collection, yet I didn't set out to collect and relate the stories with any particular themes or subjects in mind. I simply looked for entertaining examples of clever and deceitful behaviour.

One odd thing I noticed about the con men I chose to write about is that so many were really 'big' men. Lawrence Hargraves, George Cochrane and Harry Readford all stood over 6 foot 2 inches (190 centimetres) and the Tichborne claimant weighed almost 26 stone (170 kilograms). On the other hand, Peter St Albans weighed about 32 kilograms and Jack De Garis was 4 feet 11 inches tall (149 centimetres). They were all, however, 'larger than life' in some way or another.

On a more serious note, I found that certain subjects, social issues and personality traits turned up again and again, especially events to do with gold, art, forgery and horses—as well as themes of opportunity, rebellious spirit and class struggle.

I'm sure that these things are not specifically unique to our national spirit and history, but I suspect that the combination of these elements is often especially Australian.

I'll leave you to decide.

THE MONGREL

This is the best piece of 'bush verse' about a spontaneous con job—ever! My old mate Grahame Watt is one of those bush poets who always 'gets it right' when he writes about small-town characters. Grahame has a knack of capturing in verse the dry Aussie sense of humour, and that laconic, deceitful manner of spinning a yarn that seems to come so easily to many bushmen.

The Mongrel

Grahame Watt

'Who owns the mong in the corner?'
The bloke at the bar loudly said,
'He's breathing his last breath I reckon,
That poor blessed dog looks near dead!
And dogs aren't allowed, where I come from,
To frequent hotels in the town.
Who owns this excuse for a canine?
He'd be much better off if put down!'

A silence hung there for a minute,
Then a whiskery old drover spoke up.
'That's my dog, young feller, he's my dog,
I've had him since he was a pup.

'You're right, he's old and decrepit,
Like me he has not long to go.
But that mong as you call him's my best friend,
And no better mate could you know.

'For me and that dog have enjoyed life.
We both talked a language the same.
We shared the hot days and water-bag thirst
As we worked at the mustering game.
And that dog saved my life in the outback
When thrown from my horse, far away,
That dog ran for help and led the men back,
I owe him my life you could say.

'I reared him on scraps from my feed bag,
I taught him to fetch and to heel.
I'd say you're a stranger to these parts
Or you'd know just the way that I feel.
Yes, he's old, and it's cruel now to see him,
No dog should have earned such a fate.
Last Friday I picked up my rifle,
But how could I shoot my best mate?

'I even asked that young vet bloke
"How much to give my dog rest?"
"Fifty dollars", he said, "is the fee for the job."
But with money I've never been blessed.'
The stranger grew quiet at the story,
He glanced at the bar drinking crew.
He said, 'Sorry, old timer, I spoke out of turn,
I can see what that dog means to you.

'Here's fifty dollars to have him put down,
And you'll have to excuse me I fear,
I know it's hard to lose a good friend,
One so close, and so near.'

The stranger shook hands with the drover
And quickly departed the room.
A silence hung over the drinkers,
A sort of a sadness and gloom.

But then the old drover said, 'Spark up!
Things aren't that bad, for you see,
That city bloke left fifty dollars
So now all the drinks are on me!
Drink up, you blokes, name your poison,
And drink to that mong—he's a swell!
If his owner were here, well, I'd kiss him,
And shout him a few drinks as well!'

SECTION ONE:

DISAPPEARANCES AND REAPPEARANCES

THE CASE OF THE DISAPPEARING PICTURE

'The truth cannot be woven out of a string of lies.'

Fred Munoz

The Backstory

This is the complicated story of the disappearance of a work of art that was an image of Sydney as it was in 1800, drawn by a famous British artist named Edward Dayes.

Now, you may be wondering how Edward Dayes came to draw a picture of the colony of New South Wales, given the fact that he certainly never went there.

To answer this properly, we need to attempt to understand how the British public were made aware of, and accurately informed about, what was going on in the far-flung dominions of the British Empire and what life was like in those strange and exotic lands in distant parts of the globe.

During the 18th century, and the early years of the 19th century, there was a fascination in Europe for anything to do with the exotic and newly settled lands of the Pacific. Books purporting to tell the deeds of explorers and navigators, or to describe the strange and wonderful flora and fauna of those distant lands, very quickly sold out.

It was not just the scientific and academic community that was prone to this fascination. The popular press of the day soon discovered that accounts and depictions, both true and false, of life at 'Botany Bay' (as the colony was mostly known in Britain at the time) were eagerly purchased and read (and indeed believed) by a curious and often gullible public.

While some of these publications were accurate accounts, such as the journals of Captain Cook and the diaries of First Fleet officials Judge Advocate Collins, Surgeon John White and soldier Watkin Tench, others were fake accounts cobbled together by opportunistic journalists from scraps of information gleaned from the genuine accounts.

Books in this latter category often contained false information, added to 'give colour', and drawings that were simply copied from any depiction of New South Wales, good or bad, real or imagined, that the unscrupulous creators of such books could lay their hands on.

There are no better examples of this than the three books and handful of drawings attributed to the famous jewel thief George Barrington.

George Barrington was the most famous criminal ever sent to Botany Bay. He was, according to the newspapers of the day, something akin to the Scarlett Pimpernel, Robin Hood and Beau Brummel all rolled into one! He mixed freely in the best of social circles and picked pockets at the Royal Court during the Queen's Birthday celebrations in 1775. He was also a master of disguise and often dressed as a minister of religion and picked pockets and stole jewellery from wealthy women while they were actually wearing it.

London society was all agog at the exploits of this famous thief and expert pickpocket, and his exploits were the subject of millions of words in newspapers and broadsheets of the time. He was so well liked that, although he was arrested more than a dozen times and convicted at least eight times, he was actually pardoned on more than one occasion and let off lightly by judges on quite a few others. Often he was able to talk his way out of being convicted at all. His silver tongue, eloquent speeches, fashionable dress and genteel manners often convinced a jury that it was 'all a terrible mistake' or a misunderstanding, or even that he had merely found misplaced items and was returning them!

Barrington was finally convicted once too often and sent to New South Wales on the Third Fleet in 1791. He turned out to be a model prisoner and was pardoned and made a constable by Governor Phillip!

He died in 1804, but his fame lasted long after his death. He is credited with so many adventures and crimes and daring deeds that he would have needed to live three lifetimes to have done them all. 'Fake news' is not a recent innovation.

For example, while on the voyage out to Sydney, Barrington was credited by the press as having prevented a mutiny, and a long sentimental letter to his long-suffering wife begging forgiveness and swearing repentance appeared in the London newspapers, although he certainly never wrote it.

Although absent from England, his notoriety continued. In a popular broadside ballad, 'The Jolly Lad's Trip to Botany Bay', a group of convicts laugh about being transported and swear that the first thing they will do in New South Wales is take over the colony and appoint a king, 'for who knows but it may be the noted Barrington'.

He was credited with many publications, letters, journals and theatre pieces, but he certainly never wrote the books that appeared in his name. Two books called *A Voyage to New South Wales* and *A History of New South Wales* were selling in London shops in the last years of his life, and another entitled *A History of New Holland* was published four years after his death. These all sold very well and no one to this day knows who wrote any of them, though one seems to have been based on the published journals of Judge Advocate David Collins.

Barrington wrote none of them—and was also certainly not the author of the much-quoted speech supposedly given by him as a prologue at the opening of the first Australian theatre in 1796.

In the same way that some written accounts were true and accurate, while others were false and wildly imaginative, so, too, visual representations of the colony fell into two categories. Some were crudely drawn, inaccurately copied and quickly engraved and published to take advantage of the British public's fascination with Botany Bay. Indeed, some were simply made up. George Barrington almost certainly didn't draw the original pictures engraved and published in his name in London in 1802, although they are so naively composed that it could just be possible.

Some depictions of the colony at New South Wales were, however, accurate representations drawn by reasonably talented amateur artists—officials, soldiers and convicts. Some of these were then accurately redrawn by professional artists and skilfully engraved in London by the best and most respected engravers of the day.

'View of Sydney Cove, New South Wales, from an original picture in the possession of Isaac Clementson Esqr., 1802 / drawn by E. Dayes from a picture painted at the colony, engraved by F. Jukes' is probably the most important of these works. Good examples of the rare engraving have fetched almost $20,000 at auction.

Possibly the original painting was by the acclaimed convict artist John Eyre. Somehow the original painting made its way to the home of Mr Clementson in Britain, where it was carefully and artistically copied by the skilled hand of Edward Dayes before being engraved and printed by the famous London engraver Francis Jukes, whose works are also greatly valued and highly collectable.

So you can see why someone thought it was worth the risk to make it 'disappear'—i.e. steal it.

It wasn't, however, its disappearance that led its owner, Mr John Pickles, to visit the Rose Bay Police Station.

It was its reappearance.

The Story

> 'Art enables us to find ourselves and lose ourselves at the same time.'
>
> Thomas Merton, theologian and mystic (1915–68)

It was on 29 August 1994 that Mr John Pickles strode purposefully into the Rose Bay Police Station and, after some preliminaries, had quite a long conversation with Detective Police Constable Matt Dennis—during which they discussed at length the fascinating case of the disappearing, and subsequently reappearing, artwork once owned by Mr Pickles.

The artwork in question was both historically and artistically important. So, to begin at the beginning of this case, we need to wind back the clock to a time long before the re-emergence of the artefact, which was what led Mr Pickles to visit that bastion of law and order in Sydney's wicked eastern suburbs, the Rose Bay Police Station, on that late winter day.

Indeed, to understand the complexity and nefarious nature of the crime, we need to travel back beyond the disappearance of the said artefact—sometime in the middle of 1986—and even to a time long before its purchase in 1968, when Mr Pickles acquired the treasured article from a very respectable and highly regarded source—Rex Irwin's Clune Galleries in Macquarie Street, Sydney.

According to the official police report, art lover and business-man John Pickles had purchased the work, titled 'A View of Sydney Cove c.1802' sometime in 1968, by which time the engraving was already 164 years old.

The value of the picture lay in its rarity and in the fact that there was only one other published engraving depicting the colony at Port Jackson that was older than it. All other pictorial views of the colony available before 1804 had been in books.

The work that Mr Pickles had purchased in 1968 was, in fact, only the second stand-alone pictorial view of the colony ever published. Its official title, according to the Mitchell Library, State Library of New South Wales, where another example of the rare work is kept, is 'View of Sydney Cove, New South Wales, from an original picture in the possession of Isaac Clementson Esqr., 1802 / drawn by E. Dayes from a picture painted at the colony, engraved by F. Jukes'.

I intend to keep you in suspense a little longer as to the actual nature of the 'scam' or crime involved in this story while we explore what it was about the disappearing and reappearing item that gave it value and made it worth stealing.

Firstly, the image was drawn by a famous British artist, Edward Dayes, whose works are very valuable. Examples of his drawings, paintings and engravings are held in all the great British galleries. The Tate Gallery is very proud of the eight examples of his work in their collection.

Edward Dayes was born in London in 1763 and began exhibiting at the Royal Academy of the age of 23. In his rather brief lifetime, he contributed no less than 64 works of art to exhibitions held by the Royal Academy. He drew and painted landscapes from all areas of Britain, including many from the Lake District and Wales. He also painted religious subjects and produced many humorous drawings.

As a professional artist whose only source of income was his work, Dayes also painted many miniatures, was the official draughtsman to the Duke of York and Albany, and taught other aspiring artists, including Thomas Girtin.

Dayes's importance in the development of British art, however, goes far beyond the collection of beautiful works he left behind. It is his contribution as an innovator of new styles and visions in landscape painting that keeps his name and reputation alive in the world of art history today.

His two books, *Instructions for Drawing and Colouring Landscapes* and *Professional Sketches of Modern Artists*, which were published posthumously in 1805, set out in detail the principles and techniques for laying down colours and matching palettes when painting landscapes.

For many art historians, Edward Dayes's legacy resides mostly in his innovative methods of using blue and green in his palette when constructing landscapes and the influence he had on the career of Britain's greatest ever landscape artist, J.M.W. Turner.

The famed art historian and keeper of paintings at the Victoria and Albert Museum Graham Reynolds, said that the work of Edward Dayes marked 'the transition from the 18th to the 19th century' in the history of British art.

The 19th century biographer William Cosmo Monkhouse also noted the original and innovative nature of Dayes's landscapes, commenting that they were 'remarkable (having regard to the time at which they were painted) for their luminous skies and aerial perspective'.

So the original drawing for the work that Mr Pickles lost in 1986, and finally regained ten years later, was drawn by the hand of one of the most important British artists of his time. That, in itself, made it a very valuable item.

You see, Mr Pickles had never reported the picture missing— because he had been told it had 'disappeared'.

Mr Pickles told police detective Matt Dennis that 'sometime in the middle of 1986' he took it to a dealer in antiquarian artworks in Darlinghurst—a certain Mr Brian Chester—and asked him if it was possible to repair a number of small tears, an area of damage that had developed over time in the paper in the area of the clouds.

Accounts differ as to what exactly transpired in the conversation between Mr Pickles and Mr Chester. What both gentlemen did say in later accounts is that a verbal agreement was reached between them that Mr Chester would attempt some level of repair and restoration.

Mr Chester asserted later, in court, that his understanding was that he was to attempt a full restoration of the work, which involved removing the paper from the backing board, which in turn involved dissolving the animal glue that held it in place so that the damage to the paper could be repaired. This involved soaking the entire work in a bath of 'pure water'.

Mr Chester, who became the defendant in the resulting court case, also claimed that he informed Mr Pickles that, unless the work was cleaned and properly restored, there would be no point in attempting any restoration and it would eventually be lost to further deterioration and damage from fungus and 'foxing'—age-related oxidisation resulting in browning and spots on the paper.

According to Mr Chester, he also warned his client that there was a chance the work would be lost in the restoring process.

Mr Chester further testified that he told Mr Pickles that there was a 50–50 chance that 'things would not go right' and that Mr Pickles instructed him to 'go ahead anyway'.

Mr Pickles, in his statement to police, claimed to have made a phone call to Mr Chester some ten days after leaving the work with him to ask how the repairs were going.

Mr Pickles' written statement to police then reads as follows:

> Mr Chester informed me to the effect that 'When I put it in the bath it all fell apart.' I immediately asked 'Can I see it?' He said 'Oh no, it fell apart. There's nothing to see' or words to that effect. I then had a further conversation with him regarding my purchase of the print. At no time did I receive any compensation from 'Antiquarian' [the name of Mr Chester's business] or Mr Chester in relation to the damaging of my print.

Sometime during the ensuing decade Mr Pickles had one or more conversations about his artwork with a friend and business associate Simon Dewez and showed him photographs of the lost picture. Mr Pickles testified that he had a particular affection for the work and, during the many years that he owned it, had often stood and admired it, studied it closely and was particularly fascinated by the way the clouds were depicted.

He explained, in his statement to the police, that on Sunday 28 August 1994 he received a phone call from Mr Dewez, who suggested he should take a look at Lot 158, which was on view prior to being offered at auction by Goodman Auctioneers, a reputable and long-established firm situated at Double Bay.

This Mr Pickles duly did the following day, and he immediately recognised Lot 158 as his missing artwork.

> I saw that the damage to the print located in the upper middle section of the print, in the area dominated by clouds, was exactly as I remembered mine to be when I left it with Mr Chester to be repaired.

Mr Pickles then spoke to Tim Goodman, who agreed to withdraw Lot 158 from the coming auction. He then immediately proceeded, in an easterly direction, to the Rose Bay Police Station.

The resulting court case, *Police v. Brian Chester—Larceny as a Bailee* (i.e. stealing or fraudulently using property while entrusted to care for it) took place in late 1996 and was presided over by Magistrate Beveridge.

Mr Chester testified that the engraving he sent to Goodman's to be auctioned was another example of the same work, which he had purchased from an American art dealership in 1977 as part of a collection of maps and engravings. He produced a receipt, which listed only some of the items and did not include the engraving in question.

Mr Pickles told the court that he was intimately familiar with peculiarities of his print and knew that Lot 158 was his long-lost artwork in the same way that 'you would know your own dog'.

Enlarged photographs of Lot 158, now known as Exhibit 3, were compared to photographs Mr Pickles claimed to have taken when the artwork was previously in his possession.

Mr Chester countered that he believed Mr Pickles' photographs were actually copies of photographs he had taken of the example of the engraving that he had purchased from the USA in 1977 and offered to Goodman's to be sold at auction in 1994.

Expert photographic and police scientific witnesses, while not being exactly adamant, seemed to support Mr Pickles' evidence regarding the photos.

In his summing up of the case on 8 November 1996, Magistrate Beveridge was at pains to point out that the defendant appeared to be a man of good character with an excellent reputation. He said:

> He is a man of no convictions. He is a man who has, as I say, obviously very considerable business and the business in a field where I would have thought that gossip is fairly constant and where, if you did dishonest things, that that would not go untalked about by other people in the field.

In spite of what he saw as an apparent dichotomy between the defendant's good character and the alleged act of larceny, Magistrate Beveridge stated that he believed (no doubt from his experience on the bench) that committing a crime was not always inconsistent with being of good character. He stated, in conclusion, that he simply did not believe Mr Chester's version of the events:

> I think the only reasonable inference is that the defendant did put up for sale the very engraving which had been left with him by Mr Pickles, and in those circumstances, it seems to me that he has committed the necessary acts to constitute larceny as a bailee. He has taken it and converted it to his own use and I therefore find the offence proved.

At the sentencing on 17 December 1996, Magistrate Beveridge noted that:

> The Court of criminal appeal has repeatedly said in various forms of words that larceny and breach of trust should normally be expected to result in a full-time gaol sentence, and indeed have even upheld appeals against leniency where someone was sentenced to one of the alternatives to a gaol sentence.

He then went on to note that the Court of Criminal Appeal did not insist on applying gaol sentences 'inflexibly to every case', although 'incarceration does remain for those for whom nothing else is suitable'.

A prison sentence in such cases, said the magistrate, was 'the benchmark' sentence for the crime. However, he went on to say:

> Against the general background, I have got to weigh the character, which I have already commented on, and age in general circumstances of the defendant, the fact that if he went to jail, with his age, I do not mean he is ancient, but being a man well in his 50s, but with his age and background, it would be a much greater hardship for him than for most people.

He then added, as an afterthought, an observation that seems to me so obvious and unnecessary that I find it quite amusing: '... not that it is a picnic for most people.'

In sentencing Mr Chester to 300 hours of community service, the magistrate made the point that community service sentencing existed 'to avoid what many people see as a stupid system of incarceration, which does not do anyone any good'.

So Mr Chester was ordered to report to the district manager of the Bondi Junction office of the Probation and Parole Service, and Mr Pickles got back his long-lost work of art.

Mr Pickles also made an application for a copy of the transcript of the court proceedings, which he kept, along with police statements, notes and newspaper clippings relating to the case, neatly filed in an A4 display booklet with clear plastic sleeves.

No doubt Mr Pickles once again enjoyed admiring his historically and artistically significant picture for another eighteen years until, for whatever reason, the engraving was offered for sale at auction and sold again, this time legitimately, by Lawson's Auctions, on 13 November 2014.

How do I know so much about this case?

Well, oddly enough, I was the buyer who purchased the work from Lawson's Auction house and, several weeks later, the attentive staff at Lawsons forwarded to me some documentation I had failed to pick up with the picture.

It was an A4 display booklet with clear plastic sleeves containing the transcript of the court proceedings, along with police statements, notes and newspaper clippings relating to the case.

In short, it contained the entire history of the engraving—all the information I have used to tell this story.

In the art world it's called 'provenance'.

I call it a wonderful coincidence ... an amazing windfall for anyone thinking of writing a book about 'scams' in Australia ... and a darn good yarn.

Footnote: Edward Dayes's extremely gifted close friend and pupil Thomas Girtin died suddenly in his studio of heart failure and asthma in November 1802, aged 27. Dayes, whose latest series of religious paintings had not been well received, committed suicide in 1804, aged 40. His two influential books were published posthumously by friends to provide funds for his widow.

SIMPLE SISTER GOES TO SYDNEY

This is a very funny poem about the superiority of feminine guile and inner strength over male gullibility.

If you count up the number of stories published in the *Bulletin* from 1880 to 1910 about simple country folk being parted from their money by a 'spieler'—the generic singular term used for all smooth-talking con men with a clever trick designed to extract money from bumpkins—it's obvious that Sydney must have been seen as the most dangerous place on earth by country folk, whose world, it must be said, was rather small.

Ed Dyson was a very popular short-story and verse writer in the early 20th century. He was the brother of Will Dyson, the artist, and the Dyson boys grew up with the famous Lindsay family at Creswick in the goldmining district of rural Victoria. Ed's brother, Will, married Ruby Lindsay, the artistically gifted sister of renowned artists Norman, Lionel, Percy and Daryl. They were all employed on the *Bulletin* at one time or another as writers or illustrators.

Ed Dyson had a few pen names; the most amusing of them, which he used when he didn't think his verse was of any great literary quality, was 'Billy Boiling'.

Simple Sister Goes to Sydney

Edward Dyson

When Flo resolved to go to town
From brothers three a yell went up,
Predicting ruin and distress.
Bill in his horror dropped a cup.
'Gorstruth!' he said, 'in Sydney there,
What is a simple girl to do?
They took *me* down. I lost me watch
And seven quid. What 'ope for you?'

Ben turned on her in pale dismay.
'Look here, me girl, ain't you bin told
How one of them there spieler blokes
Done me for twenty pound in gold?
He was as nice a gentleman
As any in the blessed shops:
He got away with all I had,
And took a luner at the cops.'

'Me, too,' said Dave, 'that time I went
To Sydney town to see the Show
One trimmed me for me bran' new suit.
You stay where we can watch you, Flo.'
Flo packed. 'If spieler comes at me
His finish will be sharp,' she said;
And when the boys next heard of her
She'd got a bloke, and then was wed.

She wrote: 'He's rather nice, I think,
And I am putting him to work.
Next Chrissmiss we are comin' up
To see yous people back o' Bourke.'

And when he came he brought for Bill
A silver watch and seven quid,
For Dave a bran' new suit of check,
A ruby tie-pin and a lid.

To Ben he handed twenty pounds,
In nice new minted sovereigns, too.
And still the brothers gaped at him,
And still their great amazement grew.
He was a natty kind of chap,
With gentle manners, small and slim.
And when they spoke 'twas as one man.
'So 'elp me Flo,' they said, 'it's 'im!'

THE PRINCE OF BALLYHOO

The Backstory

> 'The visionary lies to himself, the liar only to
> others.'
>
> Friedrich Nietzsche

The Mildura Irrigation Colony, which was the genesis of the
town of Mildura and the district of Sunraysia, was a 'failure'
that, you could say, eventually succeeded.

In the early 1880s, the Victorian government began examining the idea of irrigation colonies on the Murray River. In 1884
Victorian Solicitor-General and Minister of Public Works Alfred
Deakin led a delegation to the United States and met the Canadian
brothers George, William and Charles Chaffey, who had successfully established three irrigation communities in California at
towns called Ediwana, Ontario and Upland.

Engineer and inventor George Chaffey, the oldest of the
brothers, visited Victoria in 1886 and, as a result, the Chaffeys
decided on the Mildura Run as a suitable location for an irrigation
colony. The brothers then sold their Californian interests at a loss
in order to invest in this new venture.

The Mildura sheep run was in liquidation. It had a frontage
of 40 miles and reached 20 miles back with river flats that were
subject to frequent flooding. One squatter called it 'the most
wretched and hopeless of all the Mallee regions' and another

'a Sahara of blasting hot winds and red driving sands, a howling, carrion-polluted wilderness'.

In 1886, after months of negotiations, the Chaffey brothers signed an agreement, which was rejected by the Victorian parliament. The property was put up for public tender but the Chaffeys decided not to tender. Instead, they negotiated with the South Australian government and on 14 February 1887 they signed an agreement securing 250,000 acres at Bookmark Plains, which went on to become the town of Renmark.

Meanwhile, the Victorian government received no suitable tenders and finally 'The Chaffey Brothers Agreement' was passed in May 1887. An indenture was signed for 250,000 acres of the old Mildura run, and the Chaffeys took possession in August.

Immediately, 50,000 acres were subdivided into cleared 10-acre blocks between irrigation channels that were offered to potential participants at £5 per acre. A further 200,000 acres were offered at £1 per acre—plus water rights to the equivalent of a 24-inch rainfall. This promised amount of water equated to 60,000 cubic feet per minute, which was approximately one-third of the Murray's lowest rate of discharge in times of drought.

Prospective settlers or investors could purchase fully irrigated blocks for £20 per acre, and Chaffey Brothers Ltd managed blocks for absentee owners for a fee of £5 per annum. Pumps, capable of delivering up to 40,000 gallons per minute to main channels, were built and installed, and the Chaffeys invested in brickworks, an engineering company, a timber mill and, in 1888, the River Murray Navigation Company.

In the early years, favourable conditions meant Mildura could rely mostly on river transport, with freight and passengers going downstream for a railway connection to Adelaide, and upstream to Swan Hill and Echuca for connections to Melbourne. There were, however, many challenges. Pests such as locusts damaged crops and there were continual problems with the irrigation. When water rates of 15 shillings per acre were introduced in 1891, settlers who had suffered three years of failed crops could not afford to pay and the Chaffeys shut down the pumps. Labourers went on strike for better wages and conditions, and were sacked. Many of the men who worked for 'blockers' were never paid.

When Alfred Deakin and members of a royal commission arrived at the company wharf aboard the SS *Pearl*, in 1894, so many settlers with complaints rushed on board that the vessel almost capsized. They were ordered to make their complaints in writing.

The problem of getting produce to markets in good condition remained until the arrival of the railway in 1903.

Added to the technical difficulties encountered in getting water to the crops was the inter-colonial bickering between New South Wales and Victoria over the rights to the Murray's water. The New South Wales premier, Sir Henry Parkes, called the Chaffeys 'trespassers'. This was because the New South Wales *Constitution Act* of 1855 stated 'that the whole of the watercourse of the River Murray is and shall be in the territory of New South Wales'.

In an hilarious footnote to this argument, years later the mayor of Echuca telegraphed the then-premier of New South Wales after the Victorian town had been flooded, requesting that the New South Wales administration come and remove their water from his town!

In spite of the problems, failures and upsets, the community struggled on. On the allotments that were owned or managed by the Chaffeys, plantings were generally successful. The brothers employed 500 men and 500 horses and, with intensive labour, good horticultural practices and an adequate supply of water, crops could thrive. If variable seasonal conditions—frosts, hail, pests and diseases—were taken into account and realistically allowed for in the management of finances, it was possible to make the scheme work ... in part.

But, in December 1895, the company went into liquidation and the Victorian government held a royal commission into its affairs in 1896.

Block holders were given tenure over their land with a five-year period to meet their dues and pay their debts, and the Mildura Irrigation Trust was created to 'conduct and control the supply of water for irrigation purposes'. Six commissioners, elected by the growers, ran the trust.

The Chaffeys' enterprise at Renmark, which had been managed

by younger brother Charles while George and William were at Mildura, also failed financially although the town developed into a successful farming settlement. George and Charles returned to the USA after the enquiry, but George's son Ben stayed in Australia and became a successful businessman and noted racehorse owner. William remained in Mildura as a fruit grower until his death in 1926; he had been elected president of the Mildura Shire Council in 1903 and mayor in 1920.

As well as the Chaffey brothers, the town of Mildura has attracted its fair share of other visionaries, schemers, flamboyant entrepreneurs, hucksters and con men of various types and degrees. Two of the most colourful of these characters have their stories told in this collection.

One of those is the notorious villain George Henry Cochrane, alias G. Maddison Harvey, whose story appears under the title 'The Tarring and Feathering of G. Maddison Harvey'.

The second character associated with Mildura who deserves to have his story told is someone who famously crossed paths with Harvey. He was, however, a very different sort of character, a horse of a different colour altogether, or perhaps just a different kind of con man. His old school friend Claude Kingston, who later became a theatre manager for the promoter Hugh McIntosh, called him 'The Prince of Ballyhoo'. His name was Jack De Garis.

The Story

> 'Sometimes I've believed as many as six impossible things before breakfast.'
>
> Lewis Carroll—The White Queen, *Through the Looking-Glass*

Jack De Garis grew up surrounded by the dreams and schemes of the Chaffey brothers and his father's evangelical visions of an irrigated paradise in rural Victoria.

In 1888 the Chaffeys proposed an irrigation scheme at Werribee, just on the western edge of Melbourne. They purchased 1500 acres of land on the Werribee River and set up the Werribee Irrigation and Investment Company. A hundred 10-acre blocks were offered for sale and 150 house blocks.

The Chaffeys' usual plan was to set up communities of small farms on land not otherwise suitable for farming and use local river systems to irrigate them. At Werribee they promised to build a weir, a pumping station and a farming college.

Despite complaints from local farmers that there was not adequate water to support the scheme, it went ahead, and George Chaffey built a large home on the property.

Australians were attracted to the idea of irrigating the inland, turning non-arable regions into fertile food-producing farmland. It had been done centuries ago in Egypt and Mesopotamia, and more recently in California, land of opportunity, by the Chaffeys and other developers.

It was a very attractive idea, but time would prove that Australia's dry climate and lack of massive rivers fed by mountain glaciers and winter snows would make such projects expensive, very difficult to achieve and, in many places, simply untenable.

There is still a debate among historians as to whether the Chaffey brothers were visionary pioneers, cunning opportunists, deluded eccentrics who believed they could achieve the impossible—or simply con men.

They have been accused of exaggerating the potential of their various schemes and promising far more than they could deliver. Some say they overestimated river flows and didn't take account of natural conditions—like the drought cycle, and pests and diseases that were prevalent and known to exist in the areas they claimed could be made into fertile wonderlands. The common yabbie, for example, could ruin irrigation channels and quite easily derail any irrigation project, and loss of water through evaporation in summer was far more than estimated.

In their famous 'Red Book' manifesto—the detailed booklet advertising and explaining their schemes—the Chaffeys stressed the wonderful possibilities and the engineering marvels that could bring them about. They did this in order to attract investors and willing participants to their schemes, but there was, critics say, no mention of plans to counter the potential dangers and difficulties.

There were 'water prophets' who came before the Chaffeys, such as Hugh McColl and Reverend Elisha De Garis, who had evangelised the idea that prosperity for Australian farmers depended on dams, canals and irrigation schemes. People wanted to believe it, and they often took up the cause and promoted the idea with very little analysis or investigation of the facts and details of what was being proposed.

At Werribee, for example, the local newspaper was on side, commenting that 'once the Californian expert gets this water on to the land, the little irrigation colony at Werribee will burst forth into Eden-like verdure and Paradisial bloom'.

It never happened.

None of the Chaffeys' schemes succeeded, but their enthusiasm was contagious, and Mildura and Renmark did eventually become successful 'small farm' districts.

Werribee failed completely. The weir was never built, nor was the college. Only a tenth of the land was ever taken up or became productive. The promised water wasn't delivered, yabbies destroyed the irrigation channels, and the Depression of 1890 meant there were no bank loans or investment capital for schemes like the one at Werribee.

———

One interesting participant in the Werribee scheme was the man who managed the project for three years, Reverend Elisha De Garis. He had migrated with his family as a child from Guernsey, one of the Channel Islands. Educated at St Peter's College, Adelaide, he studied architecture in Melbourne and was ordained as a Methodist minister in 1882, just after his marriage to Elizabeth, daughter of pioneering agricultural goods manufacturer John Buncle.

Elisha was so saddened at the effect of drought on his parishioners in farming areas that he became a strong supporter of the irrigation proposals of Hugh McColl, the parliamentarian and rural reform advocate who had an obsession with water and preached the benefits of building dams and irrigation canals in rural Victoria.

Through his regular articles for the Melbourne *Daily Telegraph,* Elisha lobbied Alfred Deakin to legislate for irrigation communities to be set up—and to visit California and meet the Chaffeys. He became chairman of the Tragowel Plains Irrigation and Water Supply Trust, the first organisation established under the new act of parliament in 1886.

Elisha was also co-founder and chairman of the Central Irrigation League, and created and edited a newspaper called the *Australian Irrigationist.* He also created and ran a farmers' co-operative marketing organisation with the grand title of 'Associated Australian Yeomanry'.

In 1887, two years after the death of Hugh McColl, Elisha resigned from the ministry (although he remained a lay preacher) and joined George Chaffey in the Werribee project.

After the scheme failed, Elisha moved to Mildura in 1891, where he worked hard to establish market gardens and build up various businesses in real estate and the growing, processing and marketing of dried fruit. He also served on the Mildura Shire Council and was shire president briefly, taking over that position from William Chaffey in 1907 before leaving the town in 1908 to move to Melbourne and run a dried fruit distribution and marketing company—to complement the family's business interests in Mildura.

Elisha's eldest son, Clement John (known as 'Jack' to his family and later 'C.J.' to his friends and business associates), was seven years old when his parents moved to Mildura. Two years later his father requested, and was granted, a special dispensation for Jack to quit school and work in the family business.

Always enthusiastic and charming, young Jack was given the task of collecting rents for the family real estate business. Historian Travis Sellars tells us:

> In the challenging role of rent collector he was successful as he
> was unconventional and people soon endeared to his irresistible

boyish qualities found it difficult to refuse payment; he also developed a knack of solving troublesome problems.

Part of the legend of Jack De Garis is that he saved money from his wages to pay his own school fees and, at fourteen, returned to school from 1899 to 1901, as a boarder at Wesley College in Melbourne where, despite standing only 4 feet 11 inches, he excelled at football. Other versions of the story say that Jack was urged to attend school again by his father.

Talking about Jack's time at Wesley, Travis Sellars says:

After a difficult induction he rose from last to dux of his class, became somewhat of a legend with his affectionate smile, and excelled in sports notably cricket and football ('easily the smallest boy who had ever played in Public School football') where his lack of height (4 feet 11 inches) and weight (6 stone 11 pounds) confounded both his coaches and the opposition.

Sellars goes on to say that Jack, whose school nickname was 'Snowy', was famously taunted during games against rival school Scotch College with cries of 'Swat that fly!'

In 1902 Jack returned to Mildura to run some of the family businesses—he was seventeen years old. Another part of the Jack De Garis legend is that he tripled the profits of the family business within two years of his return.

When his father left town to live in Melbourne in 1908, Jack was 22 and already married to Rene Vera Corbould. He took over the De Garis enterprises in Mildura and was soon adding his own ventures to those his father had set up.

In 1910 he borrowed £15,000 and built a huge state-of-the-art packing shed to process local fruit. Two years later he raised £22,000 of capital in a venture to take over a failed irrigation colony of 10,000 acres known as Pyap Village Estate in the South Australian Riverland near Loxton, on the Murray River.

The South Australian government had set up Pyap as a communal irrigation colony much earlier, in 1894. Like most other such schemes it struggled, despite funding from the state government of more than £20,000. The project got off to a bad start—the pump that was to provide the water was not delivered until a year after the families moved onto the land. The settlers, most of whom had little farming experience or knowledge, were left with no crops and thus no communal income to kick-start the venture. When the pump was installed, it broke down after a few weeks and a replacement did not arrive until the following year.

The village struggled on under poor management and was eventually abandoned in 1903. A Melbourne syndicate attempted to revive the project and failed, going bankrupt in the process.

In 1912 Jack De Garis raised the capital to buy the village and, using overhead irrigation systems, he turned it into a successful and profitable company town and moved 80 families into the stone cottages. Jack set up a school, a community library and a recreation centre, and created his own form of 'child endowment' in the form of a 'baby bonus' for settlers—similar to the one established in the same year by the federal government.

Thirty years after it was initially established, Pyap was a success!

The stage was set for Jack De Garis's finest hour.

In 1919 a sudden shortage of cargo space in ships carrying freight to British ports meant that, for four months, dried fruit from Mildura could not reach its primary market. With financial disaster looming for the growers, the Australian Dried Fruits Association (ADFA) called on the one man they knew could find a solution. That man was Mildura's local hero—the district's precocious 'wunderkind' and most successful businessman, for whom nothing seemed impossible: Jack De Garis.

Jack had a plan that would create a strong local market for their surplus product. He was hired as 'Publicity Officer' on a salary of £1500 and the ADFA raised a fighting fund with which he was to go into battle—a budget of £20,000, a huge and unprecedented amount of money for advertising and publicity at the time in

Australia. The amount was calculated as one-eighth of a penny per £1 of turnover from sales of ADFA products.

The stunts, schemes and methods used by Jack De Garis to promote the produce of the Mildura district were certainly imaginative, quirky and way ahead of their time in the Australia of 1919. Jack took to the task with rare and astoundingly creative energy and zeal. His first move was to run a competition to find a name for Mildura's products, an adjective that best described the dried fruits grown in the district.

The winning suggestion was 'Sun-Raysed'.

Jack loved the term and soon hit upon the idea of changing the adjective to a noun to describe the district itself—'Sunraysia'. He would later cement the term permanently in the nation's consciousness by cleverly calling his newspaper the *Sunraysia Daily*.

Jack's projects, gimmicks and awareness campaigns included a series of free recipe books, children's books and information leaflets distributed to schools, cartoons in national and local newspapers, and the establishment of a Sunraysia Cafe in Melbourne, staffed entirely by young girls from the district, all of whom had been, according to Jack's publicity, 'raised on Sunraysia raisins'.

The opening of the cafe was announced by sky-writing, hot-air balloons and box kites were flown over all major cities of Australia displaying Sunraysia advertisements, and a competition was launched with a prize of £1000 for whoever could most accurately calculate the number of Sunraysia sultanas in a one-pound packet. The Mildura Post Office had to take on extra staff as the entries flooded in. People all around Australia bought multiple packets and counted the contents in order to find an average until finally the £1000 went to a woman in Adelaide.

Jack made short films about Mildura and the dried fruits industry, which were played in cinemas across the country before the feature films. There were also 'serialised' guessing competitions and word games that ran in newspapers across Australia. This clever technique of getting readers to guess one word a day meant the competitions stretched out over several days or weeks.

A factory was set up in Mildura that turned surplus local fruit into 'Good Little Normie' fruit bars, and cartoon strips on wrappers and in the newspapers followed the adventures of 'Good Little Normie'. Needless to say, Little Normie was 'good' because he was consuming healthy Australian-grown dried fruit, instead of other unhealthy confectionary.

A song entitled 'The Sun-raysed Waltz', with lyrics by Jack, was heavily promoted and became quite popular in the form of recordings, sheet music and pianola rolls. Oddly enough, 1919 and 1920 saw a huge growth in home entertainment such as pianos, pianolas, sheet music and gramophones. This was due to a fear of crowds during the great influenza epidemic, which was raging worldwide and would eventually kill more people than World War I. Many theatres and dance halls were closed and people sought their entertainment at home.

The influenza epidemic, however, merely provided Jack De Garis with another bright idea. Posters appeared all over Australia with the slogan:

I fear no more the dreaded 'flu, For 'Sun-raysed' fruits will pull me through.

(Apparently, if you repeated these lines when steadily eating 'Sun-raysed' fruits, your dread of the influenza would disappear.)

It seemed there was nothing the diminutive dynamo could not do. He oozed charm and confidence and affability. His 'can do' attitude and seemingly endless store of promotional and marketing ideas and schemes were surely almost too grand and expansive to be contained in his small human frame. The ADFA and most of the locals loved him.

———

Not content with success as a farmer, salesman, entrepreneur and visionary businessman, Jack also had aspirations as an author, songwriter, dramatist, musical comedy writer, theatre producer, film-maker and aviation pioneer! He did all these things seemingly at the same time, in a few short years between the end of the war and 1923, when his marriage ended in divorce and his life suffered a drastic change in fortune.

In 1915 he had written a four-act military drama with the colourful title *Ambition Run Mad*, which had featured as a serial in the *Mildura Pioneer* newspaper and was then published by the paper in the form of booklets. Then, in 1919, Jack had organised a fairytale-writing competition as part of the Sunraysia promotional campaign. He used some of the entries to compile and edit the *Sun-raysed Children's Fairy Story Book*, published under his name by F.W. Niven and Co.

In 1920 Jack bought three regional newspapers—the *Mildura Cultivator*, *Mildura Telegraph* and the *Merbein Irrigationist*—and merged them into the *Sunraysia Daily*, which employed more than 90 staff. His newspaper, of course, further promoted the Sunraysia brand.

If you owned a newspaper in those days, you owned the means to print whatever you liked—so Jack De Garis was now not only a newspaper proprietor, he had all the technology and means to become a publisher. He could pursue his career as a publisher, editor and patron of the literary arts, and so he launched a competition to find the great Australian novel. This resulted in an avalanche of more than 400 manuscripts arriving at the now quite busy Mildura Post Office.

None of the novels were particularly good, but a Melbourne religious journalist named Frank A. Russell took out the prize with *Ashes of Achievement*, which was subsequently published by the C.J. De Garis Publishing Company. (Russell's only other published works were a report on a Eucharist conference in 1928 and a treatise entitled *Prohibition Does Work: An Australian Investigator's Opinion*, published in 1930.)

Between 1920 and 1925 C.J. De Garis Publishing produced several dozen books, novels and verse collections, with various titles such as *The White Butterfly and Other Fairytales* by Ethel Morris, *The Lost Valley* by J.M. Walsh, *The Everlastin' Ballads of Empire* by Harold Hansell, and *Sport of the Gods* by Ada Holman.

Meanwhile, the success of 'The Sun-raysed Waltz' convinced Jack that he could also pursue a career as a songwriter. He had paid composer Reginald Stoneham to create the melody for his lyrics of 'The Sun-raysed Waltz' and the two men were soon collaborating on more songs and a 'musical comedy mystery' stage production with the odd name of *F.F.F*, which was staged in Adelaide, Melbourne and Perth and promoted by the famous entrepreneur Hugh McIntosh. Unfortunately, the production was somewhat of a flop and a proposed Sydney theatre run was cancelled. Many people evidently thought the show was just another promotion for dried fruit and stayed away. However, two of the songs written for the show—'Murray Moon' and 'Sleepy Sea'—did become quite popular.

But even that wasn't enough for Jack De Garis. Jack liked to be referred to as 'an aviation pioneer' but the fact of the matter was that he never actually flew a plane anywhere. He did own several planes that set distance records around Australia while Jack was a passenger in them, but they were flown by professional pilots he had employed.

Aeroplanes were expensive in 1920 but Jack purchased three within twelve months. The first, a Boulton Paul P9, crashed; the second, a Sopwith Gnu, cost Jack almost £2000 but wasn't fast enough for his liking; the third was an Airco DH.4.

There were many returned airmen from The Great War looking for a chance to fly—and Jack employed several pilots before settling on Lieutenant Frank Briggs who, with Sergeant Stoward as mechanic and Jack as a passenger, flew the Airco DH.4 from Melbourne to Belmont Racecourse in Perth to complete the first east to west crossing of Australia by air, on 2 December 1920. They completed the trip, a distance of 2169 miles (3491 kilometres), in 19 hours and 10 minutes, making several stops on the way, and were given a civic reception by the mayor of Perth.

During January 1921 Briggs and Jack, now with Sergeant George Bond as mechanic, also flew from Mildura to Sydney in 5 hours and 30 minutes, and from Sydney to Brisbane in 4 hours and 50 minutes, as part of Jack's Sunraysia awareness-raising campaign. They then flew from Brisbane to Melbourne in a record-breaking 10 hours and 30 minutes, with stops at Grafton, Sydney and Cootamundra.

While pursuing these lofty ambitions, Jack was also putting more schemes on the ground. In late 1920 Jack had purchased, sight unseen, a 47,325 acre (19,000 hectare) property at Kendenup, Western Australia. It had previously been a large sheep run owned by the pioneering Hassell family, and then the site of Western Australia's first goldmine, which had failed to produce gold commercially.

Jack flew over to inspect the property and subsequently planned a new settlement, which would combine an irrigation community and a processing and packing business. The 350 settlers who purchased blocks, ranging from 10 to 60 acres in size, would grow mostly apples and potatoes, along with other fruit and vegetables.

The Kendenup Fruit Packing Company, owned by Jack, built a factory and dehydrating plant where the crops were to be processed. The employees working in the factory were to be housed in 80 cottages that were part of the settlement. Jack's planned subdivision of the estate included a civic centre, public parks, recreation facilities, a school and a church, as well as the factory.

Jack was in debt for more than £50,000 over the venture, but raised £25,000 by selling the various real estate components and businesses that made up the Pyap Village Estate. Still, Kendenup was seriously under-capitalised and soon Jack was in financial trouble. As usual, his reaction was to spend more money and do more publicity. He left for the United States and this advertisement appeared in the *New York Times* on 13 August 1922:

PROGRESS IN AUSTRALIA.
Growth of Kendenup an Example of What Can Be Done There.
'When railway revenue jumps from $250 to $50,000 in twelve months it is enough to make people take an interest in the cause of such a phenomenal effect,' said C.J. De Garis of Kendenup, Australia, in explaining the wonderful development of his section of Australia in which he is vastly interested. Mr. De Garis, who is at the Hotel Pennsylvania, holds the long distance record for aviation.

'We are most enthusiastic about our settlement of Kendenup, for those are the figures we can show for the last twelve months,' said Mr De Garis. 'For eighty-two years it was a sheep ranch, a tract of land comprising about fifty thousand acres, with a total population of seven people. That was sixteen months ago and the change today is unbelievable. It is now a model community of 200 houses, built of brick and concrete with tiled roofs, and the population has increased to 770 inhabitants.

'It is because Kendenup settlement has been such a success that I have come to America to interest the capitalists of your country in creating similar settlements throughout Australia. The financial success of the settlement is the best argument that I have and a shrewd captain of industry will be quick to recognize it at once. Another strong point is the fact that 100 per cent of the settlers made an unsolicited statement to the people of Australia that they were absolutely satisfied with their bargain.

'We who are interested in and responsible for this settlement have spared no pains to give the best that can be obtained. We have had the soil analyzed by experts; have ascertained what fruits and vegetables are best suited for that particular type of soil, and we have established a dehydrator for extracting moisture from the fruit which makes it imperishable.

'The system which we used in disposing of the land in our settlement of Kendenup was to cut it up into thirty-acre tracts. Seventy dollars is the average price paid an acre. The payments are extended equally over a period of ten years without interest. The climate of Australia is remarkably fine. We have not had a month without rain in forty years. The average rainfall each year is about thirty inches. Australia is a great country, and we want as many real Americans as we can get to come and settle there permanently.'

It was obvious that Jack was getting desperate and things were beginning to unravel. Many of the statements in the article were exaggerations at best and lies at worst. Some of them were simply things Jack wanted to believe. He was beginning to make the common error of the overenthusiastic entrepreneur—he was believing his own publicity.

For one thing, Jack held no aviation records, as he had never flown a plane. The record holder was Frank Briggs who had, as a result of the flight from Melbourne to Perth, been awarded the first ever Oswald Watt Medal for 'A most brilliant performance in the air or the most notable contribution to aviation by an Australian or in Australia'.

The inflow of American capital never eventuated; £250,000 was promised by one American bank but it never arrived. An Australian bank loaned £30,000 but it was too little too late. The end was inevitable. By December 1923 there were only 30 settlers left at Kendenup, the project had collapsed, and Jack lost everything and was accused of fraud.

A royal commission in Western Australia in 1923 finally exonerated him of any serious crime, but his reputation and credibility were in tatters, and his mental stability was deteriorating.

The *Sunraysia Daily* went into receivership and was later sold to a consortium of three politicians, one of whom was the future prime minister Dr Earle Page.

Jack began investing in oil exploration and speculating in land development and real estate in Melbourne with borrowed money. His energy and work ethic were as strong as ever but had taken on a manic dimension. He also somehow managed to find time to write a book based on his own life and appropriately titled *The Victories of Failure*.

Jack had married his secretary, Violet Austin, one month after his divorce became final. They had a daughter (Jack also had three daughters by his first marriage) and lived at Hawthorn but also rented a house at Mornington, on the southeast shore of Port Phillip Bay, where Jack was involved in drilling for oil.

Towards the end of 1925 Jack's brinkmanship finally failed him. Another land development scheme ran into serious financial trouble, a rather large cheque bounced and a warrant was issued for his arrest.

Jack responded by writing 70 suicide notes and faking his own death by 'drowning' in Port Phillip Bay. One of the letters was to his songwriting collaborator, composer Reg Stoneham:

You will have the papers by now, and will have seen what has become of me. The strain has been too long and too strong, and I have cracked up under it. I hope, however, for the sake of dear Vy that my new song 'Moonoloo', turns out a winner, for she will need to get every penny she can. Think as pleasantly as you can of me, who came nearer to being a big success than people think; and who consequently became the greatest failure. Regards and regrets. —De Garis

On 5 January 1925 Jack's car was found at Mentone Beach—it contained his clothes and directions to his wife about where to find the suicide notes, but no trace of a body could be found.

The tributes poured in, including this one from the *Adelaide News*, written anonymously by 'a friend':

De Garis Life Story.
Began Work at Nine.
Meteoric Rise and Reverse.

(By a Friend.)

Meteoric! That is the only description I can apply to Clement John De Garis, who is missing from his home in Melbourne in mysterious circumstances. Undoubtedly an able man with big ideas of Australia, he flashed into Australian public life during the early post-war dried-fruit boom, and as publicist, playwright, publisher, land salesman, and other things he has since starred continuously.

I met him first in 1920, when he was preparing his famous press tour through the fruit settlements of New South Wales, Victoria, and South Australia for representatives of all Australian newspapers. A quick-speaking, quick-laughing, enthusiastic man, he made immediate friends of almost every person he met and his capacity for maintaining such friendships has been well evidenced during his recent turbulent years.

Mr De Garis was born 39 years ago and had been in business since he entered Elisha, his father's, office in Mildura at the early age of nine. Later he went to Wesley College for five years, achieved particular school fame as an athlete, and, in 1905 returned as a partner to his father's firm.

'When I entered that firm,' De Garis once told me, 'I resolved to make each day's profit exceed the last, and I succeeded.'

That was until 1921.

In 1907 he became managing director of the firm, and in 1910 secured a similar post in the De Garis Sarnia Fruit Picking [*sic*] Company, Mildura.

Son of Minister.

In 1877, Mr De Garis' father, a former Methodist Minister, began his pioneer work in irrigation in Australia and 'C.J.' was ever eager to follow his lead. He purchased the Pyap estate on the Murray in South Australia and spent large sums on its transformation into a model dried fruits settlement.

It cost £23,000. The improvements, including an overhead pipe watering scheme, absorbed £47,000 in eight years. During his last four years in possession, the property had been brought to pay a net profit of £5000.

This property was sold in an endeavour to finance Kendenup.

In October, 1918, he was appointed director of publicity for the Australian Dried Fruits Association, and his salary was £1,500 for the first year, and later £2,000. He was authorised to spend an eighth of a penny in the £ of each estimated crop. In the first he over spent £11,000 in a total of £31,000, which went in films, books, posters and general publicity. But in three years the dried fruit sales increased by 5,000 tons, while crops and fruit lands increased in value £4,500,000.

That was the boom period.

Mr De Garis purchased an aeroplane and flew between Mildura and the various state capitals. He crashed the plane, but soon afterwards purchased a bigger one, employing Lieutenant Briggs as pilot; in this he made a sensational flight from Adelaide to Sydney, carrying mail for the Prince of Wales, then visiting Australia, and another from Adelaide to Perth.

He established an aerodrome at Mildura in 1921, where he then also controlled a big garage, partly to accommodate the fleet of fast cars used by himself and his various staffs including the staff of 'Sunraysia Daily,' which he established.

Keen Motorist.

I knew Mr De Garis as a keen motorist, whose high-speed tours through wild bush land I have not seen bettered. His many record-breaking non-stop runs from Adelaide to Mildura were notoriously hair-raising.

On the establishment of Kendenup, Mr De Garis was persuaded to give up flying, but he had then flown about 25,000 miles.

A prolific journalist, 'C.J.'—as he was universally called—produced many plays and short stories. One volume dealing with the Kaiser bore the title of *Ambition Run Mad.*

In 1921, however, everything changed. He became financially embarrassed, and the Kendenup settlement scheme grew unfinancial. His play *F.F.F*, lost him £2,000, and his publishing house, his 'hobby', £3,000, and by May, 1922, he was borrowing large sums at up to 12 per cent interest.

In March, 1920, he showed me that his surplus assets were more than £74,000 yet in May, 1922, he was to use his own term 'broke'.

After the recent Royal Commission's enquiry into the Kendenup (Western Australian) settlement operations, Mr De Garis made another start 'with only a pair of sleeve links' as he once remarked.

He pledged himself to redeem every debt at the face value, and to redeem the debentures of the Kendenup settlers.

By purchasing big estates at Beaumaris and Black Rock, he began to achieve success, his earnings ranging up to £1,200 in a few weeks.

Here followed a period of land selling by his Melbourne Subdivisions Company, and then trouble again apparently overtook him.

When police failed to locate a body, and none was washed up in Port Phillip Bay, some people began to speculate about Jack's ability to creatively handle troublesome situations. Then the whole affair took a sudden change of direction. The *Melbourne Argus* was first with the news, on 9 January:

MR. C.J. DE GARIS.
REMARKABLE DEVELOPMENT.
Warrant for Arrest Issued.

The mystery of the whereabouts of Mr. C.J. De Garis was in no way simplified yesterday, but late in the afternoon events took a remarkable turn. On the information of Frank Northcott, coachbuilder, of 583 Elizabeth Street, North Melbourne, Senior Detective Davey, who, with Detective McKerral, is conducting the investigations, issued a warrant for the arrest of C.J. De Garis on a charge of having, on December 22, 1924, obtained £300 by means of a valueless cheque. According to statements made by the detectives, De Garis is alleged to have given a cheque for a much larger amount than £300 to Northcott, but the police have not divulged the nature of the transaction. Northcott is said to have paid De Garis £300, subject to certain conditions, which, he alleges, were not complied with. When the cheque was presented at the bank the police say that it was dishonoured.

Although Sergeant Tennant and those who are helping him to patrol the beach and shallows at Mentone in search of a body have practically abandoned hope of finding any trace of the missing man, they continued the search yesterday. Particular attention was paid to the understructure of the pier, as it was thought possible that Mr. De Garis's body might have lodged in it. Constable Bentley carefully examined every row of piles, but found nothing.

The lack of a *corpus delicti* wasn't surprising, for Jack was actually hiding out at various country pubs disguised as an American called 'Mr Leslie' or 'Mr Young'. He then headed to Sydney using the same aliases and no doubt took great pleasure in reading his own obituaries and tributes.

One of the problems of being a well-known missing 4-foot 11-inch man is that no amount of padding, wigs or dark glasses will disguise you for long. Jack was spotted but managed to evade the police and book a passage on a ship to Auckland.

But the game was up and a quick check on his aliases and shipping passenger lists soon had the police on the trail of a 'Mr Young' or a 'Mr Leslie'. The wire service news item appeared in most national papers, including the *Singleton Argus*, on 15 January 1926:

DE GARIS ARRESTED
DENIES HIS IDENTITY

As the *Maheno* was off the heads at Auckland on Tuesday morning, the vessel was boarded by uniformed and plain clothes policemen, and an officer of the vessel pointed out the man whose arrest was desired.

One of the detectives said to him, 'Your name is De Garis'.

'It is not,' he said. 'My name is Leslie.'

He asked for the authority of the detectives, and a telegraphic copy was shown to him of a warrant charging him with having obtained £300 in Melbourne by means of a valueless cheque from Charles Northcote [*sic*]. He refused to make any statement and again denied that he was De Garis.

Before the steamer reached the wharf he was taken off in the police launch and then conveyed to the police station in a motor car.

A search of his cabin and his luggage failed to disclose anything bearing his name. On the second day out, after advice had been received from the Sydney police that De Garis was believed to be on board, a steward found in his cabin a pair of pyjamas which bore the name of De Garis. These were not there when the detectives made their search.

De Garis was charged at the police station, on the authority of the information from the Victorian police that a warrant alleging false pretences had been issued for his arrest.

CAPTAIN'S STATEMENT

Captain Norton, of the *Maheno*, stated after the vessel berthed that he was only a little way out from Sydney when he received a radio from Inspector General Mitchell that it was believed De Garis was on board his ship, under the name of 'Young.'

'Of course, I could not make a search of the ship just then,' said the captain, 'but I looked through the passenger list, and I replied by radio: "There is no person named Young aboard, as far as I know." Later on I got another message, asking if a man named Leslie were on the ship as a steerage passenger. I replied "Yes", and the second day out a steward pointed out a man to me. I had him closely watched, but in a manner that would not arouse his suspicions, nor cause the attention of the other passengers to be focussed upon him. As a matter of fact, the passenger proved to be in total ignorance of the fact that he was under observation. I took the strictest precautions to ensure that none of the passengers or members of the ship's company, outside myself and four others, were aware that there was anybody on board under suspicion. When on deck he wore a light panama hat, and appeared to be enjoying the trip.'

The *Melbourne Argus* was again a few steps ahead of the story, reporting developments that had not reached the wire service. Their information was that Jack had admitted his identity and was preparing to face the music:

At 5 o'clock yesterday afternoon the chief of the Criminal Investigation department at Melbourne (Superintendent Potter) received the following cable message from the police at Auckland:—

Chief of police, Melbourne.

De Garis, false pretences, arrested Auckland.

Admits identity.

The most sensational development following the arrest, however, was a cable message sent by De Garis to Mr. J. Woolf, chairman of the committee appointed to plan the reconstruction of the Melbourne Subdivisions Company. The message was sent from Auckland at five minutes past 4 o'clock, and was as follows:—

Joseph Woolf, solicitor, 34 Queen Street, Melbourne. Northcott's warrant executed New Zealand. Returning home first boat, defend. Cabled wife see you. Retained Allan Moody, barrister, here.

(Signed) De Garis.

De Garis's disappearance competed with the second Test match as chief topic of conversation in four States—Victoria (where he was best known), New South Wales, South Australia, and Western Australia. In November it had been known that the Melbourne Subdivisions Company, which he directed in the name of his wife, was in financial difficulties. Finally, a meeting of creditors was called and a committee was appointed to draft a plan of reconstruction. This committee was still at work when, on the morning of Monday January 5, a motor-car was found abandoned in the tea tree near the Mentone pier. In the car was a note asking Mrs. De Garis to look in a drawer at her home, and letters were found signed 'C.J. De Garis', expressing his intention to shuffle off this mortal coil by drowning himself in the bay. A thorough police search failed to find the body, and in the meantime it was found that De Garis had written dozens of letters to friends and creditors, and to the Melbourne Subdivisions Company, saying that he intended to drown himself. From the first the police did not believe that he was drowned, and on January 7 a warrant was issued for his arrest on a charge of having obtained £300 by means of a valueless cheque. On January 9 came the news from the Sydney police that a man believed to be De Garis had been staying at an hotel at Mortlake, near Sydney, disguised as an American. He was believed to have boarded the steamer *Maheno* from Sydney. At first the detectives doubted whether De Garis was on the *Maheno*, and the information received by wireless from the captain that a steerage passenger was wearing pyjamas bearing the name 'De Garis', increased their doubts, because they did not believe that a man of De Garis's intelligence could be so careless as to leave behind such a chain of clues.

'This is too much like a paper-chase,' said one of the Melbourne detectives engaged in the case. 'I cannot help thinking that there is a catch in it somewhere.' Their doubts proved to be ungrounded, and De Garis was arrested when the *Maheno* arrived at Auckland.

The *Argus* went on to report that it believed:

The process of bringing De Garis to Melbourne will not be difficult … The fact that De Garis has admitted his identity simplifies matters considerably, and Superintendent Potter said yesterday that as soon as a report is received from the Auckland police a detective will be sent from Melbourne to escort De Garis back.

According to the De Garis legend, Jack sold a block of land to the detective on the return trip to Australia, but I can find no written evidence of that. Whether it was done as they chatted on the deck in panama hats or not, I can't say.

Jack's friends put pressure on Frank Northcott to withdraw the charges and eventually that occurred. There was a meeting of creditors at which the process of establishing a public company to enable Melbourne Subdivisions Company to carry on business was begun. The amounts owing were huge by 1926 standards: £250,000 was owed to landowners who had sold land to the company; shareholders were owed £150,000; the bank £10,000; and normal business creditors £6000.

Jack had a small victory in May, when a charge of fraud and false representation brought against him in Western Australia by a settler at Kendenup was found not proven in the Supreme Court.

He threw himself into selling real estate and took out leases on land around Mornington and Hastings, where he hoped to find oil. He made valiant attempts to pay back money but the task was Herculean. He did on several occasions walk into creditors' offices and hand over cash to people to whom he was in debt. On one occasion he handed £1000 to an old friend to whom he owed much more. The friend later remarked that he felt so sorry for Jack that he would have been satisfied with sixpence.

With debts totalling more than £40,000 and little chance of ever paying back more than a few token amounts, Jack left the family home in Hawthorn on the morning of 17 August and made his way to the house at Mornington.

Before leaving he called a plumber named Scott and made an appointment at the Mornington address at noon. When the plumber arrived he found a note pinned to the door that told him instructions were under the door mat. There he found a sheet of paper that read:

> Sorry to drag you into this, but you are a plumber, and a plumber is needed. There may be danger to anyone else. The gas must be cut off outside the house. The kitchen is closed and full of gas, and you will find me there. The gas must be cut off and the door opened carefully before entering. No matches must [be] used. You had better ring the police, also my wife at Haw. 2839. Poor girl, she has no idea. Fell down on a big job yesterday. Am paying the penalty to-day.
>
> Please see parcels under mat reach destination.
>
> C.J. De Garis.

The *Melbourne Argus* reported the subsequent events:

> After reading the message Mr. Scott summoned Constable R.F. Mason and a doctor, and together they entered the house. De Garis was found lying face downwards on a table which had been drawn close to a gas stove in the kitchen, which was full of gas. His mouth was over a gas jet, which had been turned on, and the doors and windows of the room had been closed so that no gas should escape.
>
> Efforts at resuscitation were made.
>
> … Sealed letters addressed to Mrs. De Garis were found under the door mat. The body was removed to the Royal Hotel. Later

in the day it was viewed by the city coroner (Mr. Berriman), who gave the order for burial. The date of the inquest has not yet been fixed ... It is understood that the body will be brought to Melbourne today, and the burial will take place in Melbourne.

The *Argus* then gave a long obituary in which it praised Jack as a 'clever salesman, whose assets were a compelling magnetic personality and a faculty for almost ceaseless industry' and called him 'the most remarkable Australian business men [*sic*] of recent years'.

Jack, the *Argus* said, was known as a 'journalist, aviator, publicist, land salesman, company promoter, playwright, publisher, and in many other activities' whose 'enterprise and imagination several times carried him beyond the safe limits of finance, with the result that many of his ventures ended in considerable financial loss to himself and investors'.

Jack De Garis was 41 years and 9 months old.

In that short time he had achieved more than most of us could dream of in ten lifetimes. The name 'Sunraysia' is still used and recognised Australia-wide today.

On the other hand, Jack De Garis lost more of other people's money than a hundred careless entrepreneurs or cunning con men could imagine, faked his own death, and fed his own vanity to the point of self-delusion.

In his eulogy at Jack's funeral, Reverend Charles Tregear said:

Today we are laying to rest the body of no ordinary man. I will alter that, and say he was a most extraordinary man, a man with brains, wonderful vision, courage and business ability. But behind it all he was a kindly and good man.

There was no mention of 'The Prince of Ballyhoo'.

BEEN THERE BEFORE

I love this poem about a scam that doesn't work—because the 'victim' has been conned before. It's nice to know that playing the same old trick with relentless monotony eventually results in the scammers being scammed!

All small towns seem to have their standard practical joke for new chums. At Menindee, where I lived for six years, it was considered funny to send newcomers to the railway station to buy a return ticket to Wilcannia or Wentworth, so they could see the Darling River and visit another town. There was, of course, no railway line to either place, only east to Sydney or west to Broken Hill.

At Wagga Wagga the trick is to send people to watch the non-existent 'five o'clock wave' that sweeps down the Murrumbidgee River every afternoon.

No doubt the popularity of Banjo's poem has forever ruined the sport of the locals at Walgett.

Been There Before

A.B. Paterson ('The Banjo')

> There came a stranger to Walgett town,
> To Walgett town when the sun was low,
> And he carried a thirst that was worth a crown,

Yet how to quench it he did not know;
But he thought he might take those yokels down,
The guileless yokels of Walgett town.

They made him a bet in a private bar,
In a private bar when the talk was high,
And they bet him some pounds no matter how far
He could pelt a stone, yet he could not shy
A stone right over the river so brown,
The Darling River at Walgett town.

He knew that the river from bank to bank
Was fifty yards, and he smiled a smile
As he trundled down; but his hopes they sank,
For there wasn't a stone within fifty mile;
For the saltbush plain and the open down
Produce no quarries in Walgett town.

The yokels laughed at his hopes o'erthrown,
And he stood awhile like a man in a dream;
Then out of his pocket he fetched a stone,
And pelted it over the silent stream—
He'd been there before; he had wandered down
On a previous visit to Walgett town.

CONSCIOUSLY CONTRIVED NONSENSE

The Backstory

> 'Who in the world am I? Ah, that's the great puzzle.'
>
> Lewis Carroll—Alice, *Alice's Adventures in Wonderland*

This is the story of a poet who became one of Australia's most famous and popular post-modern writers. His work epitomises the surrealist, contemporary poetry that blossomed into popularity and was much praised between World War I and II. It was a form of verse that relied on techniques such as stream of consciousness, word association and image juxtaposition.

This form of modernist poetry was paralleled by the artistic movements of surrealism, modernism and post-modernism, and avant-garde, heavily extemporised, unmelodic forms of jazz music.

The seeds of these movements were sown in the early years of the 20th century, in artistic and literary philosophies such as Dadaism and modernism. Heavily influenced by philosophers and psychologists such as Nietzsche, Freud and Jung, these new forms of literature, art and music were very much the 'in thing' in academic and intellectual circles in the period between the wars.

The poet in question has been much anthologised, although his output was not great. His work has been published and republished in anthologies in the USA and Britain, as well as here in his native Australia and, as recently as 1991, his collected works were republished in *The Penguin Book of Modern Australian Poetry*.

He was, apparently, an introverted, shy and melancholic young man who lived a rather unremarkable life and kept his creative efforts very much to himself. He had migrated with his family from Britain at an early age, lived in a respectable working-class suburb of Sydney, left school without attaining his Intermediate Certificate and worked as a mechanic, before moving to Melbourne, where he was employed as an insurance salesman.

After a short spell in the armed services, he contracted a life-threatening medical condition, which he neglected to have treated. He descended into melancholy and, after an apparently failed romance, returned to Sydney, where he was nursed in his final days by his only Australian relative, a sister who later discovered his poetic output when sorting out his affairs and belongings.

The seventeen poems she discovered are among the most analysed and discussed poems ever written in the history of Australian literature.

There is one other fascinating thing about this poet—he didn't exist.

His name was Ern Malley.

Ern appeared in a blaze of glory in June 1944 and disappeared in a puff of smoke several weeks later. His poetry, however, refuses to go away.

The Story

> '… deceiving others. That is what the world
> calls a romance.'
>
> Oscar Wilde—*The Picture of Dorian Gray*

The Ern Malley hoax, perpetrated in 1944, came as a result of war in more ways than one.

During World War II, two soldiers in the intelligence unit headquarters of the Australian Army, in Melbourne's Victoria

Barracks, had plenty of time on their hands and applied their creative intelligence to concocting some 'bad poetry', rather than to inventing schemes designed to defeat the Imperial Japanese forces to the north of the continent.

What they did was an act of war against what they saw as pretentious academic elitism. They reacted against the promotion and praise of unrhymed verse that relied on the reader making associations between images and words to provoke an emotional or aesthetic response. This response, the champions of this new style contended, defied any old-fashioned literary analysis or syntactical logic.

In other words, the two soldiers were trying to debunk 'modern' poetry and make fools of those who promoted it at the expense of more classical and consciously creative styles of verse writing.

What they did, when they concocted the Ern Malley hoax, would take the battle between the opposing camps of literary and artistic philosophy into a very public arena.

On one side of the argument were the forces of 'old-fashioned' rationalism and realism in literature and art, proponents of the notion that painting, writing and music required structure and meaning in the classical sense of the words.

On the other side were the avant-garde modernists, who were more inclined to the notion that music, art and literature were forces that operated on the mind in ways unknown, not always explicable or logical. Words and images and sounds were some of the ways humanity reached into its collective subconscious to experience some understanding of the human condition—joy and sorrow, empathy, beauty and enlightenment.

Writers, artists and academics were forced to take sides, come out from their academic hiding places and join one or other of the two opposing 'armies'.

Some critics and academics were ambushed and fought back against the odds. Others conducted a brave rear-guard action against the attack, while the main target of the exercise attempted to attack on a new front.

Many others (if you'll forgive the mixed military, naval and political metaphor) leapt from the trenches of academia, nailed their colours to the mast and jumped on their soapboxes.

Some attempted to remain neutral with a foot in each camp, which proved to be the most difficult stance of all. Some were conscientious objectors.

Like all wars, there were casualties and quite a bit of post-traumatic stress syndrome. The Ern Malley hoax is, I have to admit, my personal favourite of all the scams and cons ever perpetrated in Australia.

There is no deep or meaningful personal reason for this. There are simply two bits of the story (neither of which is relevant to the main academic argument) that make me laugh out loud whenever I read them. The story contains two of my favourite characters in Australian literary history: Ethel Malley and Detective Vogelesang.

One of these characters is fictional but the other was a real person. Oddly, however, the fictional one is totally realistic and recognisable to me, while the real one appears too comical to be true, but you can judge for yourself.

The three main protagonists on the 'conservatives side' were all poets. The two young men working in army intelligence at the Victoria Barracks in Melbourne, were both born in Sydney.

James McAuley was a schoolteacher educated at Sydney University, where he was an excellent student and lived a rather Bohemian lifestyle, evidently doing a lot of drinking while smoking cigarettes and playing jazz piano. On leaving university he developed more conservative attitudes, becoming vehemently anti-Communist and converting to Catholicism. He developed a hatred for the modernist movement in poetry and eventually became editor of the conservative literary magazine *Quadrant*. At the time of the hoax, he was a lieutenant in the army.

His co-conspirator, Corporal Harold Stewart, had dropped out of university to study poetry. Like McAuley, Stewart was an admirer and protégé of the poet A.D. Hope. Although he had experimented with modern verse as a young man, Stewart had also come to despise the 'modernist' style of writing, dismissing it as pretentious and shallow. He spent the last part of his life living in Japan, having apparently decided to shun Western culture. He did, however, produce some critically acclaimed translations of Japanese haiku poetry into English.

The third member of the triumvirate was not actually involved in the creation of the 'fake' poetry, although he certainly encouraged the idea and took great delight in the embarrassment it caused when the hoax succeeded.

A.D. Hope OBE CBE was a poet steeped in the scholarly traditions of classical English literature. During his lifetime he was called many interesting things, including 'the 20th century's greatest 18th century poet', 'Australia's greatest living poet' and, in a sarcastic reference by Douglas Stewart to the erotic nature of much his verse, 'Phallic Alec'.

Hope was the son of a Presbyterian minister and, after spending his early childhood in the Southern Highlands of New South Wales and Tasmania, moved to Sydney and attended Fort Street Boys' High School and Sydney University, before completing this university education on a scholarship to Oxford.

He became lecturer in English at the Sydney Teachers' College, which is where he met young James McAuley. It was while holding this position, during World War II, that he precipitated and encouraged the Ern Malley hoax.

After the war Hope became a lecturer in English at Melbourne University, before establishing the post of Professor of English at the Canberra University College, which later became the Australian National University.

A.D. Hope was, on the one hand, a poet steeped in the tradition of Alexander Pope and John Dryden, a writer of beautifully crafted, often satirical, rhymed verse that never deviated from the structural and metrical dimensions of classical poetry.

He was also, however, a poet with a distinctly Australian, albeit scholarly, voice and he was a major influence, along with others like Kenneth Slessor and Judith Wright, in the establishment of a tradition of Australian poetry writing that gave Australians an alternative, far more contemporary, national poetic vision than that established fifty years previously by Banjo Paterson, Henry Lawson and other *Bulletin* poets.

Hope was once asked in an interview what poets could do for Australia, to which he replied, 'merely justify its existence'.

Like many other literary academics, Hope held very strong opinions about the nature and purpose of poetry, and was capable of displaying a quite nasty streak in defending his opinions and attacking those who disagreed with them. He certainly had very little time, or respect, for the person he saw as the leader of the opposing view in the academic war about the value and quality of modern verse.

The leader of the opposition was a charismatic and opinionated young intellectual from Mount Gambier named Max Harris. He was the only child of a salesman and a well-read, refined bridge-and-croquet-playing mother with the better-than-fiction name of Claris Harris.

A voracious reader with an encyclopaedic mind, Max Harris was the *enfant terrible* of the modernist movement.

Harris stridently and confidently championed the cause of the 'new poetry' and briefly edited the university newspaper *On Dit*. He had been ceremoniously dunked into the Torrens River in 1941 after a student mock trial condemned his anarchist views as 'unpatriotic' during wartime.

He served three months in the army, during which he read the complete works of Proust instead of digging latrines, and was released to do 'special research work' and aircraft watch.

By 1944 Harris had married his girlfriend from school days, against her parents' wishes, and was spending a lot of time in Melbourne, where he had helped establish the Contemporary Art Society, Reed and Harris Publishing, and a magazine called *Angry Penguins*. The first edition of *Angry Penguins* in 1941, funded by Claris Harris, had contained the views that led to his dunking in the Torrens.

The link to Melbourne was a result of Harris's association with wealthy Melbourne lawyer John Reed who had, with his wife,

Sunday Ballieu, established a rural retreat for artists and writers at their old dairy farm in the outer Melbourne suburb of Bulleen, in the Yarra Valley.

The name of the farm was 'Heide' and the group of artists associated with it became known as the Heide Circle. They included Joy Hester, Albert Tucker, John Perceval, James Gleeson, Arthur Boyd and most famously Sidney Nolan, who painted much of his Ned Kelly series of paintings at Heide.

Angry Penguins was an 'occasional' magazine co-edited by Max Harris and John Reed—it was supposedly a quarterly but only nine editions were ever published, between 1941 and 1946. There were 'newsletters' for subscribers in between editions. The title of the publication came from a line in one of Harris's poems.

The magazine promoted modern art, architecture and philosophy, and published the poetry of overseas poets like Gabriel Garcia Marquez, James Dickey and Dylan Thomas, as well as local poets like Geoffrey Dutton and Harris himself.

The now famous 'Autumn 1944 Edition' of *Angry Penguins* was dedicated entirely to the poetry of Ern Malley and featured a Sidney Nolan painting on the cover, which was inspired by one of the poems.

The poems were concocted by McAuley and Stewart from randomly selected lines from various books they had lying on their desks at the Victoria Barracks, including Shakespeare and an army manual on mosquitoes. Most of it was written in one afternoon, they claimed, and they had only three 'rules'.

Firstly, there should be 'no coherent theme ... only confused and inconsistent hints at a meaning'. Secondly, 'no care was taken with verse technique, except occasionally to accentuate its general sloppiness by deliberate crudities'. Finally, it was intended that the poems should not specifically imitate Max Harris's verse but 'the whole literary fashion as we knew it'. There were even hints and jokes in the poems like these lines from 'Sybelline':

> It is necessary to understand
> That a poet may not exist, that his writings

Are the incomplete circle and straight drop
Of a question mark.

The two young poets had been discussing the idea of writing 'nonsense' and passing it off as modern poetry for a while. Their friend and mentor A.D. Hope had written a scathing review of Harris's surrealist novel *The Vegetative Eye* in 1943, in which he said Harris could not write and was 'morally sick'. Hope suggested that a hoax such as they had discussed, would be a good way to debunk the pretentious Heide group and 'get Maxy'.

It worked.

McAuley and Stewart invented Ern and his sister and their biographies, aged the 'manuscript' using some dirt and exposure to sunlight, and sent it off to *Angry Penguins*. Their intention was to wait until the ruse had played out and then allow a young cadet reporter on the Sydney *Sun* newspaper, a friend of Stewart's named Tess van Sommers, to have the 'scoop' and tip a huge bucket of humiliation on the whole modernist movement.

The 'Autumn Edition' of the magazine actually appeared in mid-winter due to wartime publishing delays. It was beyond the wildest hopes of the hoaxers, reading their eagerly awaited copy in June 1944, to see that Harris lauded Malley as 'a poet of tremendous power, working through a disciplined and restrained kind of statement into the deepest wells of human experience'.

No matter what one might think about the whole affair, the pretentious nonsense of Max Harris's review of the poems is still funny. In among references to 'vast Homeric metaphors' and 'the felicity of language' being 'integral to the "analytic" experience itself' is the claim that Malley, as a poet, 'did not aim at revelation of all Truth, of inferring a valid Weltanschauung from his own range'. You can't help laughing at stuff like that.

Like many hoaxes, the Ern Malley con took on a life of its own and became something quite different to what it was intended to be.

One of Harris's lecturers from Adelaide University, Brian Elliott, accused Harris of inventing the whole thing and writing the poems and the review 'tongue-in-cheek'.

The university newspaper headline read 'LOCAL LECTURER CRIES "HOAX"—IS MALLEY, MALLEY OR MALLEY, HARRIS—OR WHO?'

Max Harris realised very early that he had been duped and admitted to John Reed that he should have exercised 'more restraint'. He then made his own investigations via friends in Sydney and it came to light that Ethel Malley's address was actually the home of Harold Stewart's family.

Meanwhile, Tess van Sommers had jumped the gun as soon as the magazine appeared and told other reporters, who immediately 'stole' the scoop and published what they knew in the Sydney magazine *Fact*. This magazine also published the confession by McAuley and Stewart that they had concocted the whole thing.

In early September 1944 newspapers around the nation reported the next twist in the story. This version is from the *Melbourne Argus* on 6 September:

INDECENCY ALLEGED IN PUBLICATION
'Angry Penguins'
ADELAIDE, Tues: In a courtroom crowded with young men and women today, Maxwell Henry Harris, of Churchill Ave, Glandore, was charged before Mr L.E. Clarke, SM, with having sold, offered, or distributed certain indecent passages in a publication known as The 1944 Autumn number of *Angry Penguins*. It was also alleged that Harris edited part of the publication and was a co-publisher. The hearing was adjourned until September 26.

Mr D.C. Williams, of the Crown Law Department, who prosecuted, said that it was claimed that certain passages in the book were immoral, indecent, or obscene, or all three. Defendant was a member of the firm of Reed and Harris. When interviewed by Detective Vogelesang, and asked if he was editor of the publication, Harris replied: 'Not exactly. There is a committee of four. I am one, and the others are John Reed, Mrs Sunday Reed, and Sidney Nolan, all of Templestowe Rd, Heidelberg, Melbourne. Articles are submitted to us, and if we accept we send them to Melbourne, where the book is printed.'

Continuing, Mr Williams said that the issue of *Angry Penguins* in question stated that it was to commemorate the Australian poet Ern Malley, who did not even exist. In parts the so-called literature in the publication was impossible to understand. Sex was dragged in without any apparent reason or real excuse.

The philistines had invaded the palace.

The hoax had opened the door to the wowsers, who were now free to attack the arts and academia generally and without restraint.

In a bizarre twist to the story, Detective Vogelesang, of the South Australian police, alerted by all the fuss, had found time to read *Angry Penguins*. In his evidence Detective Vogelesang said he considered it 'was immoral to have a conversation with a friend about sexual intercourse' and he objected to 'any descrip-tion of the female parts in poetry'. He (hilariously) added that he thought the word 'genitals' was immoral and was sure that the word 'incestuous' was indecent, although he 'did not know what it meant in its relation to the poem'.

Harris defended himself with his usual wit and told the court that he thought the Bible was more salacious than Ern Malley's poetry, but all to no avail. The magistrate decided that Mr Harris had 'too great a fondness for sexual references' and sentenced him to six weeks in prison or a £6 fine.

When the whole affair was long over, James McAuley, at least, showed remorse about the way the hoax had led to an attack on the arts generally. He always maintained the affair wasn't a personal attack on Harris and they were later reconciled. Harold Stewart, apparently, remained hostile towards Harris all his life.

Harris, to his credit, took it all on the chin and maintained the defence that McAuley and Stewart had subconsciously and inadvertently created some beautiful and meaningful poetry. The other members of the Heide circle and many international poets and followers of the avant-garde and modernist movement in the arts supported him in this opinion.

Max Harris AO went on to be an influential publisher, column-ist and bookseller, having helped create the 'Mary Martin' chain of stores, which he sold to Macmillans in the late 1970s. He was instrumental in fighting censorship and wowserism and helped create the liberal and artistic atmosphere that blossomed in South Australia in the Dunstan era. He died in 1995.

Personally, I think the hoax was brilliant and the 'poetry' of Ern Malley was truly awful. I find the often-praised random images, such as 'the new men are cool as spreading fern' and 'the black swan of trespass on alien waters' to be meaningless, pretentious nonsense. I know, however, that many other perfectly sane and intelligent people feel differently—and that's fine, too.

Interestingly, the most praised poem of the collection, 'Durer: Innsbruck, 1495', is the only one that wasn't created randomly. The hoaxers used an unfinished poem of McAuley's to create it.

While the poetry is awful, as it was intended to be, the real genius of McAuley and Stewart lies in the creation of Ethel Malley.

Ethel is a brilliantly well-observed and totally believable fictional character, and reading her letters to Max Harris makes me laugh out loud. It is much more fun than ploughing through the pretentious nonsense that makes up her brother's poetry. Perhaps it's because I grew up knowing so many respectable working-class women just like Ethel that I find her so funny.

Evidently it was Harold Stewart who more or less 'created' Ethel. He did a brilliant job of giving her a voice in the letters that constantly implies 'It's none of my business, but ...' For example:

Mother died in August, 1933, and I could not stop Ern from leaving school after that, as he was set on going to work. I have always thought that he was very foolish not to have got his intermediate, but he was determined to go his own way.

Speaking of her lack of knowledge of her brother's life in Melbourne, Ethel writes:

From things he said I gathered he had been fond of a girl in Melbourne, but had some sort of difference with her.

The euphemisms 'been fond of' and 'some sort of difference' bring tears of laughter to my eyes. It could be my mother talking over the fence to our neighbour in 1956.

In her first letter to the editor of *Angry Penguins*, Ethel writes that she was 'going through' her 'brother's things' after his death and found 'some poetry he had written'. She, being 'no judge of' the poems herself, still felt that she 'ought to do something about them' and, on the advice of a friend, was sending 'some of the poems for an opinion'. The letter goes on:

> It would be a kindness if you could let me know whether you think there is anything in them. I am not a literary person myself and I do not feel I understand what he wrote.

Of course, no one else 'understood what he wrote' either, as that was the whole point of the exercise. Ethel's turn of phrase and self-deprecating tone is brilliant. I love Ethel Malley and agree with Michael Heyward, author of *The Ern Malley Affair*, when he says:

> Ern Malley mocked the romantic myth of the proletarian artist but Ethel anticipated by a decade that formidable icon of the Australian suburban sensibility, Edna Everage.

Ern's poetry is as boring and pretentious today as it was in 1944; Ethel's letters are still very funny and worth reading.

Albert Tucker commented that the worst thing about the Ern Malley affair was that the hoaxers, by not coming to Harris's aid after the hoax succeeded, had:

> ... let the philistines take over and use it against the entire contemporary movement, making the whole business socially and culturally vicious.

In one of her letters to Harris, Ethel had given him the copyright of the poetry and James McAuley always maintained that he couldn't in all consciousness claim copyright of something he had written to defraud, and was happy for Harris to have the right to use the poems.

In 2003, however, with all three men having died, Curtis Brown, literary agents for McAuley's estate, threatened legal action against a publisher, Tom Thompson, who represented Harris's estate and attempted to claim copyright over the poems when Michael Heywood's book *The Ern Malley Affair* was being reissued.

Heywood said he'd been advised by the Australian Copyright Council in 1993 that Ethel's letters and McAuley's unsigned comments carried no legal weight and copyright had to be assigned formally in writing. He therefore sought permission to use the poems in his book from the estates of McAuley and Stewart, not from Thompson. There was no problem with him or others being granted permission to use the poems, but there was an objection from Curtis Brown to Thompson claiming he had copyright and sole right to licence the poetry to others.

It's hard to say exactly what the Ern Malley poems represent. Some claim they are the best poetry the two hoaxers produced, which seems rather insulting to two poets who did both write other poetry of perfectly acceptable quality.

Commenting on the artistic counter-claim that he and McAuley had inadvertently and subconsciously created valid poetic works, Harold Stewart wrote:

> One of the greatest brain washing effects of modern civilisation is the corruption of the sense of beauty and the sense of humour which often go together. People simply cannot tell the difference between what is beautiful and what is ugly.

The poetry of Ern Malley, according to Stewart:

> … does not represent an effusion or eruption from the subconscious or the unconscious of either James McAuley or myself.

It was, according to its co-creator, 'consciously contrived nonsense'.

TO THE IMPRESSIONIST SCHOOL

It seems that every new movement, school or development in artistic style and convention is looked upon with horror by the practitioners and exponents of the previous one.

More accurately, perhaps, we should say that those who have come to admire and understand the previous accepted conventions of art are often aghast when new ways of conceptualising and constructing paintings and drawings arrive on the scene.

I am reminded of the fact that, throughout the 1920s, the paintings of the Australian 'moderns'—Roland Wakelin, Roy de Maistre, Grace Cossington Smith et al.—were not accepted in the mainstream Australian art scene. Eyes and minds were attuned to the impressionist view of the world and the 1919 exhibition of 'musical' paintings by Wakelin and de Maistre caused shockwaves of non-acceptance. The Society of Artists refused to accept other works by these artists for exhibition and Wakelin's masterpiece, 'Down the Hills to Berry's Bay' was criticised for taking modernism 'too far'.

This witty piece of doggerel by *Bulletin* poet W.T. Goodge pokes fun at the arrival on the art scene of the impressionist movement, which twenty years later would, ironically, be accepted by the art world as 'mainstream'.

To the Impressionist School

W.T. Goodge ('The Colonel')

I'd love to be an artist, an artist free from guile,
And wear long hair and a great big stare,
And a transcendental smile.
I'd love to paint a picture, a picture full of thrill,
Of a knock-kneed horse on the Randwick Course
And the moon behind a hill.
I'd love to paint a portrait, a portrait full of soul,
Of the cross-eyed girl with her hair in curl
And a neck like a barber's pole.
I'd love to paint a landscape, a landscape bold and free,
With a Vandyck cliff and a crimson skiff
On a lilac-tinted sea.

GOODBYE, MR CASTRO

The Backstory

> 'Truth is stranger than fiction, because fiction
> is obliged to stick to possibilities; truth isn't.'
>
> Mark Twain—*Pudd'nhead Wilson's New Calendar*

The Tichborne family claimed to have arrived in Britain with William the Conqueror and were granted land on the south coast. It was just over a century later that the 'Tichborne Curse' came into being, along with the tradition of the 'Tichborne Dole'.

The story goes like this.

Back in those days, Lady Day, which was originally known as Our Lady's Day, was considered to be the first day of the year.

In medieval times the religious calendar was divided into four quarters; Lady Day was the first day of the spring season and was celebrated at the vernal equinox. Each 'first quarter day', as they were sometimes known, was marked by a solstice or equinox—Midsummer Day, Michaelmas Day, Christmas Day and Lady Day.

The practice of beginning each year on 1 January only arrived in Britain with the Gregorian calendar in 1752. Before that time, Lady Day, 25 March, was New Year's Day. This made much more sense in farming communities and rural areas. It was a natural time of transition in the farming year, the perfect time for rents to be paid and tenants to leave farms or begin working on new ones. It was a time when farming work was all done, crops were harvested, animals slaughtered, and the cycle of land use was ready to begin again. Yearly leases and rentals of rural property ran from Lady Day to Lady Day.

The lady in question was, of course, the Virgin Mary, and Lady Day was the time for the celebration of the Feast of The Annunciation—the moment when Mary was told she would bear a son by Immaculate Conception. It was the day of the vernal equinox, nine months before the birthday of Christ on Christmas Day.

It was supposedly around the time of Lady Day in 1180 that Lady Mabella Tichborne, sick and dying, pleaded with her husband to bless her passing by establishing a charitable tradition that would ensure the tenants and villagers on their estate would never go hungry.

The 12th century version of Sir Roger Tichborne was a military man not noted for his compassion and his wife was fearful that he would not provide well enough for the estate's villagers and tenants.

Sir Roger was not keen on the idea of handing over the food harvested on the private part of his estate to a bunch of grubby commoners, villagers and tenant farmers, but he could hardly deny the wishes of his pious and dying wife. He informed her that, for her to gain favour in the hereafter, any such charity should come from her efforts.

He would, he said, give away annually all the food produced from an area of land that his wife could encompass at night while her torch burned.

Now, had Lady Mabella been younger and fitter, she might have dashed around the entire estate like an athlete carrying the Olympic torch. She was, however, bed-ridden and dying and the best she could do was to crawl around 23 acres of the estate before the torch went out.

Not long afterwards, Lady Mabella herself went out and no doubt had an express passage to heaven due to her wonderful act of charity. She did, however, live long enough to place a curse upon the house of Tichborne, should the charitable tradition ever be discontinued.

Like all good medieval curses, it was quite specific.

Should the tradition ever be stopped, she prophesied, the family would produce a generation of seven sons who would produce seven daughters and the family name would die out and the house of Tichborne would fall.

The fields encircled by Lady Mabella have been known locally since that day as 'The Crawls' and the annual Lady Day distribution of food is known as the 'Tichborne Dole'.

The dole continued happily until 1796. Originally, it took the form of 1400 loaves of bread, which were distributed to whoever turned up. If you turned up and all the loaves were gone, you were entitled to tuppence. Over the centuries the tradition changed to giving out a gallon of flour to every adult applicant and half a gallon to every child. As the Tichborne family and many of their tenants have remained staunchly Catholic to this very day, this has meant that many local families over the centuries have received an awful lot of flour on Lady Day.

In 1621 King James I, in appreciation of Sir Benjamin Tichborne's support in keeping Hampshire loyal upon his accession in 1603, bestowed upon the family the hereditary title of baronet and exempted the village of Tichborne from anti-Catholic regulations. To this day a Catholic requiem mass is held on St Peter's Day each year in the village's Anglican parish church, one of only three Anglican churches in the UK to incorporate a Catholic chapel.

In the decade leading up to 1796 there were complaints from people in the district that the dole was attracting many itinerant, undesirable characters. In response to these complaints the local authorities, who had obviously not read enough fairy stories and folktales, prevailed upon the family to end the tradition.

I'm sure I don't need to tell you what happened next.

The old manor house collapsed in 1803 and a new one had to be built. At the time, Sir Henry Tichborne was the Eighth Baronet. He was the eldest of the seven sons of the Seventh Baronet, also called Henry. The Eighth Baronet had seven daughters but no sons and, when he died in 1845, his brother Edward became the Ninth Baronet.

Meanwhile, in 1836, somebody evidently remembered the curse and the Tichborne Dole was resumed.

Edward had never expected to inherit the title and had changed his surname to Doughty as a condition of inheriting a large estate from a childless aunt who wished the name Doughty to carry on after her death. Edward Doughty did have a son, but he had died in 1835 aged six years old. The Doughtys also had a daughter, Katherine, of whom more later.

Edward Doughty died in 1853 and another of the seven brothers, James, became the Tenth Baronet. James had two sons. The younger, Alfred, born in 1839 after the dole was restarted and the curse lifted, eventually became the Eleventh Baronet on his father's death in 1862.

Roger, the older son, who was born in 1829, before the dole was resumed and the curse lifted, was shipwrecked and lost at sea in 1854.

Or was he?

What has all this got to do, I hear you cry, with Australian scams, rorts and cons?

You would be surprised.

You *will* be surprised.

Now, read on ...

The Story

> 'I know who I WAS when I got up this morning, but I think I must have been changed several times since then.'
>
> Lewis Carroll—Alice, *Alice's Adventures in Wonderland*

Perhaps the strangest attempted con with an Aussie connection is the famous case of the 'Tichborne Claimant'. This case culminated in two trials in British courts, the second of which was, for a long time, the longest in British history.

What amazes me about the case is that it demonstrates how easily people can make the seemingly obvious into something else—and how other agendas can muddy the waters and distract people from simply applying logic and common sense to a situation.

While it appears to be a British story about titled gentry and famous court cases and class rivalry, it is actually a very Australian yarn. The events that led to this famous and extremely odd court case and controversy, the 'wonder of the age' in Victorian times, could only have happened here in Australia.

The 'Tichborne Affair' is very genuinely part of our Australian colonial history.

Let me explain the basic features of the case and introduce the main characters—later it gets complicated, so pay attention!

Part 1: The Wapping Liar

Arthur Orton was born in the East End of London in the dockside suburb of Wapping in 1834, the eighth child in a family of twelve. His father was a butcher who supplied meat and other products to ships, and bred Shetland ponies. As a child Arthur was already quite 'stout' and would be known in his youth as 'Fatty', 'Fatboy' and 'Bullocky'.

When he was six Arthur survived a fire that burned through shops and houses in Wapping for more than a day and killed three people. This left the plump little boy traumatised with a condition that made him twitch so badly it was misdiagnosed as St Vitus's dance and he was treated with cold baths.

As sailing seemed to 'cure' the condition, he was apprenticed as a cabin boy aboard a ship called the *Ocean* and went to sea just after his fourteenth birthday. By the time the *Ocean* arrived in Valparaiso, in Chile, six months later, the plump fourteen-year-old had had enough of a sailor's life; he deserted and made his way inland to a village called Melipilla, where he was taken in by a family named Castro.

Although he arrived in the village dressed in rags and penniless, Arthur told everyone his father was Queen Victoria's butcher and the young lad lived, apparently happily, as a member of the Castro family for over a year, in which time he learned to ride horses and to rope and work with cattle. These skills would come in handy later, during his life in Australia.

Evidently the villagers had a whip around and collected enough money to pay for Arthur's passage back home in June 1851. Perhaps they had heard enough stories about Queen Victoria's butcher—Arthur's greatest skill in life was telling stories.

Back in Wapping, now aged sixteen, he worked as a butcher with his father for less than two years before heading off, with a consignment of Shetland ponies, to seek his fortune in far Van Diemen's Land. However, he had stayed home long enough to acquire a girlfriend, fifteen-year-old Mary Ann Loder and, no doubt, tell her lots of stories about his life as a Chilean cowboy.

Arthur wrote long, sentimental and quite articulate letters to Mary Ann, which were full of rather rudimentary spellings and signed with a strange symbol—a crescent and stars. He told her Hobart was a dreadful place and he was heading for the goldrushes in Victoria. He seemed very excited about news of the battle between the miners and the army at Eureka Stockade and told her that 'diggers and solgers are fighting like tagers [sic]'.

Arthur seemed always to attract trouble. He went to work for a butcher in Hobart and was charged with selling diseased meat. Arthur was acquitted but his employer took the rap, and Arthur moved on.

He borrowed money from an old family friend, an ex-convict named Euphemia Jury, who was related to one of Arthur's sisters by marriage and was now the wife of a publican in Hobart. Euphemia loaned him £15 to set up a butcher's stall in Hobart's new meat market, and he wrote to her promising to soon repay it, along with some other money he had inadvertently taken by mistake at the same time as he was given the loan.

Failing to repay debts was second only to storytelling in Arthur Orton's list of personal character traits and, after the market stall failed, the money was never repaid.

Instead, Arthur departed the colony sometime in 1856. He'd

arrived in Van Diemen's Land but he actually left Tasmania—the colony having changed its name on 1 January 1856 in order to leave behind the awful history of brutality, genocide and lawlessness associated with the name 'Van Diemen's Land'.

The name lived on, however, in the 'Vandemonian trail', a wellworn migration path that led from Tasmania via Port Albert to Gippsland and on to the goldrushes at Omeo and Kiandra in the Victorian High Country and Beechworth and Mansfield, and thence to the developing grazing districts of the Riverina.

Port Albert, established by the explorer Angus McMillan in 1841, was named after the prince who Queen Victoria had married in 1840, her German first cousin Albert of Saxe-Coburg and Gotha. The port became the gateway to Gippsland, a fertile area developed as a cattle-raising district. Many ex-convicts, sons of convicts, ex-bushrangers, gold seekers and other 'Vandemonians' made their way along this trail to the cattle-grazing country and goldfields of Victoria during the boom years of the 1850s.

It was a crazy decade. In 1850 Melbourne's population was less than 29,000; it was half a million by 1860, a not insignificant increase of 1700 per cent in ten years.

Arthur worked at horse-breaking and made his way from Port Albert to Boisdale, 65 miles away, where he was taken in and employed by the Foster family, who owned cattle properties in the district. Mrs Foster was kind to Arthur and gave him medicine for sore throats and loaned him books. In 1857 he took the lonely job of stockman, living in a hut at the Fosters' highland property 55 miles away, at Dargo.

Here, two odd events occurred that were to be very significant in the later stages of this saga.

Arthur had been living alone for almost a year. Mrs Foster sent him books to read and he apparently gained some romantic notions and ideas from the novels he read.

One day, when his mail and supplies were delivered to the hut, he received a letter with a broken seal. This provoked him to do something a little odd and seemingly over-reactive. As he had no Bible in the hut, he inscribed an oath in a book of Mrs Foster's, which apparently had a cross embossed on the cover as part of the decoration. The book was a romantic novel about class struggle and ambition in Ireland, written in 1829 by Gerald Griffin and titled *The Rivals*.

The inscription was an oath sworn 'on this book although not a Bible' and it stated that Arthur Orton would find the man who broke the seal and punish him 'according to the laws of my countrie [*sic*]'. It was signed and dated 11 March 1858.

The significance of the letter, and the level of anger displayed over it, has never been explained.

A few days after the letter arrived, two guests appeared at the hut and stayed overnight. One was Harry Clare, a prospector believed to have a stash of money hidden somewhere. The other was another Vandemonian named Tom Toke. The men were apparently prospecting together. Toke was later charged with Clare's murder and found in possession of his watch, horse and quite a lot of money. As no body was ever found, Toke was acquitted.

In the meantime, however, Arthur suddenly deserted his post as stockman and returned to Boisdale and went to work at a hotel livery stable in town.

Not only did he 'repay' the Fosters' kindness by leaving their cattle unguarded, he sued them for unpaid wages. When the case came before the court in Sale, he was awarded £10 of the £160 he'd claimed.

It has been suggested that Arthur deserted his post rather than be called as a witness in the murder trial. However, he did not leave the district but worked at various stables, breaking in and trading horses, including one he apparently named Tichborne because it was high-spirited. He also told people his real name was De Costello and his family were Spanish nobility.

In May 1859 he was listed in the Victorian Police Gazette as 'Arthur Ortin', wanted for stealing a chestnut mare. The mare was later found wandering in the bush near Port Albert, not long after the paddlesteamer *Shandon* left for Melbourne.

Three days after the *Shandon* had berthed in Melbourne, a man known only as Arthur, apparently a native of Chile, gained employment with a butcher named McManus at the Reedy Creek goldfields near Kilmore on the Sydney Road. He worked there for six months and then did casual work around the town. In November 1859, after some horses went missing and a reward was posted for information about them, Arthur disappeared. The horses were found nearby.

'Arthur from Chile' was never seen again in Australia, nor was Arthur Orton, or Arthur Ortin.

Part 2: The Wagga Wagga Butcher

Tom Castro, full name Tomas de Castro, was a butcher in Wagga Wagga, where he had set up a shop in a slab hut behind a hotel in 1864.

He had previously worked for quite a while riding the mail run from the village of Boree to Narrandera. This mail run was an extension of the one from Hay, part of a network of mail runs and coach services operated by James Gormly.

Previous to that Tom had worked in Hay as a butcher and delivery man for about six months, before leaving hurriedly after a courtship failed to end in marriage when an unpaid debt evidently forced Tom's departure for Wagga Wagga.

Previous to living in Hay, Tom had been employed at John Burrows' butchery in Deniliquin, for eighteen months. At Deniliquin he boasted of being the heir to a fortune and was in court over an unpaid promissory note for the purchase of a mare named 'Goldie'.

Tom had made his way to Deniliquin from Bendigo, where he had briefly worked as a bullock driver. He had arrived in that town in early January 1860; just a few weeks after 'Arthur from Chile' disappeared from Kilmore.

In Wagga Wagga in April 1863, Tom Castro sold Goldie for £20, after racing her unsuccessfully and having to borrow money to shoe her for a race. He worked in various capacities and spent some time prospecting at Tumut, before establishing his own butchery.

Tom was noted for using a large American-style saddle and boasting about his horsemanship, although poor Goldie had been unshod for some time when he went to race her at Wagga Wagga and needed a good few inches taken off her overgrown hooves. He was laughed at by local horsemen and was several times thrown off while attempting to break in horses. While recovering from one fall, he met Mary Ann Bryant, an illiterate, pregnant servant girl recently arrived in town from Goulburn.

The couple set up home in a windowless hut near Tom's shop in Gurwood Street and, in January 1865, after Mary Ann had given birth to the daughter she was carrying when they met, the couple were married in a private ceremony by a Wesleyan minister. Tom signed 'Tom Castro', son of 'a Chilean merchant', and Mary Ann made a cross.

The business struggled along. Tom loved gambling and drinking and one of his best mates was Dick Slate, a reasonably well-educated native of Hampshire, who disappeared from town after a local farmer had been 'bushwacked'—ambushed, attacked and robbed while drunk—one night and died as a result of the attack. At some point after chatting to Dick, Tom carved the initials 'RCT' on a flask and a tree.

Tom was an avid reader and spent much of his time visiting the local bookshop and reading novels by Captain Marryat, Gerald Griffin and others, many with plots about missing heirs and lost fortunes. His favourite novelist was Mary Elizabeth Braddon, a prolific author of 80 novels including the hugely popular *Lady Audley's Secret*, which involved upper-class secrets, class discrimination, bigamy and adventures on the Australian goldfields.

Braddon's brother, Edward, was a long-serving British officer in India and, odd as it may seem, was very briefly the premier of Tasmania in 1888, having emigrated there after his retirement from the military.

After reading one of Mary Elizabeth Braddon's novels entitled *Aurora Floyd*, Tom Castro paraphrased a passage from the novel in his pocket notebook:

Some men has plenty money and no brains. And some men has plenty brains and no money. Surely men with plenty money and no brains were made for men with plenty brains and no money.

The notebook contained a few other interesting things, as we shall find out later.

During his time as a butcher in Wagga Wagga, Tom was involved in a court case to do with stolen cattle. He had helped a man named William Allen to take the cattle across the Murrumbidgee River and Allen had sold two of them to Tom. Again, someone else took the rap, Allen got five years, and Tom got off.

During the court case he met local solicitor, William Gibbes, who was also involved in acting against Tom on behalf of a client to whom Tom owed money. They discussed the possibility of Tom's bankruptcy and other things. In the course of these conversations, Tom claimed to 'own property in England' which could solve his debt problems.

In August 1865 William Gibbes read notices that were placed in Australian newspapers seeking information about the possible whereabouts of Sir Roger Tichborne, who was believed to have drowned in 1854, but was rumoured to have survived.

He immediately went to see Tom Castro.

Part 3: 'Smallcock' Tichborne

Born in Paris in 1829, Roger Charles Tichborne was brought up in France and his first language was French. His mother, Henriette, was the illegitimate child of a French duke's daughter and an upper-class Englishman who was in Paris under house arrest during the Napoleonic Wars.

Roger's uncle Edward was the Ninth Baron Tichborne but he had no sons and so, when he died in 1853, Roger's father, James, inherited the title and Roger became the heir to the baronetcy and the family fortune, which was a very lucrative inheritance including large land holdings in Hampshire and real estate in London.

Roger's parents' marriage was not a happy one: they lost two daughters in infancy and lived apart after the birth of a second son, Alfred, when Roger was ten.

Roger was not sent to England until he was fifteen and, as a result, spoke English with a strong French accent. French was his native tongue.

His father, despairing of the boy's foppish mannerisms and the way his mother spoiled and protected him, sent him to Stonyhurst Jesuit College for two years and then bought him a commission in the 6th Dragoon Guards Regiment, based in Dublin.

Roger was teased and bullied at school and again while in the Dragoons, and not just for his slight build, narrow chest and French accent. In the Dragoons, his nicknames were 'Froggy' and 'Frenchy' but, more commonly, 'Smallcock'.

Roger had a small and 'inverted' penis, which made him a figure of fun in the officers' quarters and must have made his life hell at school. It was said that he had a penis 'like a horse' but this did not mean what it might mean in today's crude schoolboy parlance. The comparison to a horse was nothing to do with size; it was a reference to the fact that Roger's penis withdrew inside his body, like that of a horse, when not erect.

I'm not telling you this out of mere prurient, salacious interest; it is really important later on—honestly.

You don't have to be a rocket scientist or doctor of veterinary science to figure out that Roger's time in the army was probably not the happiest period of his short life and, after three years, he sold his commission and left for South America.

It was not only the fact that he was rather unfit for the rough and tumble of the army that caused Roger to decide to move on in life; there was another quite surprising reason, given his apparent 'unmanliness' and shortcomings—and this is a big part of the story. There was a failed 'romance' involved.

While on leave from the 6th Dragoons (which would have been as often as possible, one imagines), Roger often stayed with his uncle, Edward Doughty, the Ninth Baron Tichborne, and he evidently developed a very strong relationship of some sort with his cousin, Katherine Doughty.

Katherine's parents liked their nephew but thought the idea of first cousins marrying was not wise, despite the fact that Queen Victoria was at that time happily married to her first cousin and busy producing a series of nine children. The liaison was banned.

The Tichborne family was Roman Catholic (another interesting and relevant element of the story) and first-cousin marriage was frowned upon in the Catholic church, so there was more than one reason for the marriage being disallowed. There is some evidence that Roger asked the family to request a papal dispensation but the idea was also vetoed by his aunt and uncle.

It is believed the cousins kept meeting in secret, although forbidden to do so.

It was soon after this disappointment that Roger sold his commission and headed to South America. He had a lot to put behind him: his obsessive and neurotic mother, the disappointment of a failed romance, a banned marriage, and bullying at school and in the army.

Arriving in Valparaiso, he found letters waiting for him. These informed him that his uncle had passed away and his father was now the Tenth Baron Tichborne, which meant that he was the heir to the title and estates.

Roger had a servant named John Moore with him and spent ten months travelling in South America before paying off his servant when he became ill in Santiago. Roger then travelled on alone. (During this time he may even have visited the village of Melipilla, between Valparaiso and Santiago, which had been the happy home of Arthur Orton until just two years previously.)

Moore wrote to Roger's father complaining about his treatment at the hands of the young 'gentleman' who was, apparently, a lazy and rather inept traveller. Roger had hunted and fished, sent specimens home, and attempted taxidermy on an albatross, somehow managing to impale his eyelid with a fish hook in the process.

After crossing the Andes and arriving in Buenos Aires, Roger took a passage to New York via Jamaica on a ship called the *Bella*. The *Bella* was lost at sea. An empty lifeboat and wreckage was found drifting off the Brazilian coast and Roger was presumed to have perished.

He was officially declared dead in 1855.

His younger brother, Alfred, inherited the Tichborne title in 1862 when their father died. Alfred himself died only four years later, aged just 27, and a son, born four months after Alfred's death, became the Twelfth Baron Tichborne at birth in 1866.

So, the Dowager Lady Tichborne, having never recovered from the loss of her adored older son, Roger, had now lost Alfred as well. She was probably not of the soundest mind to begin with, having grown up as a privileged but illegitimate child, suffered through an unhappy marriage, and borne four children and now lost them all.

Henriette's marriage to James Tichborne had been arranged by her father, Henry Seymour.

Henry Seymour, young James Tichborne and James's father (also a Henry) had all been captured in the Napoleonic War and kept under house arrest in Paris, where Seymour managed to seduce the daughter of the Duke of Bourbon—Henriette was the result.

Henriette was raised in an atmosphere of luxury and privilege, but as a little bastard in a noble French family was somewhat of an embarrassment to all concerned. She was still unmarried at age twenty, so her father suggested a marriage of convenience to James, son of his old mate Henry Tichborne and his fellow internee during the war. James was a rather unattractive chap, unmarried at age 47, and it seemed a good solution to various problems.

Henriette is often portrayed in the Tichborne saga as 'deranged by grief' at Roger's disappearance. What many chroniclers miss is evidence that she was a deranged, neurotic and difficult woman well before her son's disappearance.

While in South America, Roger wrote to the family's business manager, his friend Vincent Gosford, saying how wonderful it was to be away from his mother and commenting:

> I am very sorry my mother's character is so disagreeable, it must make Tichborne a kind of hell for my father and everyone in the house.

In a later letter, giving instructions in the event of his father's death (James Tichborne was past 70 when he became the Tenth

Baronet), Roger told Gosford to ensure his mother was looked after but insisted that she could not live at Tichborne when he became baronet as it would be 'quite impossible' for him to 'put up with her character'.

This seems to me to be a very important element in later developments, often missed by those telling the story. Henriette wasn't just a deluded old lady saddened by grief who wanted her son to be alive. She was a woman who had been, for most of her married life, impossible to live with and was, quite possibly, barking mad. She disliked England and the English, was disliked by the Tichborne family, and was a self-indulgent, spoiled and rather stupid woman. She had disapproved of the friendship between her son and Katherine Doughty and expressed a wish that he should marry a French or Italian girl. On the other hand, Sir Henry had told his son, in a letter, 'If you marry a foreigner, you will regret it the rest of your life.'

The dowager decided to spend considerable amounts of money on advertising for any news of her long-lost and much adored older son. She visited Portsmouth Harbour and handed out coins to sailors as she enquired about any news of survivors of the *Bella* or ships in the vicinity of the wreck. Apparently there was a rumour that some passengers and crew survived the wreck and were picked up by a ship heading to Melbourne.

Whether this rumour was simply a case of maritime Chinese whispers, or some cruel attempt by persons unknown as a result of the dowager's enquiries to get her to spend money in futile investigations, we will never know.

This is the advertisement as it appeared in Australian newspapers:

PERSONS ADVERTISED FOR

A handsome reward will be given to any person who can furnish such information as will discover the fate of ROGER CHARLES TICHBORNE. He sailed from the port of Rio Janeiro [*sic*] on the 20th of April, 1854, in the ship *La Bella*, and has never been heard of since, but a report reached England to the effect that a portion of the crew and passengers of a vessel of that name was picked up by a vessel bound to Australia—Melbourne it is believed—it is not known whether the said ROGER CHARLES TICHBORNE was amongst the drowned or saved. He would at the present time be about thirty-two years of age; is of a delicate constitution, rather tall, with very light brown hair and blue eyes. Mr Tichborne is the son of Sir James Tichborne, Bart., now deceased, and is the heir to all his estates. The advertiser is instructed to state that a MOST LIBERAL REWARD will be given for any information that may definitely point out his fate. Gentlemen in a position to refer to shipping reports may be able to find some record of the saving of the shipwrecked persons from *La Bella*, and a very careful search, if with a successful result, will amply repay anyone who will take the trouble to reinvestigate the matter. All replies to be addressed to Mr Arthur Cubitt, Missing Friends Office, Bridge Street, Sydney, New South Wales.

Now, even the less astute among us will realise that advertising that there is a 'most liberal reward' to be had for 'any' information is likely to attract certain types of individuals to concoct 'information'.

The reply that came, via Mr Cubitt, from the office of solicitor William Gibbes in November 1865 was, however, totally beyond Lady Tichborne's wildest hopes.

Apparently, a client of Mr Gibbes had informed the solicitor that he not only had information concerning Roger Charles Tichborne; he was in fact (you guessed it) Sir Roger Charles Tichborne *himself*!

Part 4: Who Do You Think You Are?

Although it was reported that the claimant was physically much larger than Sir Roger, had a different build, lighter hair, totally differently shaped ears and was an often unwashed, greasy and apparently poorly educated butcher who spoke no French, these discrepancies did not appear to bother Lady Tichborne, who, as we have learned, was rather at odds with the family into which she had married.

For more than a decade after he was officially declared dead, she had obsessively refused to believe Roger had drowned. She was so desperate to find him that she sent for the claimant Tom Castro, who arrived in London in December 1866. But quite a few things occurred in the intervening year.

Tom Castro, William Gibbes and Mr Cubitt made a plan. Castro's identity was to be kept secret until some things were sorted out between them. Gibbes had Castro write a will as Sir Roger Tichborne before he would proceed with advancing him money and taking the claim further.

After an exchange of letters between Cubitt, Gibbes and the Dowager Lady Tichborne, the reward of £250 was claimed and various increasingly larger amounts of money were forthcoming for the claimant's travel and living expenses from Wagga Wagga to Goulburn, then on to Sydney and finally by ship to London.

Castro and his wife, along with her daughter, Annie, and their new daughter, Mary Agnes Theresa, travelled to Goulburn and stayed with Mary Ann's family. There they remarried in a Catholic church with Castro signing as 'Roger Charles Tichborne'. Mary Ann again used the cross.

In the meantime, a strange coincidence became apparent: two ex-Tichborne employees were living in Sydney. One was an Irish gardener named Guilfoyle, who met the claimant and seemed to accept his *bona fides*. The other was a much more important character in the plot, a gentleman of West Indian descent, Andrew Bogle, who had served the Doughty family for many years and was living on a pension of £50 a year, provided by Lady Doughty.

Bogle, who had a certain affection for Roger Tichborne as a lad and admitted that he had long hoped that he had survived, was convinced almost immediately that the claimant was Sir Roger. When they met, the claimant asked, 'Is that you, Bogle?'

Now, it may occur to the more cynical of you that a well-dressed black man appearing in the claimant's hotel in Sydney might be rather obviously assumed to be the man in question. Bogle, however, was chuffed and delighted to be recognised and, apparently, replied in the affirmative, adding, 'How stout you've got!'

The colony was abuzz with the news that a long-lost nobleman was among them and, with the typical sycophantic vigour of the times in the Australian colonies, the claimant was accepted as genuine almost without question and fawned over and doted upon.

This gave him, and his 'team'—consisting of the solicitor Gibbes, Bogle and others—the chance to begin raising money and organising financial backing in order that the claimant could travel to Britain and claim his inheritance.

Basically, it worked like this: credit, loans and bills for expenses were all to be paid back in full when the claimant received the vast estates and wealth that he obviously seemed to deserve. No one in Sydney appeared to have had the slightest doubt that this would happen.

The claimant established a pattern that would remain as his template for the entire period of his 'claim': the best food, wine and alcohol, cigars, accommodation, clothing and transport—all on credit.

In Sydney certain bankers and wealthy 'friends' were enticed into 'investing' in the venture. Throughout the entire process the claimant's team used this practice. Later in the story there were actually 'Tichborne Bonds' that sold in the hundreds of thousands. They were to be redeemable, with a dividend, when the title was finally claimed.

In the next stage of the claim, part of the team left Sydney via Auckland and Panama on a ship called the *Rakia*. They consisted of the Castro family minus daughter Annie, Bogle and his son (who would work for the claimant for years and never be paid), a secretary with the wonderful name of Truth Butts, and a nurse-maid for Theresa, named Rosina McArthur.

A passenger who travelled on the ship remembered later that a coarse fellow who spoke like a Cockney and dropped his aitches spent the journey telling everyone he was returning home to claim his estates.

The ship arrived in London on Christmas Day and Bogle took care of arrangements, accommodation and introductions, etc. Soon, with Bogle's help, the claimant was meeting family acquaintances and others who had known Sir Roger. He visited the Tichborne estates in Hampshire and amazingly convinced some he met of the truth of his claim and acquired some powerful supporters, including the Tichborne family's former solicitor, Edward Hopkins, who became an ally.

Through his contact with the Tichborne family, the claimant was able to thoroughly research Sir Roger's life and strengthen his claim.

Several weeks later, having secured the aid of a London solicitor, John Holmes, and delayed the inevitable as long as possible, which annoyed the Dowager Lady Tichborne no end, the claimant travelled to France to meet her.

The meeting was held in a darkened room, as the claimant was either feigning illness or was so nervous that he was genuinely ill.

This was the most important moment of the entire marathon drama.

The bereaved mother claimed to recognise her son in the darkened room and, after her acceptance, settled him and his family in England with a handsome allowance. She wrote to her daughter-in-law:

> I have fully recognised him—as it is really him—and I cannot conceive those who knew him very well will not recognise him.

This was not what her daughter-in-law Theresa wished to hear. It meant the end of the £1000 a year she received as mother of the Twelfth Baronet, Alfred's son Henry, who had been born four months after his father's death.

Holmes had now taken over as the 'ringmaster' of the proceedings. He had Lady Tichborne sign a document at the British Embassy acknowledging the claimant as her son Roger. The news was spread all over the world and Lady Tichborne accompanied the team back to London.

Roger's old tutor in Paris, Father Chatillon, was brave enough to go against the wealthy old woman's wishes and declared the claimant was an imposter.

Other members of the Tichborne family were also not convinced. Lady Doughty, wife of Edward and Roger's aunt, had declared the claimant an imposter as soon as she had been shown the first photograph to arrive from Australia. Lady Tichborne, of course, had looked at the same photo and declared it was Roger.

Thanks to detectives the family had sent to follow the claimant, and investigate him in Australia, they came to believe that Tom Castro from Wagga Wagga was, in fact, London-born Arthur Orton.

Foolishly, the claimant even visited Wapping as soon as he arrived back in London, on Boxing Day 1866, and made enquiries about Orton's family and Mary Ann Loder at the local pub, where the owner had commented on his likeness to Orton's father and asked if he was Arthur Orton. The claimant said he wasn't but had known Orton in Australia and had a letter for Mary Ann.

However, it seems that claiming to be a baronet, and acting like one by spending money, is enough to make many people accept that you are one. The claimant travelled in an expensive carriage and ate and drank only the best food and wine and smoked the best cigars. He quickly gathered a coterie of sycophantic supporters who revelled in his generosity. He dined often with his supporters and eventually weighed almost 27 stone (170 kilograms).

Those who opposed his claim to be Sir Roger mostly had no financial interest in it being true. Obviously, the Tichborne family invested heavily in disproving the claim, eventually spending about £100,000 to fight it.

Katherine Doughty, now Lady Radcliffe and mother of a large family, never believed the claim. She met the claimant twice in very guarded and chaperoned situations. On the second occasion, she cleverly took an aunt and a female cousin, wearing veils, to meet the claimant.

The real Sir Roger should have known them by their voices and general demeanour and from his childhood memories. The claimant failed to identify them and panicked, saying, 'Too many veils!'

When the ladies attempted to converse in French, Sir Roger's native tongue, about shared experiences, the claimant again panicked and cried out, '*Non, non!*'

The ladies then rose, and Sir Roger's cousin, Carolyn Nangle, terminated the brief visit with the words, 'Goodbye, Mr Castro!'

In July 1867, the illiterate Mary Ann Castro, now styling herself as 'Lady Tichborne', gave birth to a boy. This potential heir to the title was named Roger Charles Doughty ... Tichborne, of course.

On 31 July the first steps in the legal battle were taken. The claimant's team made a claim in Chancery, the equity court, to freeze the money being collected from rents on Tichborne estates and other sources of income until the rightful title could be determined.

It was now all or nothing. There could only be one winner. If the claimant won, the Tichborne estates were entirely his.

The Tichborne family hired a famous detective.

As Sherlock Holmes was busy being a fictional character, they turned to Jack Whicher, 'the prince of detectives', and one of the founders of Scotland Yard, who had successfully solved several famous puzzling cases.

Whicher soon uncovered evidence of the claimant's Boxing Day visit to Wapping, along with evidence that he had contacted the Orton family and was paying them to deny that he was Arthur.

Seven months after the Chancery lodgement, the saga took a sudden turn. Just before noon on 12 March 1868, Lady Henriette Tichborne was found dead by a servant; she had been writing a letter to one of the claimant's supporters.

At the inquest the claimant demanded an inquiry into possible 'foul play' and claimed he knew that a servant had been offered £1000 to 'get rid of him'.

The gentry were appalled that this vulgar upstart, supported by a now-deceased madwoman, should intrude into the grief and affairs of a noble family. They were further appalled at the funeral when the claimant and the ex–family servant Bogle displaced Henriette's two half-brothers, Alfred Seymour and Lord Arundell, as chief mourners.

The *Pall Mall Gazette* reported that these two respected members of the upper class had been:

> … extruded by the Australian claimant, a large and corpulent man, supported by a Jamaican negro.

One of the most fascinating elements of the Tichborne affair, and one that is hard for modern readers to understand, is that it quickly escalated into a contest that was really nothing to do with the claimant's true identity.

It was now class warfare, with xenophobic and racist overtones on one side and claims of unfair privilege and elitist snobbery on the other!

The established nobility, and those who believed in gentility and tradition, were shocked that a vulgar colonial could assume to be as good as, or one of, the British upper class. The Tichbornes were one of the oldest families in Britain.

On the other hand, many working-class people, along with some liberal-thinking, anti-establishment figures and newspapermen, liked the idea of a common man taking on the privileged snobs.

Why shouldn't a normal bloke—a butcher who didn't speak proper—not have a lovely carriage and drink champagne and smoke cigars?

As the claimant's team grew and grew, more and more people were relying on the inheritance to eventually be paid, to receive their invested money back, or to reap some reward for their involvement.

The whole affair was spinning out of control as the newspapers devoted thousands of columns of print to reporting the smallest details. The public took sides, as people do in such cases.

Australians struggling to understand how this happened in Victorian England might relate it to the way modern sensational cases, such as those of Lindy Chamberlain and Schapelle Corby, polarised the nation and were grist to the mill of the media, rumour mongers, cartoonists, comedians, social philosophers, social reformers and politicians.

Imagine something a thousand times more sensational and popular—and you have the 'Tichborne Affair'.

There were plays and pantomimes about the case, souvenir dolls, posters, cards, handkerchiefs, books, cartoons. The claimant was bigger news and far more 'popular' as a public figure than the royal family. Music hall songs and skits about him were written and performed all across Britain and a comic miniature version of him became one of the greatest variety acts of all time.

Meanwhile, the legal pantomime continued, commissions of inquiry were established by Chancery in South America and Australia, and both sides had detectives and investigators active on those continents.

The claimant finally agreed to go to South America and be part of the investigations. He sailed to Argentina via Portugal and stayed many weeks in Buenos Aires, but declined to travel overland to Chile for fear of bandits. This proved to be a very wise decision. Bandits attacked the coach he had been booked to travel on and all on board were murdered.

In Buenos Aires the claimant 'hung out' with legendary adventurer and linguist Richard Burton, drinking heavily with the famous writer and a young diplomat named Blunt.

Blunt, attached to the British consulate, had been at school with Sir Roger's younger brother, Alfred, who had briefly been the Eleventh Baronet before drinking himself to an early death. In letters home Blunt accepted that the claimant bore a resemblance to Alfred.

The claimant's reluctance to travel to Chile and face the commission disgusted some of his most powerful supporters, and several, including his solicitor John Holmes, changed their minds and declared the claimant to be a fraud.

Back in Britain people were becoming impatient. The claimant's staunch supporter Edward Hopkins had died and, with Dowager

Tichborne also gone and the commissions of inquiry gathering evidence, things were looking grim.

There was no stopping the momentum now; the claimant was forced to take his claim to court.

Part 5: *Tichborne v. Lushington*

The first trial lasted almost a year, from 11 May 1871 to 5 March 1872. *Tichborne v. Lushington* was a civil trial to establish the claimant's right to the Tichborne inheritance. The estate had been leased to Colonel Lushington, who had allowed the claimant to visit and was merely the 'name' taken to court as he had legal ownership of the estate at the time. If the claimant's right to the estate could be established, his identity would be proven.

Nearly one hundred people spoke in the claimant's defence; most of them by now had a pecuniary interest in proving that the claimant was Sir Roger Tichborne.

The holes in his story soon became obvious, particularly his inability to speak French.

Evidence against the claimant was comprehensive. The court cases have been documented at length in various books and accounts over the years, ranging from those written by popular authors such as Bram Stoker (author of *Dracula*) and Mark Twain, to later recent excellent books by Australians Robyn Annear and Paul Terry.

Let me summarise a few salient pieces of evidence:

- The claimant was acknowledged by Lady Tichborne and he seemed to be able to recall fragments of information from the personal life of Roger Tichborne. Mr Ballantine, appearing for the claimant, described the dowager as:

  . . . an extremely beautiful woman of strong good sense, a perfect woman of the world and perfectly able to form a sound judgement.

  Sir Roger's former servant, John Moore, bewildered by the claimant's ability to recall incidents from Moore's time with Sir Roger in South America, said he now believed he was Sir Roger.

This was countered by the defence's suggestions that the claimant had been 'coached' and fed information and that Lady Tichborne was far from being a person 'of sound judgement'.

John Moore somewhat undermined Ballantine's claim that the dowager was of sound mind when he agreed that he had once said of her:

She would believe anything ... if they sent over an Egyptian mummy and ticketed it 'Roger Titchborne' [sic] she would acknowledge it as her son.

- The claimant had been physically and psychologically altered by his ordeal at sea, hence, expert witnesses claimed, his ears had changed shape, he had forgotten his native tongue and his personality had been altered by his low and impoverished later life. The defence argued that this was nonsense.
- The claimant had written a will in Wagga Wagga as Sir Roger Tichborne, in which he bequeathed property that the family had never owned and put his mother's name as Hannah Frances—right initials, wrong names.

The claimant countered that he knew the will would be deemed false, but when the solicitor William Gibbes would not forward him any money or help in the case until he made a will, he decided to make one that would not stand up to scrutiny.

Defence council then asked if this was the same Gibbes the claimant had described in letters to Lady Tichborne as 'the best friend I have in Australia'.

The claimant replied that he was not attempting to defraud Gibbes but wrote the will knowing it to be untrue.

- A detective sent to Australia by the Tichborne family returned with a pocket notebook once owned by Tom Castro. It contained the paraphrased quote from the novel previously mentioned, *Aurora Floyd* by Mary Elizabeth Braddon; various attempts at signing Sir Roger Tichborne's name in different ways and with different spellings; the name and address of Mary Ann Loder in Wapping; and the 'stars and crescent' symbol used by Arthur Orton years before in letters to Mary Ann Loder. It also contained the note:

I, Thomas Castro do hereby certify that my name is not Thomas Castro at all. Therefore, those that say it don't know anythink [*sic*] about it—R.T.C.

The only argument offered against the notebook was that there appeared to be two different types of handwriting used. It was proposed that the claimant might have owned the book after Arthur Orton and they were two separate men. (This led to salacious speculation that either Orton, or Castro, or Roger Tichborne had been murdered in Australia by either Roger Tichborne, or Tom Castro, or Arthur Orton ... or somebody else!)

- The claimant finally swore under oath that a mysterious letter, left by Roger with the family's solicitor and estate manager in 1852, contained instructions to be followed in the event of Katherine Doughty being pregnant.

In other words, the claimant said he had 'deflowered' his cousin. When asked if he meant he had seduced his cousin, he replied, 'I most solemnly swear to my God I did.'

Lady Radcliffe (née Katherine Doughty) was later called as a witness and, when asked if there was any truth to the claimant's evidence, she replied, 'Certainly not. Not one single word.'

This was the absolute hiatus of the class warfare element of the case. Either the claimant had impugned the honour of a titled, respected married lady and proved himself to be no gentleman at all, or the upper classes were no better than the common, immoral working-class folk, fornicating outside of wedlock and then lying to protect their privilege!

It was a no-win for the claimant. Either way, he was certainly no 'gentleman'.

The support for the claimant disappeared in certain quarters but was polarised even more in the press and with the public.

- Finally, Sir Roger had been tattooed as a youth. The claimant had no tattoos.

In March 1872 the jury informed the judge they had heard enough—and they found against the claimant.

The establishment came down hard and fast on the claimant, who was arrested the same day on charges of perjury. Deeply in debt—despite thousands of bonds being sold at £65 each to support his case, loans and gifts of money, as well as that provided by the late Lady Tichborne—he did not have the bail money, which was set at a staggering £10,000.

The claimant's trail of debt—promised unpaid wages to servants, legal bills, hotel bills, extended credit, etc.—led all the way back to Wagga Wagga. Virtually nothing had been paid for since the claim began.

From a cell in Newgate Prison, the claimant appealed to 'every British soul who is inspired by a love of justice and fair play and who is willing to defend the weak against the strong' to donate money for his bail.

Amazing as it may seem, the money was raised. Half was donated by a member of parliament and staunch 'claimant supporter', Guildford Onslow. The affair was now a political *cause célèbre*.

The resultant perjury trial, *Regina v. Castro*, was the longest in British history until 1996.

Part 6: *Regina v. Castro*

Defending 'Tom Castro', who continued to be known as 'Sir Roger' by most of Britain, was an interesting fellow, Dr Edward Kenealy, who had an axe to grind. He hated Catholics and campaigned endlessly against Roman Catholicism.

The Tichborne family were famously Roman Catholic—perhaps the wealthiest and oldest Catholic family in Britain. One of the family had been hung, drawn and quartered for his role in the religiously inspired plot against Elizabeth I.

Kenealy's opening address lasted for a month.

While on bail, the claimant attended massive rallies in his support and gave demonstrations of pigeon shooting, at which he was rather good. A typical event would see him compete against the local pigeon-shooting champion, then attend a rally at which various public figures and local dignitaries gave speeches in favour of his claim.

The court held commissions of inquiry in various towns in Australia and South America and witnesses came from around the globe to testify. Witness after witness swore that the claimant was Arthur Orton, including Mary Ann Loder and others from Wapping, the wife of Tomas de Castro from Melipilla, Euphemia Jury from Hobart, and the now-widowed and remarried ex–Mrs Foster from Boisdale (who added that there was no 'Tom Castro' in the employ of the Fosters, ever—just Arthur Orton).

The old evidence was trawled over. Lady Katherine Radcliffe testified, when asked about the claim of seduction, that 'Roger would never have thought of such a thing'.

Vincent Gosford, the Tichborne estate manager, said the letter left by Roger in 1852, and written in his presence, contained matters relating to property and a sworn promise by Roger to build a church should he be allowed to marry Katherine upon his return from South America, but nothing more.

In a desperate attempt to prove the case for the defence, Kenealy used two pieces of sensational so-called 'evidence'. He produced a witness who claimed he had been on the ship *Osprey*, which rescued Sir Roger, and he asked the claimant to show the jury his penis.

Kenealy claimed that the defendant had an inverted penis, which was a rare enough deformity to prove he was Sir Roger 'Smallcock' Tichborne.

He made this claim after the court had been cleared of women and children, and the jury (all male in those days, of course) dutifully trooped into the barristers' robing room, where the claimant dropped his daks and gave them a good look.

The defendant's penis did, indeed, appear to be 'inverted'. Whether this proved that he was Sir Roger, or was merely due to the fact that he weighed more than 26 stone and the presence of a stomach that size in any male causes the penis to disappear, we will never know. (Courtesy of my good friend 'Dr Google' I am informed that, 'In some cases, abdominal fat all but buries the penis', according to Ronald Tamler, MD, PhD, co-director of the Men's Health Program at Mount Sinai Hospital in New York City.) A doctor who Kenealy claimed would testify that the claimant had the same condition declined to appear for the defence.

The second piece of evidence involved a wait for a seafaring witness to arrive 'from overseas'. The claimant took advantage of the break to continue his fund-raising tour, talking about his adventures in South America and Australia to huge and enthusiastic sell-out audiences in theatres around the country.

The seafaring witness was a certain 'Jean Luie', steward of the *Osprey*, who told a story about a deranged Englishman saved from a drifting lifeboat.

All was going well for the defence until, after two adjournments, the prosecution produced a witness named Mrs Lundgren. She testified that 'Jean Luie' was, in fact, her husband, Carl, a convicted liar, thief and con-artist now bigamously married to another woman and recently released from prison. He had never been on a ship called the *Osprey*.

With his star witness back in prison on multiple charges of bigamy and perjury, Kenealy's case collapsed.

During the course of the case, Kenealy had tried a number of approaches. At one point he had claimed his client was 'stupid but genuine'. The argument was that Roger had been a depraved, drunken, low-life imbecile—and the claimant was too! He hinted at insanity and possibly venereal disease.

Another ploy was to attempt to prove that another English-born butcher working in Tumut was actually Arthur Orton. This character, William Cresswell, was an excellent cricketer who had gone mad in Tumut and threatened an auctioneer with a knife after writing a crazy letter about some grievance and insisting the auctioneer sign it. Cresswell then ran naked down the main street. He was an inmate of Parramatta Insane Asylum at the time of the trial and may well have been from Wapping—or anywhere else. Not even his Australian wife knew where in England he was from.

All Kenealy's attempts and approaches had failed.

The claimant was convicted and became simply 'Arthur Orton', sentenced to two terms of the maximum penalty of seven years for perjury.

Part 7: Big Tich

The case was over but the Tichborne phenomenon would continue for another 30 years.

The sentence of two maximum terms, to be served separately, not concurrently, was seen by many as the establishment taking revenge on an upstart, vulgar butcher who dared to assume he was worthy of privilege equal to his betters.

Edward Kenealy started a newspaper, *The Englishman*, which attacked the judges and those he saw as the political enemies of the claimant. The attacks led to him being struck off as a barrister in 1874.

In 1875 Kenealy was elected to parliament at a by-election in the working-class seat of Stoke-on-Trent. Prime Minister Benjamin Disraeli had to change parliamentary procedure when Kenealy took his seat in the Commons, as no other member would officially 'introduce him'.

Kenealy tried to have the Tichborne case examined by a royal commission and moved a motion to that effect. The vote was lost 433 to 3. Kenealy then lost his seat at the general election in 1880 and died the following year.

Arthur Orton served ten years in prison, getting out in 1884.

He immediately went back on the theatre circuit, aided by his eldest daughter, Mary Agnes Theresa, who had always been known as Theresa but was now calling herself Agnes. She had been well educated at boarding school at the expense of the claimant's supporters and was a capable young woman who spoke several languages.

The act, billed as 'The Greatest Attraction in Europe', consisted of the claimant telling his story with photos to prove he was Sir Roger Tichborne, describing his life in prison and attacking those who had 'cheated' him out of his 'rightful' inheritance. At first, business was good and support for his cause was rekindled; there were more pigeon-shooting matches with prize money and, for a time, a wave of public curiosity brought in the money.

Gradually 'Sir Roger' became a curiosity rather than a working-class *cause célèbre*. He made plans to stand for parliament in Kenealy's old seat but could not raise the £100 deposit required.

He began touring with a travelling show called 'Captain Trans-field's Circus'. At first crowds were good but slowly interest waned and a tour of Ireland was cancelled. To make matters worse, an eleven-year-old sensation known as 'Young Nimrod' started beating the claimant, and everybody else, at pigeon shooting.

Around this time the claimant met popular music hall performer 'Nellie Rosamund', a male impersonator, dancer and singer of witty songs whose real name was Rosina Enevers. The two became soulmates and lovers and toured together. Nellie's big hit was a song poking fun at the gentry, 'The La-di-dah Brigade', which fitted in well with Sir Roger's 'schtick'.

Rosina became pregnant and Agnes quit in disgust at her father's 'immorality'.

The couple visited New York in 1886 and a daughter was born there, only to die from cholera three weeks later. The death certificate listed her parents as Sir Roger and Lady Tichborne. They would go on to have four more children, all of whom died in infancy—at least one, and possibly all three, of congenital syphilis.

Of course, they could not have been legally married as the claimant had never divorced Mary Ann Castro, who had continued to call herself Lady Tichborne while the claimant was in prison. During that time she gave birth to a further four children to various fathers, adding to the four she'd produced with the claimant and the one she'd been carrying when they first met, Annie, who had been left behind in Goulburn.

A court had legally relieved the claimant of any responsibility for his wife when presented with the evidence of her adultery and drunkenness. He had attempted to care for her but she continually pawned whatever was provided for her. She ended her life in the workhouse.

The other three children from the claimant's marriage to Mary Ann changed their names and disappeared from the story. Only Agnes stayed loyal and claimed her father was Sir Roger Tichborne until her death in 1926.

The claimant and Rosina returned to London in 1871. They unsuccessfully ran a tobacconist shop for a while, and then 'Sir Roger' appeared in pubs as a curiosity. They lived together in poverty until 1895, when a series titled 'The Claimant's Confession' appeared in several issues of the magazine *People*.

In a sworn affidavit, the claimant admitted he was Arthur Orton from Wapping and told how he and friend Dick Slate and solicitor William Gibbes had concocted the fraud in Wagga Wagga, based on Slate's knowledge of the Hampshire Tichbornes and the advertisement seeking information about Sir Roger.

He further claimed his intention was to get as much money as possible in advance and desert his wife once the ship reached Panama. This fits in perfectly with a claim by the girl hired as Theresa's nursemaid for the voyage, oddly also named Rosina (McArthur), that the claimant had unsuccessfully attempted to seduce her and get her to run off with him when the ship reached South America.

The articles went on to say that it all changed when he reached Sydney only to find that Guilfoyle and Bogle amazingly accepted him as Sir Roger. After that, the deception took on a life of its own and he went along for the ride.

The confession was made for payment and the claimant soon withdrew the confession and returned to the claim that he was Sir Roger.

Having wasted away in poverty to a mere 18 stone (115 kilograms), the claimant died of heart failure, in bed beside Rosina, at about 5 a.m. very appropriately on April Fool's Day 1898.

Rosina reported his name to the police surgeon who attended as 'Sir Roger Tichborne' and his death certificate and coffin plate both bore that name.

Rosina later claimed in *The Standard* that they had been promised £3000 for the confession and only paid £400. She maintained it was a false confession.

The *London Daily Mail* reported, tongue-in-cheek:

> The Judges of the High Court were two years in determining that the living Tichborne was Orton. The Registrar of Births and Deaths determined in two minutes that the dead Orton was Tichborne.

There are many odd things about the Tichborne case that have never been satisfactorily explained and will probably never be. I find it weird, for example, that the claimant was attracted to two different women called Rosina and two women called Mary Ann.

One odd consequence of the case is that the claimant inadvertently gave a commonly used word to our vernacular. There was a very popular comedian and dancer on the music hall circuit during the late 19th and early 20th centuries who was famous for his hilarious acrobatic big-boot dance, in which he wore 28-inch (71-centimetre) shoes although he was only 4 feet 6 inches (137 centimetres) tall.

As he resembled a miniature Tichborne claimant, he dressed like the claimant and was known as 'Little Tich'—the term became popular and is still used today to describe anything, or anyone, small, as in 'a titchy little thing' or 'he's just a little titch'. It is believed he actually performed on the same bill as the claimant several times.

In his confession, the claimant declared:

> The story really built itself ... and in that way it grew so large that I really could not get out of it.

He never did 'get out of it'; he eventually got lost in it.

Some reports of the story erroneously say that the claimant's 'tombstone' was inscribed 'Sir Roger Charles Doughty Tichborne'. This is quite wrong. The cemetery records show that name for a person buried in a pauper's grave. It's the name Rosina gave the police surgeon when the claimant died and thus was the name under which he was buried and it was, apparently, inscribed on the coffin.

There was no tombstone.

If there had been one, the most appropriate inscription I can think of would have been simply, 'Goodbye, Mr Castro'.

The Tichborne Dole continues to this day.

Footnote: Although clay 'pigeons' (clay discs thrown by hand or propelled by a sprung trap) had been used since the early 19th century in shooting contests, 'live' pigeon shooting, where birds were released from cages or thrown up by hand, remained popular until the 1900s and this was the sport at which the claimant excelled. At the first modern Olympics in 1896 clay targets were used but at the second, in Paris in 1900, live birds were used and over 300 were killed. In 1904 at St Louis the Olympic shotgun event switched back to clay pigeons.

THE BATTLER

The romantic concept of the 'swaggie' or 'sundowner' is an iconic part of Australian mythology and one of the most popular images used to identify our nationality. Tramping along with corks around his hat and a swag on his back, he is seen as some sort of stoic pioneer. He is also the hero in our national song, 'Waltzing Matilda'.

There is, however, another side to the character of the swaggie— a less romantic one. That version is of a man avoiding work at all costs and using the notion of 'tramping the bush in search of work' as a clever cover as he cons his way from station to station, living on handouts from sympathetic, hard-working country folk, arriving at 'sundown' to avoid having to work for his supper and a place to doss for the night.

This is the notion behind the amusing story told here in rhyme by that master of character writing, C.J. Dennis. 'Den' was the creator of the 'Sentimental Bloke' and many other wonderful characters in the 3000 poems and sketches he wrote while contributing a piece a day to the *Herald Sun* newspaper in Melbourne, from 1922 until his death in 1938.

The following story is told from the point of view of the gullible station owner.

The Battler

C.J. Dennis ('Den')

> 'Could you give me a bite to eat?' said he,
> As he tarried by my back door.

And I thought of the dull, lean days that be
As I glanced at the clothes he wore:
Patched in places, and worn and old,
Yet cosy enough to fend the cold.
And I caught the glint of his gay blue eye,
Sure sign of his slogan: 'Never say die'.

'Could you spare me a trifle to eat?' said he;
'For it's tough on a man these days.'
Then, somehow or other it seemed to me,
Some trick of his voice, or ways,
Stirred half lost thought. But I let it go,
As he said that his tea was 'pretty low':
And his sugar-bag, too, was 'well-nigh out'.
'Tho' I'd hate', he added, 'to put you about.'

'Could you do with a couple of chops?' said I.
'Some eggs and a ration of bread?'
'Why, mister, that would be comin' it high!
It's a feed for a king!' he said.
So with this, and a trifle of sugar and tea,
Tucked under his arm: 'Thanks, boss', said he.
'It's hard on the roads when yer out of a job ...
D'yeh think yeh'd be missin' a couple o' bob?'

'One minute!' I bade him, as memory stirred.
'Have I ever seen you before?'
'Seen me?' said he. 'Why, upon my word!
For the half o' my life or more,
I been comin' round nigh every year.
An' I never yet drawed a blank—not 'ere.
An' I'll say this for yeh: you ain't too bad
As a regular customer—best I've 'ad.'

SECTION TWO:
LARGER THAN
LIFE

BOUND FOR BOTANY BAY

The Backstory

> 'It ain't leaving old England we cares about,
> Or cos we mis-spelled what we knows,
> It's because all us light-fingered gentry
> Hops around with a log on our toes.'
>
> *Bound For Botany Bay*, from the music hall show
> *Little Jack Shepherd* 1885, described at the time as
> an 'Old Air' arranged for the show
> by Wilhelm Lutz

Recently, Bill Gates, in praising the book *The Better Angels of Our Nature*, by Canadian psychologist Steven Pinker, theorised that '… the world is getting better. Sounds crazy, but it's true. This is the most peaceful time in human history.'

He is probably right, if we leave aside warfare and terrorism. *Civil* unrest and crime were far more prevalent in the past, especially in most so-called 'civilised' parts of the world, than they are today.

In the social upheaval that came with the Industrial Revolution, British cities grew and crime increased. The *Enclosure Act* of 1773 took away the right of access to farmland for common people, who either starved or moved to the cities. The ports of Britain became crammed with 'hulks'—unseaworthy vessels used as makeshift prisons. The loss of the American colonies in 1776 made matters worse, as transportation across the Atlantic was no longer an option.

Throughout the 18th century, approximately 50,000 British criminals were transported to the American colonies, mostly to Maryland and Virginia, where they were auctioned to plantation owners as indentured workers to work in the fields beside African slaves. While the African slave trade provided approximately 47 per cent of the migration to the American colonies in the 18th century, the transportation of convicted criminals contributed a not-insubstantial 9 per cent of migrants to America.

The factors discussed above led to severe laws and punishments for what would seem to us today petty crimes, or not crimes at all. The rationale was to maintain some social stability and deter the less fortunate from turning to crime. There were 222 crimes punishable by death in Britain in 1800, and over 10,300 criminals were 'hanged by the neck until dead' between 1791 and 1892, just in England and Wales.

Capital crimes included impersonating a Chelsea Pensioner, begging without a licence, damaging Westminster Bridge, being out at night with a blackened face, robbing a house of goods worth more than 40 shillings, shoplifting goods worth more than 5 shillings, forgery, sodomy, poaching game, damaging a forest, stealing a letter, returning from transportation, living with Gypsies for more than a month, and impersonating an Egyptian. These last two were actually laws designed to persecute Gypsies and prevent others from consorting with them and forming 'outlaw' gangs.

This was a time when cruelty and capital punishment were considered to be 'necessary' in the justice system. It is also fair to say that the upper and middle classes were fearful of the working-class masses. There was a certain admiration among the poor for criminals like highwaymen and colourful characters like pickpocket George Barrington. They were often made into heroes in the newspapers, ballads and broadsheets of the day. When highwayman John Rann was found not guilty of theft in London in 1774, he was mobbed by a crowd of adoring fans outside the court.

Those condemned to die were hanged in public until 1868 and hangings were popular events. Prisoners were paraded in carts to the gallows and hanged in batches of up to twenty at a time. Crowds of many thousands watched the executions. When the famous highwayman Jack Sheppard was hanged in 1724, after four escapes from prison, 200,000 people were reputed to have watched his execution.

In general it is true that cities were quite unsafe places to live in Britain in the 18th and even the 19th centuries, and attitudes towards punishment and cruelty were far different from today's 'politically correct' ideas about fairness and individual rights and dignity. Until 1835, when it was banned by law, the practice of 'gibbeting'—leaving the bodies of those executed to hang in chains after death—was a common practice and was thought to deter others from crime. The body of Francis Morgan was left hanging in chains on a gibbet on top of Pinchgut Island, a tall rock in Sydney Harbour that was later levelled to make Fort Denison. His skeleton was still greeting new arrivals as they sailed into Sydney Cove four years later.

Francis Morgan is, incidentally, one of my favourite convict murderers. He was transported in 1793 and was sentenced to death for the bashing murder of Simon Raven on Sydney's north shore in 1796. Until 1796 hangings had taken place at a spot near the shore in the Rocks area and at Parramatta. Governor Hunter thought a tall rock in the harbour was a more suitable location and Francis Morgan was the first to test the theory. When asked if he wanted to confess or pray for forgiveness, he evidently replied that death was a morbid subject and he had no desire to confess his sins. 'The only thing worth mentioning,' he is reputed to have commented, 'is what a superb view of the harbour I have from up here. I am sure there are no waters in the world that compare to it for beauty.' He was right.

In 1787, when the First Fleet set sail, general attitudes to human rights and justice were very different to those we hold today. Slavery was still legal, free men could be 'pressganged' (i.e. kidnapped) and made to serve in the Royal Navy, and flogging sailors was deemed an essential part of running a sailing ship.

Half of the 120,000 men serving in Royal Navy at the Battle of Trafalgar in 1805 had been 'impressed' into the navy and flogging sailors with the 'cat-o-nine-tails' was legal until the 1860s. Caning or birching sailors was still legal in the Royal Navy in World War II. These punishments were decided 'ad hoc' by officers—there were no trials or procedures necessary. Times were tough.

Things didn't get any better after the Napoleonic Wars ended in 1815 either; they became worse. There was a depression in Europe after the wars and returning soldiers had no jobs or welfare system to help them, just the workhouse. Army pensions were restricted to those over 65 with twenty years' service, or to permanent army men severely wounded.

The vast majority of soldiers and sailors returning from fighting for Britain on the Continent had no pensions and no jobs, and could be executed for begging. The Corn Laws, passed to protect British farmers from foreign competition in 1819, made bread prices soar and crime increase. Laws that benefitted land owners had harsh effects on those who had little and lived in poverty. As crime increased the legal recourse of transportation to 'Botany Bay', as New South Wales was commonly called in Britain, was more necessary than ever.

There were, of course, many thousands of genuinely wicked people among the 162,000 felons transported on 806 ships to the Australian colonies from 1787 to 1868. No doubt there were also many who were innocent, or simply victims of class warfare and social change.

Probably quite a few of the 162,000—perhaps a few thousand—were what we might call 'con artists', and I'd like to introduce you to my three favourite, larger than life, convict con men.

The Story

> 'One of the many lessons that one learns in prison is that things are what they are and will be what they will be.'
>
> Oscar Wilde

Thomas Barrett, James Daley and that wonderful artist Joseph Lycett are three of the memorable characters who set the scene for our continuing history of fraud, forgery and lies. Their sad lives demonstrate that, for the convicted felons who inhabit our history, and the pages of this book, 'things are what they are and will be what they will be'.

Thomas Barrett was a petty thief, amateur engraver and counterfeiter. In September 1782, when he was in his early twenties, he was apprehended running from the house of a lady named Ann Milton in London and found to have in his possession a silver watch and other items valued at 72 shillings. He was sentenced to death at the Old Bailey on 11 September and the sentence was immediately commuted to transportation for life to the American colonies.

Barrett, along with 178 other convicted felons, left the port of Dover aboard the transport *Mercury* in March 1784, bound for the colony of Georgia. After just a few days' sailing, however, Barrett was apparently one of the ringleaders of a mutiny in which the convicts took charge of the vessel and attempted to sail to Ireland.

Adverse weather caused them to abort their plan and they returned to the Port of Torbay, in Devon, where some of them managed to abscond from the vessel before they could be apprehended.

Most of the runaways were rounded up and tried for crimes including mutiny and being 'criminally at-large'. Of the 108 re-arrested, two were hanged and a further 24 were tried for mutiny.

Barrett was again sentenced to death but reprieved after evidence was tendered to the court that he had intervened to save the life of a crew member and had also prevented the captain's ear from being taken off with a pair of scissors by other mutineers. He spent four years on the prison hulk *Dunkirk* at Plymouth before joining the convict transport *Charlotte*, as part of the First Fleet 'bound for Botany Bay'.

There were 67 convicts from the *Mercury* mutiny on the First Fleet.

Barrett spent his time on the voyage to Rio engraving cheap coins that had been rubbed flat and made into love tokens for fellow convicts to give to the female convicts aboard the *Charlotte*.

When the fleet arrived at Rio, it became apparent that he had been able to make more than just a few love tokens. Surgeon General John White, also a passenger on board the *Charlotte*, noted in his journal:

> 5th August. Still calm. This morning a boat came alongside, in which were three Portuguese and six slaves, from whom we purchased some oranges, plantains, and bread.
>
> In trafficking with these people, we discovered that one Thomas Barrett, a convict, had, with great ingenuity and address, passed some quarter dollars which he, assisted by two others, had coined out of old buckles, buttons belonging to the marines, and pewter spoons, during their passage from Teneriffe.
>
> The impression, milling, character, in a word, the whole was so inimitably executed that had their metal been a little better the fraud, I am convinced, would have passed undetected. A strict and careful search was made for the apparatus wherewith this was done, but in vain; not the smallest trace or vestige of any thing of the kind was to be found among them.

Barrett had managed the forgery while under the constant scrutiny of marines, and apparently without access to any kind of a furnace.

Governor Arthur Phillip was somewhat of a celebrity in Rio, having served with distinction for many years in the Portuguese navy, and it was obviously a rather embarrassing affair, as White explained:

> The officers of marines, the master of the ship, and myself fully explained to the injured Portuguese what villains they were who had imposed upon them. We were not without apprehensions that they might entertain an unfavourable opinion of Englishmen in general from the conduct of these rascals; we therefore thought it

necessary to acquaint them that the perpetrators of the fraud were felons doomed to transportation, by the laws of their country, for having committed similar offences there.

Surgeon General John White was obviously impressed by Barrett's skill and, on arriving at Botany Bay, commissioned the convicted amateur engraver. White gave Barrett a silver kidney dish from his personal medical equipment and asked the convict to create a medallion commemorating the voyage of the *Charlotte*.

Barrett, over the following week, skilfully produced a silver medal about 3 inches (74 millimetres) in diameter that shows the *Charlotte* at anchor in Botany Bay on one side and has the following inscription neatly engraved on the other:

Sailed, the Charlotte from Spit Head the 13 of May 1787. Bound for Botany Bay in th Island of New Holland. Arriv'd at Teneriff th 4 of June in Lat 28.13 N Long 16.23 W. Depart'd it 10 D. Arriv'd Rio Janiero 6 of Aug in Lat 22.54 S Long 42.38 W. Depart'd it th 5 of Sepr, arriv'd at the Cape of Good Hope the 14 Octr in Lat 34.29 S Long 18.29 E, Depart'd it th 13 of Novr and made the South Cape of New Holland the 8 Jan'y 1788 in Lat 43.32 S Long 146.56 E. Arriv'd at Botany Bay the 20 of Jany. The Charlotte in Co in Lat 34.00 South Long 151.00 East. Distance from Great Britan miles 13106.

At an auction held by the coin and medal dealers Noble Numismatics in 2008, the Australian National Maritime Museum acquired the medal with a bid of $750,000. When the buyer's premium was added, the medal actually cost almost $1 million. It was good news for retired Melbourne dentist Dr John Chapman, who had purchased it for $15,000 in 1981. A copper version of the medal, also made by Barrett for John White's servant William Broughton, was sold privately in 2013, also by Noble Numismatics, having failed to reach the auction estimate of $500,000.

Barrett could have done with $1.5 million in 1788. Less than a month after arriving at Sydney Cove, he and three others, driven by hunger no doubt, robbed the government food store, taking an amount of 'beef, butter and pease'. Two were 'banished to some uninhabited place', and one was flogged and forced at gunpoint to hang the fourth, as an example to the assembled community.

No prizes for guessing the identity of the fourth food thief. Surgeon General White noted in his journal that the prisoner was 'taken to the fatal tree' and there:

> Barrett was launched into eternity, after having confessed to the Rev Mr Johnson, who attended him, that he was guilty of the crime, and had long merited the ignominious death which he was about to suffer, and to which he said he had been brought by bad company and evil example.

Thus, Thomas Barrett, designer and engraver of artworks that would become worth in excess of $1 million, gained a further permanent distinction in our history—being the first man hanged in New South Wales and the first European executed on Australia's east coast.

I suppose that, if you are sentenced to death three times, you are probably lucky to be hanged only once.

James Daley (aka James Dealey and James Daly) was only 21 when he was sentenced to seven years transportation at the Old Bailey on 26 May 1784 for stealing clothing worth 54 shillings.

Like Barrett, Daley spent time on the hulks waiting for the American War of Independence to be decided before being sent on the First Fleet transport *Scarborough* to the penal settlement of New South Wales.

It seems he acquired a girlfriend from among the female convicts for, in August 1788, he reported that he had found an 'inexhaustible source of wealth' in gold 'some distance down the harbour', in the vicinity of what is now Hunter's Hill, where the only inexhaustible source of wealth these days is real estate.

He asked to see the governor and said he merely wanted a free pardon for himself and his girlfriend and some money and land, and then he'd reveal the whereabouts of the find.

Major Ross was in charge of the colony at the time, as Governor Phillip was out exploring. Ross told Daley he'd get nothing of the kind and ordered him to show an officer of the marine corps the location of the gold.

This didn't please Daley and he led the officer into the bush and then ran away. On his return, after a brief 24 hours of freedom, he was given 50 lashes but stuck to his story and produced a sample of rock with traces of gold showing quite clearly.

Once again Daley was taken to the area where he claimed he'd found the gold. On the way, when told that he would be shot if he ran again or if the gold was not found, he developed a pair of very cold feet and confessed that he had 'told a falsehood'.

The 'gold-bearing rock' was made up of clay into which he had inserted some filings from a gold guinea coin and a brass belt buckle, before baking it in a fire. Daley produced the remains of the coin and the buckle, and received a further 100 lashes for his trouble.

Some of his fellow convicts believed he really had found gold and had changed his mind about revealing its location.

No doubt, if that was true, Daley hoped to serve out his time and then make the most of his find. After all, he had less than three years to serve, having been sentenced in 1784. As he recovered from his lacerated back in August 1788, he and his girlfriend were possibly contemplating a happy future after he had served out his sentence.

Sadly, however, it was not to be. In December 1788, for entering the hut of another convict and taking a handkerchief by force, James Daley became the fifth person hanged in New South Wales.

Joseph Lycett was a professional portrait artist and painter of miniatures who was born in Staffordshire in 1774. As well as being a very accomplished and competent artist, he was also, sadly, an incurable alcoholic and habitual forger.

Convicted of forgery in 1811 and sentenced to fourteen years, he was not transported until 1814 when, as luck would have it, he sailed to Sydney on the *General Hewitt*, which happened to be also carrying Captain James Wallis of the 46th Regiment to a tour of duty in New South Wales.

Wallis was an enthusiastic amateur artist and the two men became friends. Upon their arrival in the colony, Wallis secured a job for Lycett as police clerk and all went well for eighteen months. Both Wallis and Lycett drew and painted many landscapes of the colony.

Then, in May 1815, hundreds of very well-counterfeited 5-shilling postal notes turned up all over Sydney. A copperplate press was found at Joseph Lycett's premises and he was convicted of forgery and sent to the penal coalmining settlement at Newcastle.

Newcastle was the hell-hole of the colony at that time and many convicts died there from the harsh conditions and savage discipline. Luckily for Lycett, however, James Wallis was appointed commandant at Newcastle in June 1816.

Lycett worked on plans for a church, which Wallis designed, and was given a conditional pardon on Wallis's recommendation. He then worked as a government and private artist in the colony from 1818 until 1821, painting landscapes, flora and elegant houses. He was given an unconditional pardon at the end of 1821, after Governor Macquarie had sent three of his paintings as a gift to Lord Bathurst.

Lycett returned to England in 1822 and published twelve sets of views of New South Wales and Van Diemen's Land, which were published together as *Views in Australia* in 1825.

In 1828 it seems that he forged bank notes (from the Stourbridge Bank) while living at Bath and, when caught, attempted to cut his own throat rather than face another prison term. After his life was saved, he was taken into custody and hospitalised and had his throat stitched, but apparently he tore open the wound in his neck and died. Another account says he was wounded by a sword during his arrest and died of septicaemia.

Joseph Lycett is now considered to be the most important colonial artist of his day, renowned for his elegant brushwork and eye for detail.

In a *Sydney Morning Herald* interview with reporter Janet Hawley on 11 April 2016, John McPhee, an art historian and Lycett expert, called the artist 'a con man with persuasive charm, a forger, heavy drinker, womaniser, an appalling business-man and a pretty stupid crook'.

In 2016, Lycett's paintings of flora specimens, now the property of the Botanic Gardens Museum in Sydney, were valued at $2 million.

JIM JONES AT BOTANY BAY

As I have said previously, what was really happening in the midst of social change and upheaval in Britain in the 18th and 19th centuries was a 'class war', between the 'haves' and the 'have nots'. In the cities, hungry people stole bread and, in rural areas, hungry men like Jim Jones went out at night poaching game.

I love the anger and resentment that the author of this poem has invested in the voice of Jim Jones, a true 'victim of society' whose regional accent and vehemence are so accurately captured in the verse. Sadly, however, we have no idea who the author was.

Jim Jones at Botany Bay

Anonymous

O, listen for a moment, lads, and hear me tell my tale—
How o'er the sea from England's shore I was compelled to
    sail.
The jury said, 'He's guilty, Sir,' and says the judge, says he,
'For life Jim Jones, I'm sending you across the stormy sea;
And take my tip before you ship to join the iron-gang.
Don't run away at Botany Bay, or else you'll surely hang—

Or else you'll hang!' he says, says he, 'and after that, Jim Jones,
High up upon the gallows-tree the crows will pick your bones.
You'll have no chance for mischief then; remember what
    I say.
They'll flog the poaching out of you, out there at Botany Bay.'
With the storms a-raging round us, and the winds a-blowing
    gales.
I'd rather drowned in misery than gone to New South Wales.

The winds blew high upon the sea, and the pirates come
    along,
But the soldiers on our convict ship were full five hundred
    strong,
They opened fire and somehow drove that pirate ship away.
I'd have rather joined that pirate ship than come to Botany
    Bay.
For night and day, the irons clang, and like poor galley slaves
We toil, and toil and when we die must fill dishonoured
    graves.

But by and by I'll break my chains; into the bush I'll go
And join the brave bushrangers there—Jack Donohoo
    and co.
And some dark night when everything is silent in the town
I'll kill the tyrants one and all and shoot the floggers down;
I'll give the law a little shock; remember what I say.
They'll yet regret they sent Jim Jones in chains to Botany Bay.

A WILD AND UNPROFITABLE UNDERTAKING

The Backstory

> 'Three things cannot long stay hidden. The sun,
> the moon, and the truth.'
>
> Buddha

Australian history was simple when I was in primary school. It was a list of 'facts' detailing the achievements of certain white European 'gentlemen' over the previous 200 years. For example:

- Captain Cook 'discovered' Australia.
- Blaxland, Wentworth and Lawson were the 'first' men to cross the Blue Mountains.
- Edward Hargraves 'discovered' gold in Australia.

Throughout my adult life I have been prone to bouts of disillusionment, dismay, sadness and nostalgia as I came to realise, albeit slowly and reluctantly, that history was just a little more complex than my primary-school teachers suggested.

Although I knew that a Dutchman once nailed a plate to a tree on an island off the coast of Western Australia, I was astounded to learn that many of his countrymen had explored and mapped much of Australia's northern, western and southern coastlines more than a century before Captain Cook was even born.

My mind was sent reeling when I stumbled upon the possibility that the Portuguese Captain Cristovao de Mendonca had explored and mapped the entire eastern coast of Australia from Cape York to Warrnambool a century before the Dutch arrived on the other side!

Imagine my deep sense of betrayal when I found evidence to show that an Irish ex-convict, James Byrne, was probably the first European to cross the Blue Mountains west of Sydney. Later, I was astounded to find further evidence that John Wilson, another ex-convict, probably crossed the mountains further south well before Byrne, and that Lieutenant William Dawes (who arrived on the First Fleet, no less!) certainly explored well into the mountains and may have crossed them quite early in the colony's history, with the help of his Aboriginal friends.

It took me days to recover my equanimity when further research revealed that those three famous explorers, Blaxland, Wentworth and Lawson, had actually paid Byrne to guide them across the mountains and didn't even have the good grace to mention his name in their account of the expedition—referring to him only as a 'servant' and 'kangaroo hunter'.

My heart was saddened, and my faith in natural justice deeply shaken, as I contemplated the perfidious nature of 'gentlemen' like the three above mentioned—and primary-school teachers.

Along with all this, it also became apparent to me, at some point in my post-school development, that the indigenous population of Australia had been exploring and surviving quite successfully on the continent for the previous 60,000 years.

I was so deeply moved by this revelation that I decided to write a scholarly treatise on the subject, in the form of a limerick, which amazingly and hilariously later found its way into a primary-school textbook. Here it is:

> There once was a captain named Cook,
> Who sailed south, to take a quick look.
> There he found a land,
> Stuck a flag in the sand,
> And that's how native title got took.

But, I digress.

One of the greatest lies we were ever told in primary school was that Edward Hargraves was the man who discovered gold in Australia, and should be regarded as a hero because this wonderful discovery was responsible for a giant leap forward in the history of civilisation as Australians know it.

It simply isn't true.

The Story

'Gold is money. Everything else is credit.'

JP Morgan, financier, (1837–1913)

Edward Hammond Hargraves was born at Stoke Cottage in the village of Alverstoke, near Gosport, in Hampshire, on 7 October 1816.

Edward was the third son in a family of fifteen children. His father was a low-ranking military officer and it seems that young Edward spent some time being educated at Brighton Grammar School and Lewes Grammar School before going to sea as a cabin boy at the age of fourteen.

He was tall, strong and robust and evidently made a good sailor. As an adult he stood at least 6 feet 3 inches (some reports say 6 feet 6 inches) and weighed up to 18 stone in later life. He arrived in Sydney in 1832, aboard Captain Lister's ship *Wave*. He had served with Captain Lister for a considerable time and was friendly with the captain and his wife and young son.

In Sydney, Hargraves joined the crew of the ship *Clementine*, which headed north to collect *bêches-de-mer* and hunt turtles in Torres Strait. During this voyage the ship's captain, David Parry-Okeden, inherited a large sum of money and left the ship to buy property and become a pastoralist.

The voyage ended in Batavia (modern-day Jakarta), where the ship was sold and most of the crew—20 of the 27—died of typhus (some reports say yellow fever). Hargraves, however, was possessed of a strong constitution and, having survived the rigours and dangers of life at sea, returned to Sydney as a crewman on the *Red Rover*, from London, via Capetown and Hobart, in 1834.

Back in New South Wales he made his way across the Blue Mountains and worked for some time on Captain Hector's property 8 miles from Bathurst, before deciding to follow the example set by Captain Parry-Okeden by taking up 100 acres of land near Wollongong and attempting to become a farmer.

Although he never stuck at anything for very long, Hargraves was, it seems, possessed of a good deal of self-confidence and had the ability, as do many successful people, to make his own luck— often by making good use of people he met throughout his life.

He was no great success as a farmer but he was, it seems, 'lucky in love' and in 1836 at St Andrew's Church in Sydney, he married Elizabeth Mackay. Elizabeth came with a substantial dowry, which included a number of cottages at East Gosford, a privately developed township north of Sydney, in which her father had invested.

The happy young couple then secured a small place in Australian colonial history by establishing the first general store south of Wollongong, which they sold in 1839 when they decided to move to East Gosford and start a new business—another general store that also operated as an agency for the General Steam Navigation Company. Hargraves used part of his wife's dowry to build a pub, The Fox Under The Hill, and became a publican as well as a storekeeper and agent for the General Steam Navigation Company.

By 1843 Edward and Elizabeth had four children and perhaps the tall opportunist was finding family life rather tedious. The pub had failed and he was forced to forfeit the property, leaving Elizabeth to run the store while he took up land in the Manning River district further north.

Apparently he was back with Elizabeth by the beginning of 1849—not for long, but at least long enough to father the fifth and last of their children, Emma Maria, named after Edward's favourite sister, who had died a decade earlier.

By the time baby Emma was born in September 1849, her footloose father had already sold up most of his property, paid some of his debts, and departed for the California goldrush, leaving his pregnant wife to mind the store—and look after their kids. Hargraves had left Sydney on a British ship, the *Elizabeth Archer*, in July 1849 and returned from San Francisco in November 1850 aboard a ship called the *Emma*.

Perhaps the more observant readers among you may have noticed a certain wistful irony in the fact that Hargraves left Australia on a ship bearing the name of his wife and chose to return on a vessel that shared its name with the daughter he had never seen. But it was not a desire to see his new daughter and be reunited with his wife and family that brought Edward Hargraves scurrying home from California after just fifteen months.

Hargraves had left Australia determined to make his fortune on the Californian goldfields, but found the work hard for a man of his size and admitted himself that he had little aptitude for the actual work of mining. He had, however, found some friends whose willingness to share their knowledge and skill with him was to prove very useful. Big Edward always did have a way of making good use of his friends.

The two friends in question were fellow passengers on the *Elizabeth Archer*. One of them, Simpson Davison, was an experienced miner with a good understanding of geology. The other was Enoch Rudder, who was travelling to California with his two sons in the hope of making his fortune by way of a new gold washing machine that he had invented and designed.

The men teamed up for a time and travelled together to the diggings on the Sacramento River, Marysville and Foster Bay. Hargraves tried his luck at several of these places with no success; he was far more adept in getting his two experienced and knowledgeable companions to share their understanding of the geology and mineralogy involved in the business of finding gold. Perhaps, more importantly, they had a lot to tell about the history of gold discoveries in the Blue Mountains area of New South Wales, an area with which they were all somewhat familiar. They also showed Hargraves how to construct and operate a cradling machine, a device that uses water to wash alluvial gold from soil.

All this information was to be very useful to Edward Hargraves in the not-too-distant future.

What brought him back was the knowledge that the New South Wales government had changed its attitude towards the possibility of the existence of large amounts of payable gold in the colony.

Previous to 1850 the colonial administration had suppressed any news of gold discovery for fear of convict riots, uncontrollable population movements and civil unrest. Transportation had ended in 1840, however, and there was a recession in the colony in the 1840s. And now thousands of men were leaving for the California Rush, which began in 1848. Perhaps it was time for a change of policy.

So in 1849 the New South Wales government asked the Colonial Office in England to allow exploration to begin, with the purpose of exploiting any mineral resources that could be found, and requested a geologist be sent to supervise the process. The Colonial Office agreed and a reward was then offered for the first person to find 'payable gold' in New South Wales. At the same time Samuel Stutchbury, who had been in the colony previously as naturalist to the Pacific Pearl Fishery commercial expedition to New South Wales and the Pacific Islands, was appointed as supervisor and arrived in November 1850.

As soon as he heard the news, Edward Hargraves knew where his fortune lay—and it wasn't in California. He had a plan and he took the first available ship home, which happened to be the *Emma*. He left on 23 November and arrived in Sydney in January 1851, just two months after the arrival of Samuel Stutchbury.

Hargraves had no intention of making his fortune by finding and mining gold. He had another plan in mind. He later wrote:

> It was never my intention ... to work for gold, my only desire was to make the discovery, and rely on the Government and the country for my reward.

In the process of achieving this ambition, Hargraves lied, exaggerated, twisted the truth and ruthlessly befriended, manipulated and used people whom he later betrayed and cast aside. In the end, the part he played in 'discovering' gold was minor, but he managed to claim the reward and the fame—it was actually a clever con job.

You see, it had been a very poorly kept secret since the 1820s that there was 'gold in them thar hills' west of Sydney and the Great Dividing Range.

Let's take a look at the evidence.

Convict James Daley claimed to have found gold within months of the First Fleet arriving and there are accounts of convicts finding traces of gold along the roads they were building across the Blue Mountains as early as 1814, and later in the 1820s, but these accounts are unsubstantiated.

A Russian naturalist named Stein, part of the Bellinghausen scientific expedition which visited New South Wales in 1820, made a twelve-day trip to the Blue Mountains and claimed to have found gold-bearing ore.

James McBrien, the colony's assistant surveyor, made notes in his journal in February 1823 stating that he had found alluvial gold while exploring and surveying along the Fish River to the east of Bathurst.

In 1837, newspapers reported that a Russian stockman had found gold and silver ore 30 miles from Segenhoe in the Hunter Valley.

So it was common knowledge there was gold in the colony when, in 1839, the Polish count, explorer and geologist Paul Strzelecki reached Sydney, via New Zealand. He spent four years making a geological survey zig-zagging back and forth across the colony as far as the Southern Alps, where he climbed what he took to be highest peak and named it after the Polish democratic leader, Tadeusz Kosciuszko. In 1845 Strzelecki became a British subject, and published in London his *Physical Description of New South Wales and Van Diemen's Land*, for which he received the founder's medal of the Royal Geographical Society.

Strzelecki later reported that when he told the New South Wales governor, Sir George Gipps, of his discovery of alluvial gold near Hartley in the Blue Mountains, and at Wellington in the central west, Gipps 'frightened' him into 'saying nothing about it'.

Instead, Strzelecki took mineral samples to show English geologist Sir Roderick Murchison, who examined them and concluded that gold 'would be found in the Eastern Cordillera of Australia'. When Murchison was made president of the Royal Geographical Society in 1844 he predicted the existence of gold in Australia's Great Dividing Range in his first presidential address. His ideas were published in a feature in the *Sydney Morning Herald* on 28 September 1847, paraphrased as 'gold will be found on the western flanks of the dividing ranges'.

Another geologist and friend of Murchison's, Reverend William Clarke, also arrived in the colony in 1839. He spent two years prospecting between Hartley and Bathurst and found numerous samples of gold-laden quartz. Clarke reported his finds to some members of the New South Wales Legislative Council. When he showed the samples of gold to Gipps, however, the governor evidently responded by saying, 'Put it away, Mr Clarke, or we shall all have our throats cut.'

The governor's attitude was understandable, but the policy of denial could not last long. After a government enquiry was held in 1853 into the management of the Australian goldfields and the legitimacy of claims by Hargraves and others, Clarke was awarded £1000, followed by another £3000 in 1861, and credited as the 'scientific discoverer of gold in New South Wales'.

But long before that official declaration, in an area known as Lewis Ponds or Yorkie's Corner, where two creeks converge 10 miles east of the township of Orange, there was local knowledge of gold being discovered by shepherds over many years. One shepherd, the eponymous 'Yorkie', had his hut there and found a nugget, which was displayed around the district. At least two other shepherds working in the area—a Mr McDonald, working on property owned by William Lane, and a Mr Delaney, working for Henry Perrier—were also known to have found gold in the area.

In December 1845, a shepherd had arrived at the George Street jewellery shop owned by goldsmith Mr E. Cohen and sold him a 4-ounce gold nugget embedded in quartz, which was, for quite some time, displayed in a window of Cohen's shop.

This prompted an amateur geologist and mineralogist with the delightful name of William Tipple Smith, who owned an iron foundry and lapidary business in George Street, to make a few trips west of the mountains. Smith sent mineral samples he had obtained to Sir Roderick Murchison early in 1848 and Murchison contacted the secretary of state, Earl Grey, suggesting a mineral survey of the area where the samples had been taken. It was felt, however, that a goldrush would threaten the colony's economy, especially the lucrative wool trade. It was feared shepherds and shearers would all desert their jobs and head for the goldfields.

Mr Smith then went to see the colonial secretary in Sydney, Edward Deas Thomson. He showed him rock samples and a nugget weighing more than 3 ounces and promised to tell the administration the location of the find in return for a reward. (There is some suggestion that this was actually Yorkie's nugget, though Smith claimed he found it himself.) When Governor Fitzroy was informed about the offer, he declined to take it up.

But that wasn't the end of Edward Deas Thomson's role in the saga. Just after his interview with Mr Smith, in 1849, he was a guest of Thomas Icely, an influential landowner who had property at Carcoar, near Blayney, southwest of Bathurst. The property was being mined by the Belubula Copper Mining Company and the copper miners had discovered samples of gold several weeks before. These were also sent off to Sir Roderick Murchison, who had become convinced as early as the mid-1840s that gold could be found west of the mountains in New South Wales and had suggested the idea of sponsoring Cornish miners to migrate to the colony to search for gold in the area. (Ironically, there were already Cornishmen there who would have a part to play in the events that were to follow.)

Meanwhile, the gold continued to appear. In May 1850, the *Bathurst Free Press* reported that a shepherd named M'Gregor had found a significant amount of gold at Mitchell's Creek, near the town of Wellington, over the past several years. The paper was adamant:

> Neither is there any doubt in the fact that Mr M'Gregor found a considerable quantity of the precious metal some years ago, near Mitchell's Creek, and it is surmised he still gets more in the same locality.

So, who knew there was gold to be found west of the Great Divide before 1851?

Well, various governors certainly knew. Charles Fitzroy, the incumbent at the time, knew, as did his predecessor George Gipps. It is more than likely that Richard Bourke, Ralph Darling and Thomas Brisbane also knew, because James McBrien, the colony's assistant surveyor, knew in 1823, which meant that John Oxley, the surveyor-general at the time, knew.

Landowners such as Thomas Icely, William Lane and Henry Perrier knew.

Explorers and fossickers, including Strzelecki, the Reverend Clarke and William Tipple Smith, knew.

Shepherds like Yorkie, McDonald, Delaney and M'Gregor around Wellington, Orange and Bathurst knew.

Lots of locals in those areas knew and that's probably how Simpson Davison and Enoch Rudder—Hargraves' Australian friends in California—knew (and they told Hargraves what they knew).

Anyone who looked in Cohen's jewellery shop window in George Street knew.

Colonial secretary Edward Deas Thomson certainly knew, as did famed British geologist Sir Roderick Murchison and the British secretary of state, Earl Grey.

You might be tempted to ask, 'Who didn't know?!'

So, how did a man like Hargraves, a man whose knowledge of geology and mining was very limited and all second-hand (as was his knowledge of the discoveries made over the previous decades just west of the mountains), manage to claim the reward and the fame for 'discovering' gold in Australia?

It's a very good question.

The answer is a little complex.

———

As soon as Hargraves disembarked on 17 January 1851, he began lobbying the colonial administration for government funding to finance a gold-prospecting expedition across the mountains. Not only did he want the reward from the colonial government for finding the gold—he wanted the colonial government to pay him to find it!

Ever the optimist, Hargraves had boasted, 'There is as much gold in the country I'm going to as there is in California, and Her Most Gracious Majesty, the Queen, God bless Her, will appoint me one of her Gold Commissioners.'

The response from the Fitzroy administration was a resounding 'no'. The newly appointed Inspector General of Police, William Spain, called the concept 'a wild and unprofitable undertaking'.

Hargraves later reflected on the whole exercise of seeking government assistance by saying, 'one and all, however, derided me, and treated my views and opinions [as those] of a madman'.

Not everyone thought him mad, however, and he did have friends in Sydney.

Always adept at using others, especially friends, to gain his own ends, Hargraves raised enough money for a one-man expedition. Chief contributor was an old friend, William Northwood, who threw in £100.

Equipped with a horse and supplies, and an invitation to visit Thomas Icely at Carcoar (and without bothering to visit his own family at Gosford), Hargraves wasted no time in crossing the Blue Mountains. He kept going past Bathurst and met Icely near Blayney.

Hargraves had decided to start his quest by following up information he had gleaned about the shepherd M'Gregor's finds near Wellington. He told Icely his plan and the two men discussed possibilities. As Hargraves seemed in a great hurry to achieve his goal, Icely suggested that he head straight to the inn at the small settlement at Guyong 6 miles to the north of Blayney, rather than staying with Icely at Carcoar.

This was an attractive option for Hargraves—for several reasons—but unfortunately he got lost for a few days and didn't manage to reach the hotel until 10 February.

One reason Hargraves was happy to head north to stay at Guyong was that it put him much closer to Lewis Ponds, or Yorkie's Corner as it was known locally, and he knew gold had been found there in the past. The main reason he liked the plan, however, was that it put him back in contact with some old friends—who were sure to come in useful. Based on Icely's description of the inn at Guyong, Hargraves thought he might find a welcome there.

The owner and licensee of the inn was none other than Mrs Susan Lister, now widow of Captain John Lister, for whom Hargraves had worked as a cabin boy and sailor. Hargraves had first arrived in Sydney as a crewman on Lister's ship, the *Wave*, and knew the family well, having sailed with Mrs Lister and her young son on several voyages, including the one to Sydney.

In 1838 the Listers had settled in Sydney and embarked upon a number of unsuccessful business enterprises. The first was a shipping agency, which went bankrupt. That was followed by a stint for John as captain of a coastal trading vessel that foundered in Moreton Bay. The crew was rescued by Aborigines, but the vessel was lost.

Then, in 1846, the family took up the licence of a pub, on the Wellington road out of Bathurst, with the rather long-winded name of The Robin Hood and Little John Inn. But in 1850 Captain Lister was killed by a fall from his wagon and his widow took the family a little further west to run the pub at Guyong, which was rather confusingly named The Wellington Hotel, although it was 60 miles from the town of Wellington, which was of course named after the Duke of Wellington … as was the pub at Guyong. It was here, six months later, that Hargraves found them.

Most accounts of Hargraves' discoveries mention that he was assisted by a young man, John Lister, who he met at Guyong.

Those accounts fail to make the connection—John Lister was a long-lost 'friend' whom Hargraves had played with and told yarns to when Young Lister was a toddler on his father's ship. Here was somebody else to use and manipulate!

Once Susan Lister had recognised and welcomed Hargraves, and Hargraves had chatted to young John about some of the rock samples he noticed around the pub, the fortune-seeker decided to postpone his trek to the town of Wellington to follow up leads about M'Gregor's finds. Instead, he decided to stay a while at the pub, which was close to the area he had heard so much about— known as Lewis Ponds or Yorkie's Corner.

This seemed a good plan because, oddly enough, the hotel just happened to be run by the widow of his old boss, who just happened to have a healthy and useful son aged 23, who just happened to know quite a lot about fossicking for gold in the local area.

Within two days the change of plans proved to be a stroke of sheer genius—or incredible good luck.

On 12 February John Lister guided Hargraves down Lewis Ponds Creek to a place called Radigan's Gully, some 2 miles from Yorkie's Corner. It was here that the supposedly 'amazing' discovery was made.

In fact, the reason for choosing this site was merely that the summer had been so hot that there was little water around and this was the only place that provided sufficient water for Hargraves to do some panning. Apparently Hargraves went through the process six times and on five occasions tiny specks of gold were found.

This was enough for the ever-optimistic Hargraves to proclaim to his young companion, 'Where you walk over now there is gold'.

On a piece of paper torn from the corner of the *Empire* newspaper, he wrote 'Gold discovered in the alluvial at Lewis Ponds Creek this 12th day of February, 1851' and added his signature.

Quite carried away by this rather insignificant find and an overwhelming sense of his own importance, he then apparently proclaimed to his audience of one: 'This is a memorable day in the history of New South Wales. I shall be a baronet, you will be knighted and my old horse will be stuffed, put in a glass case and sent to the British Museum.'

Hargraves was well aware of the fact that a few tiny specks did not constitute 'payable gold', but he had found something and that was the main thing. He had a credible witness, although it no doubt also occurred to him that he was now in partnership with the Listers, who had provided horses, equipment and local knowledge for the day's expedition.

He could deal with that problem later. For now, he had evidence, a witness and a plan. His plan was to cheat.

Hargraves had to make it appear that he'd found substantial amounts of gold at one location and he knew how he could do that. He had to find significant amounts from as many places as possible and put it all together and say it came from the same place.

He had an idea that the best place to search locally was along tributaries of the Macquarie River, one of which was the Fish River, where the colony's assistant surveyor McBrien had found gold in 1823. John Lister suggested they enlist the help of the Tom family, who lived in the nearby Cornish settlement. James Tom joined the prospecting team while Hargraves headed north to try his luck in the creeks around the township of Wellington, as he had originally planned.

None of the fossickers had any luck and, on his return, Hargraves showed James's brother William Tom, a carpenter, how to construct a 'California-style' cradle to speed up the process of washing earth to find alluvial gold. William built the cradle in the front room of the family home and Hargraves demonstrated how to use it. The four men made a verbal pact that no one would say a word until they could produce convincing evidence of a find that produced £1 worth of gold a day. They also agreed that any profits would be shared equally.

Sadly, none of the agreements were put in writing.

Hargraves and John Lister went east and panned along the Fish and Campbell rivers unsuccessfully. Hargraves then made his way back to Sydney, leaving the other three to search and cradle the local creeks while he, supposedly, set off for Moreton Bay in Queensland to try his luck there.

Meanwhile, James, William and a third brother, Henry Tom,

tried out the cradle successfully, obtaining sixteen grains of gold for three days' work.

Back in Sydney, Hargraves immediately broke the promise he had made to his partners and visited Colonial Secretary Edward Deas Thomson, claiming to have found payable gold and asking for £500 as an advance on the reward. He was asked to put his request in writing, which he did (neglecting to mention Lister or the Tom brothers).

Edward Deas Thomson's reply, dated 5 April, said in part:

> I am directed by the Governor to inform you that His Excellency cannot say more at present than that the remuneration of the discovery of gold on the Crown Lands, referred to by you, must entirely depend on its nature and the value when made known.

Hargraves also broke his promise of secrecy by sharing the news of his discovery with his friend from his California days Enoch Rudder, who wrote to the *Sydney Morning Herald* on 4 April 1851, announcing that 'someone' had discovered a goldfield 'extending over a tract of country about 300 miles in length'. Hargraves had plans which included the involvement of Rudder, but whether he approved the leaking of the news or not is uncertain.

Meanwhile, west of the Great Divide, events were moving forward very satisfactorily.

On 7 April, John Lister and William Tom, acting on local information about the location of the find made by the shepherd Delaney, panned at the junction of Lewis Ponds Creek and Summer Hill Creek—in other words right 'in' Yorkie's Corner— and William Tom found a nugget weighing more than half an ounce.

Over the next five days they used the cradle and found around 2 ounces. Then John Lister walked down the creek a little way and found a nugget weighing 2 ounces in the submerged roots of a tree. They also found a heart-shaped nugget that weighed a quarter of an ounce.

John Lister wrote to Hargraves telling him the news, and Hargraves promptly returned to Guyong on 5 May. The 4 ounces of gold, worth about £13, was shared equally between the four men and then Hargraves said he wanted it all in his possession when he represented the partnership to the colonial officials—so he paid the three other men for their share of the gold, promising that they would be included as equal partners in his dealings with the government.

The next day Hargraves' friend Enoch Rudder arrived and melted and combined some of the gold to make a larger nugget.

The Tom brothers and John Lister begged Hargraves not to disclose the find until they could stake some official claim and ensure their right to work the area, but on 8 May Hargraves made his way to Bathurst and met with some of the town's influential citizens and showed them the gold—the larger natural nuggets and the one created by Rudder.

Hargraves referred to the gold as 'his' find and officially made the discovery public. He then waited until the government geologist Samuel Stutchbury arrived three days later and took him to the creek where he was able to produce twenty grains of fine gold from three hours of cradling.

The *Bathurst Free Press* reported on 17 May as follows:

The existence of gold is therefore clearly established, and whatever credit or emolument may arise therefrom, Mr. Hargraves is certainly the individual to whom it properly belongs.

The goldrush era had begun.

Stutchbury wrote to the colonial secretary on 19 May:

Gold had been obtained in considerable quantity. The number of persons at work and about the diggings (that is occupying about one mile of the creek) cannot be less than 400, and of all classes ... I fear, unless something is done very quickly, that much confusion will arise in consequence of people setting up claims.

Hargraves was awarded £10,000, appointed as a special Commissioner of Crown Lands, and given the use of a covered wagon, two horses and two policemen.

Not to be completely outdone by New South Wales, the new colony of Victoria, which had come into existence on 11 November 1850, also decided to award Hargraves £5000, and actually paid him £2381 of the money. The reason they stopped paying was that news began spreading that the Tom brothers and John Lister were hotly disputing the validity of Hargraves' claim. The remainder of the Victorian reward was never paid.

It was, however, all rather late. Hargraves had been too clever for his 'partners', and the horse, as the saying goes, had well and truly bolted.

———

Hargraves travelled to Britain where he gave talks as an expert on geology and gold discovery, was made a member of the Royal Society and met Queen Victoria in 1854. He produced a book, *Australia and its Goldfields*, which sold very well, as did life-sized prints of the 'discoverer of gold' painting by T. Balcombe (at 3 bob a print!). The book—except for the parts about Hargraves and his wonderful achievements—was almost certainly ghost-written by his far more knowledgeable friend Simpson Davison.

The city of Sydney gave Hargraves an official reception at which he was presented with a 'pure gold cup' supposedly valued at £500. The money for the cup was raised by public subscription, to which Hargraves had donated substantially himself. In a fitting and hilarious footnote to that affair, Hargraves later melted the cup down and found it to consist mostly of lead and copper!

His effrontery knew no bounds. He even claimed to have given the goldfield its name, Ophir, when it was actually William Tom Senior, a Wesleyan lay preacher, who suggested the name. It was taken from the name of King Solomon's legendary mine in the Old Testament and related to the First Book of Kings, chapter 9, verse 23: 'They came to Ophir and they fetched from thence gold'.

Hargraves not only lied, and betrayed and cheated his partners, but it seems he could not stand anyone else being credited with any part of the 'discovery'. He even had the audacity to ask John Lister to sign the following letter and send it to the *Sydney Morning Herald*:

Gentlemen—A report having been spread abroad by some malicious person who evidently is jealous of Mr. Hargraves' great discovery to the effect that I was the party who made it and communicated it to him, I beg leave most unreservedly to contradict this false report, although having been upwards of two years searching for it at one time with two geologists, and mineralogists who told me there were indications but could not find the gold. Mr. Hargraves, during his explorations, called on me as an old friend of my late respected father, and in course of conversation he told me this was a gold country, and if I would keep a secret, he would combine [with] me. This I agreed to—he was as good as his word, and scarcely ever made a failure,—where he said gold was to be found, he found it. I neither understand geology or mineralogy—but I was convinced my friend Mr. Hargraves knows where and how to find gold, and all honour and reward in the late discovery belong to him alone. Indeed, few men would have done what he has, intersecting the country with blacks, sometimes alone, sometimes with my friend Mr. James Tom, and during his explorations, had rain set in, from the imperfect manner in which he was equipped, starvation and death must have been the result. Trusting you will give this publicity in the columns of your valuable journal.

I am, Gentlemen,

Your most obedient servant,

John Hardman Lister

P.S.—I have also heard it reported that Mr. Hargraves had not acted fairly towards me,—I beg most distinctly to state that in all transactions with that gentleman, he has acted strictly honourable with me and friends in the secret of the great discovery. Mr. Hargraves is now no longer connected with me or my party at Ophir, and wherever he may go he has my best wishes, and I believe of all who have known him in the district of Bathurst.

Naturally, John Lister not only refused to sign the letter, but he openly refuted the claims it made and sent it on to the *Bathurst Free Press* with the following reply:

I could not subscribe my name to the untruths it contained ... I also assert in plain words that Mr. James Tom and I never travelled with Mr. Hargraves with any other understanding than that we were his prospecting colleagues and concerned equally with himself in any favourable results that might accrue from our journey or journeys.

I find it puzzling that a man as cunning and manipulative as Hargraves could be so deluded about his own wickedness and so besotted with his own sense of importance that he would think that a man he had betrayed and cheated would help him to establish himself in the position he had cheated the other man to gain!

It took 40 years for the other partners in the discovery to get any real justice. But it was too little too late.

William Tom had, on their behalf, written to the colonial secretary Edward Deas Thomson in June 1851, but all Thomson could say was that Mr Hargraves had made no mention of any partners at any stage in his communications with the government.

They wrote again in December, directly to Governor Fitzroy.

Both letters were published in the *Bathurst Free Press* in January 1853, together with an article that made certain accusations.

Finally a government select committee, chaired by the colonial secretary, addressed their claims during June and July 1853.

Hargraves gave evidence, as did the other partners, but by this time Edward Hargraves was acknowledged as a hero of almost legendary status in the colony and Thomson was very sympathetic to his version of events.

Nevertheless, John Lister, William Tom and James Tom were awarded a £1000 reward to be shared between them for 'having played a part' in Mr Hargraves' discovery of payable gold.

Simpson Davison and Enoch Rudder (who had played a part in the deception regarding the amount of gold found) were also 'forgotten' in Hargraves' version of events, and did not remain his friends for long. Both published their own accounts of their adventures in California, in which they claimed that Hargraves' specious declaration—that he recognised the similarity in terrain and geology between California and the district around the Ophir Goldfield and knew there was gold there—was, in fact, based on their knowledge of geology, their knowledge of both areas and their observations, which they had discussed with Hargraves while in California.

In his book Davison also questioned the integrity of the colonial secretary and asked why he was so slow in considering evidence that cast doubt on Hargraves' claims.

But, while his former associates had good reason to be bitter, Hargraves revelled in his fame and celebrity status. Some 20 miles from East Gosford he built a grand house called Noraville that was partly a replica of Stoke Cottage, where he was born. When he was staying at Noraville, rather than his other residence at Forest Lodge in Sydney, he flew a flag to indicate he was 'in residence' like a member of the royal family.

His travels and lavish lifestyle saw him practically broke in less than ten years, so he used his Masonic connections to attempt to get the remainder of the Victorian reward and to lobby the New South Wales parliament to pay him an annuity—and was finally granted £250 a year in 1877.

Invited by the Western Australia government in 1862 to advise them on finding gold in that colony, Hargraves explored and confidently reported that gold would never be found there. His stunning lack of mining knowledge would be proven later when, between 1892 and 2012, more than 10,000 tonnes of gold was mined in Western Australia, which still produces 70 per cent of Australia's gold each year.

The controversy about Hargraves' claim never went away and finally, in August 1890, a second select committee was appointed to again investigate the affair. John Lister and the Tom brothers were now old men, and John Lister died from influenza on the day he was to give evidence. His son, daughter and sister all died of the same disease within the following week.

Lister's sister, Mrs Bates, said in her evidence that the gold her brother and Hargraves found in 1851 consisted of 'three specks and they were so small I could not see them distinctly with the naked eye'. The gold found by John Lister and William Tom, on the other hand, amounted to more than 4 ounces.

In December 1890 the second select committee into the claims made by Lister and the Tom brothers announced that they were 'undoubtedly the first discoverers of payable gold in Australia' and that, given the 'substantial improvement in trade in the colony' that their discovery had brought about, 'the petitioners had not been adequately rewarded'.

While their claims were finally justified, the New South Wales parliament did not give assent to the committee's findings and no additional reward was paid.

A memorial column, unveiled at the Ophir Goldfield by the Minister for Mines in 1923, states that those responsible for the discovery of payable gold in Australia were Edward Hammond Hargraves, John Hardman Australia Lister, James Tom and William Tom.

Hargraves died of pneumonia at Forest Lodge in Sydney on 29 October 1891. Although he had received more than £12,000 in rewards and an annuity of £250, he left an estate of just £370. Even in death he was the subject of publicity-seeking sensationalism, with a story being circulated that he had died in a riding accident.

The Tom brothers made some money exhibiting the original 'California-style' cradle and the heart-shaped nugget at agricultural shows for a time. The heart-shaped nugget is now owned by the Orange Historical Society.

As late as 1924 the younger sister of the Tom brothers, Selina Webb, who had been a witness to many of the events and conversations as a fifteen-year-old, was still writing to the press to tell her side of the story.

Yet somehow it became a 'fact', that millions of little Australians have learned: Edward Hargraves discovered gold in Australia.

History was all so much simpler in primary school.

SWINGING THE LEAD

Banjo subtitled this poem 'Army term for malingering' and it is true that malingering, derived from the French *malingre* (literally meaning 'to be wrongly weak'), is a form of 'swinging the lead'.

'Malinger', however, quite specifically means to feign illness or injury in order to avoid work or duty, whereas 'swinging the lead' is a more general term that can also apply to workers pretending to work, or taking a long time to perform a task, in other words to shirk from work (nice rhyme). In the 1600s 'shirk' meant to 'practise fraud or trickery' but the word changed its meaning slightly over the years until Webster defined it as 'to evade the performance of an obligation'. This more accurately fits the true colloquial meaning of 'swinging the lead'.

Aussies would have called it 'bludging' when I was kid.

'Skiving' or 'skiving off' from work is another term often heard in the past in Australia to describe the practice of avoiding work, and that's actually of French origin also, via the USA! The French verb *esquiver* literally means 'to dodge', but by inference and usage it translates as 'to slink away'. Strangely enough, it became a popular slang term in colleges in the US in the 19th century, used by students to describe the practice of not studying or not attending lectures, and was used in the same context here in Australia when I was a student.

'Swinging the lead', meaning that a person is pretending to work (or claiming to be ill) when they are not, has a very clear-cut maritime origin. In the sailing days, one of a deckhand's duties was to check the depth of water by 'sounding'. This involved dropping a lead weight attached to a rope with knots marking its length to the bottom of the ocean or river or waterway to check the depth of the water.

Lazy sailors could make the weight descend as slowly as possible by swinging the lead to and fro several times before dropping it into the water, instead of just dropping it straight down. This slowed its descent considerably as the swinging motion continued all the way to the bottom, thus giving the sailor more time to do nothing while appearing to be working.

Banjo's poem about a soldier trying to 'con' his way out of facing the enemy (and failing to manage it) was written towards the end of WWI, in April 1918, and appeared in the magazine *The Kia Ora Coo-ee*, which was distributed to Australian and New Zealand troops fighting in Europe.

'Taubes' were a type of German aircraft that dropped bombs on the allied trenches.

Swinging the Lead

A.B. Paterson ('The Banjo')

> Said the soldier to the Surgeon, 'I've got noises in me head
> And a kind o' filled up feeling after every time I'm fed;
> I can sleep all night on picket, but I can't sleep in my bed.'
> And the Surgeon said,
> 'That's Lead!'

> Said the soldier to the Surgeon, 'Do you think they'll send
>   me back?
> For I really ain't adapted to be carrying a pack
> Though I've humped a case of whisky half a mile upon my
>   back.'
> And the Surgeon said,
> 'That's Lead!'

'And my legs have swelled up cruel, I can hardly walk at all,
But when the Taubes come over you should see me start to
    crawl;
When we're sprinting for the dugout, I can easy beat 'em all.'
And the Surgeon said,
'That's Lead!'

So they sent him to the trenches where he landed safe and
    sound,
And he drew his ammunition, just about two fifty round:
'Oh, Sergeant, what's this heavy stuff I've got to hump
    around?'
And the Sergeant said,
'That's Lead!'

MR COLLINS AND THE WHITE BULL

The Backstory

> 'The question isn't who is going to let me; it's
> who is going to stop me.'
>
> Ayn Rand

There is a white bull at the centre of this story, although, unlike the one in the 1959 hit song for Tommy Steele, he was a rather large white bull—certainly large enough to be noticed—and 'once upon a time', way back in 1871, he almost sent Harry Readford to jail. It took a miscarriage of justice to save him.

This particular 'not-so-little white bull' was the property of Bowen Downs station, in North Queensland.

The Bowen Downs region was named in honour of Queensland governor Sir George Bowen by the explorer William Landsborough, the man who was sent to find Bourke and Wills, and later became the Queensland Commissioner for Crown Lands.

In 1860 Landsborough and Nat Buchanan explored the area and, when the district was opened for settlement and the newly formed government of Queensland issued grazing licences, they applied for a pastoral lease over a large tract of country along the Thomson River. They mortgaged the property to the Scottish Australian Investment Company and Landsborough's friend Edward Cornish. Buchanan became the first manager and overlanded 3000 cattle to the property in 1862. But after a few bad seasons Buchanan abandoned his one-eighth share to the Scottish Australian Investment Company and walked out.

So, apart from Landsborough's small share, Bowen Downs was completely owned by the Scottish Australian Investment Company, whose address was Sydney. The company owned fifteen huge properties in Queensland, ranging in size from 40 square miles (10,000 hectares) to 1500 square miles (4 million hectares).

Bowen Downs was a huge cattle run fronting more than 200 kilometres of the Thomson River, with good Mitchell-grass plains stretching away from the river. The property was managed by Robert Morehead and Matthew Young, who were part owners as well as the Queensland representatives of the Scottish Australian Investment Company, but it was run by overseers. By 1870 the drought had broken, and after several good seasons the property had restocked very well, with large numbers of 'cleanskins' (unbranded cattle) running wild over the 100 square miles.

Some modern accounts claim that the station carried more than 60,000 head of cattle in 1870. This is fanciful in the extreme, given that in 1865 Nat Buchanan walked off the property in a time of severe drought. Cattle don't breed like rabbits and there had been no store cattle to buy during the drought. After several good seasons, 16,000 might be nearer to the mark.

Whatever the numbers were on Bowen Downs, Harry Readford reasoned that 1000 of them, including a rather large white bull, would not be missed—until it was too late.

The Story

> 'Cattle duffers on a jury might be honest men enough,
>> But they're bound to visit lightly, sins in those who cattle duff.'

> Melbourne *Punch* magazine (July 1885)

Of all the rorts and acts of bush skulduggery in our colonial past, the sheer audacity of Harry Readford's theft of 1000 head of cattle probably takes the prize for daring and originality, not to mention skill and bushmanship! He and two companions (maybe four; we don't really know) took the cattle from North Queensland 1500 kilometres down the Channel Country and through outback desert where no stock had ever been before, and delivered them into the colony of South Australia—where Harry knew their brands would be unknown.

It was a feat comparable to the greatest overland cattle treks in our history and the skill and audacity it demonstrated led to one of the most obvious and infamous miscarriages of justice in Queensland history. (And there have been plenty of those!)

The greatest rort involved in the whole episode was not the reckless cattle stealing and remarkable journey. It was the mind-boggling effrontery with which jury foreman James Nimmo gave a straight-faced 'not guilty' decision which meant that an obviously guilty-as-sin Harry Readford walked free from the Roma Courthouse.

Henry Arthur 'Harry' Readford was born in December 1841 near Mudgee, the youngest of the eleven surviving children of an Irish convict and his Australian-born wife. He was a strong massively built bushman, 1.9 metres tall. Harry worked at various jobs in the bush and on the Hawkesbury River, and by the late 1860s he had headed north and was living on a small cattle property in central north Queensland, where he was involved in a carrier business with three other men, carting goods from the railhead at Tambo to the large cattle property Bowen Downs.

It seems the venture was a success for Readford and his friends, William Forrester, William Rooke (or Brooke) and George Dowdney. Harry also supplemented his income by working as a stockman for Forrester, who owned a station called Balaclave between Readford's property and Bowen Downs, and by stealing cattle in partnership with local property owner John McKenzie and a man named James McPherson, who worked for McKenzie.

Apparently, the epic cattle heist and cattle drive through the Channel Country to another colony was dreamed up by Readford after talking to Dowdney and Rooke, who had travelled through that part of the country from South Australia previously. Harry and the others had been stealing cattle successfully for a while and had almost been caught a few times. So Harry suggested a big 'one-off' job that would make them rich.

Cattle duffing had increased dramatically in the 1860s in Queensland due to higher cattle prices and the issuing of grazing licences over huge areas of good grazing land to large companies whose principals lived in Sydney, Brisbane, Melbourne or the UK.

Many locals, especially those struggling to make a living with smaller holdings, felt aggrieved by the government policy of allowing absentee ownership of land. They also resented the wasteful grazing practices and the poor way that overseers ran these huge properties. They thought locals and 'Australians' should own and profit from the natural resources of the country. (Sound familiar?) These strongly felt sentiments would later save Harry from prison and bring about a miscarriage of justice that shocked the Queensland establishment to its core.

Harry realised that Bowen Downs Station was so big that parts of it were rarely, if ever, visited by stockmen. Harry and his mates would be able to build a set of stockyards in a remote corner of the station and herd a large mob of cattle there without anyone ever knowing what they were doing. They also had cattle from Bowen Downs hidden on the McKenzie property.

Early in March 1870 the men started moving the cattle onto William Forrester's property. At this point Harry revealed his 'master plan' to take a massive mob of cattle across the outback, and McKenzie and McPherson refused to be part of the scheme. They only wanted to continue stealing small numbers of cattle and keep their duffing on a small scale. But Rooke and Dowdney, who had travelled up from South Australia using the same route Harry proposed taking, thought the scheme was possible—they were 'in'.

At Forrester's cattle camp the cleanskins were branded with various local brands to make the herd look like a typical mob of store cattle (cattle rounded up for market or fattening—not breeding stock). Many of the Bowen Downs herd were already branded 'LC', which stood for 'Landsborough and Cornish', the original partners in the station.

In late March Harry set off with a large mob of the stolen cattle down Coopers Creek and the Strzelecki Track, via the Channel Country. He was accompanied by Rooke and Dowdney and perhaps two others, stockmen James Johnson and Harold Merrick, for part, or all, of the journey.

Harry had decided to steal a valuable white bull, known as 'Whitey' or, more officially, 'The Duke of Marlborough'. The bull's presence, it was thought, would keep the herd, which contained many cows and heifers, quiet and tractable. It was a good idea but ultimately a mistake.

Harry Readford never talked much about the experience, although he did, rather strangely, give a newspaper interview after selling the cattle, as we shall see. He revealed that he was nervous for the first month of the trek and climbed a tree or hill every morning to look for any signs of pursuit. After that first month, he knew they were relatively safe—any dangers lay ahead of them, not behind them.

For most of the trek they kept the cattle together, but sometimes split the herd into three smaller mobs to get better feed. Harry and his accomplices and the cattle covered 1300 kilometres in three months, which included detouring around floodwaters and dealing with local Aborigines, who they found mostly friendly. It is uncertain whether they had Johnson and Merrick with them or managed the whole trek with just three men—it would have been an incredible task for three, or even five, men to achieve!

What makes the story even more remarkable, and the feat more believable, is the fact that they had incredible good luck with the seasons. The Channel Country and Strzelecki Desert were experiencing unusual wet weather and good seasons, and the biggest problem the cattle duffers had with water was avoiding it!

They arrived safely in June 1870, at the general store at Strzelecki Creek, also known as Artacoona Native Well, in north-eastern South Australia.

Harry, posing as 'Henry Collins', attempted to trade two cows for clothes and provisions at the general store. He told the store-keepers, two brothers named Walke, that the cattle were from a station called Wilbe Wilbe in New South Wales and belonged to him and his brother Lawrence Collins, which explained the 'LC' brand. (Harry did actually have a brother named Lawrence.)

But Allan Walke was suspicious and demanded the white bull as part of the deal. With the heist almost completed, Harry reasoned they no longer needed the bull, so he exchanged it and two cows for clothes and sorely needed provisions. Harry signed a receipt 'Henry Collins'.

After resting a few days, the last stage of the journey via Mount Hopeless to Blanchewater Station east of Marree was easily accomplished. Blanchewater was owned by the Hon. John Baker, a Conservative member of the South Australian parliament who had briefly been premier—for six days in 1857.

The cattle were sold for £5000 to station manager Mr J. Mules, who may have believed Readford's story, or simply been only too happy to buy 1000 head of cattle cheaply in the best season the country had seen since European settlement—no questions asked. There was feed for fattening and the Adelaide market needed beef.

Readford was paid with a promissory note cashable in six months time and made out to 'Henry Collins'. The men then proceeded to Adelaide, where the note was sold off at a discounted rate to a money dealer. On their way down through the Flinders Ranges to Adelaide, 'Henry Collins' gave an account of his exploits—part fact, part fiction—to a newspaper reporter in the township of Blinman.

The newspaper reported that Collins, 'the owner of Wilbe Wilbe Station', had overlanded cattle and 'just sold them at Blanchewater after a trek of four months', which had 'involved repeated detours of more than 50 miles to escape floodwaters'.

It wasn't until September that stockmen at Bowen Downs noticed tracks of cattle that had left the station. They followed the tracks to the neighbouring property belonging to John McKenzie.

The police became involved. McKenzie was implicated in the thefts, and he and two other men were arrested and charged with stealing 100 head of cattle from Bowen Downs. McKenzie and a man named McGrath were tried at the district court in Roma in early 1871 and, despite an overwhelming case and many witnesses testifying against them, a sympathetic local jury found them not guilty.

It seems amazing that it was only while this investigation was underway in late 1870 that mustering on Bowen Downs led to the realisation that many more cattle were missing and local rumours started circulating that suggested certain 'possibilities'.

Bowen Downs' manager Boyd Morehead, Robert's son, had even been told about a huge mob of cattle being moved through the Channel Country, but the clue had been dismissed as irrelevant as the prosecution of McKenzie and McGrath was in progress.

The information had come from a bushman named John Costello, who noticed the tracks of a huge mob around the part of the Channel Country known as Wombunderry Channel, 400 kilometres south of Bowen Downs. Costello was exploring with the idea of taking out a lease there, which he later did. The bushman assumed, quite rightly, that a mob that big had to come from Bowen Downs, but his information went unheeded until mustering on the station brought to light the missing numbers and the secret stockyards were discovered in October 1870.

The trail was now six months old and fading, but Bowen Downs sent stockmen Edmund Butler, John Vernon and John Craigie to follow it, track down the missing cattle and unravel the mystery. They found the white bull at Artacoona and traced some of the cattle to the Adelaide markets. South Australian police had already arrested a drover taking cattle branded 'LC' down a stock route to Adelaide. Morehead and Young's agents, auctioneers Elder Smith, found other cattle similarly branded in the Adelaide market.

Morehead travelled to Adelaide by steamer and arrived on 17 February 1871 and the Blanchewater connection was exposed.

A warrant was issued for the arrest of 'Henry Collins' and Harry Readford's name started to be associated with the affair, but the connection wasn't made until John Craigie remembered being in Adelaide on family business in July 1870 when he'd met Readford unexpectedly and been surprised to hear him called Mr Collins. Then it was noticed that Collins' description matched Readford.

But where *was* Harry Readford?

He had left Adelaide soon after meeting Craigie, on 20 July 1870, aboard the steamship *Aldinga*. Returning via Sydney to Mudgee, he had married childhood sweetheart, Elizabeth Scuthorpe, there in April 1871.

Meanwhile, in light of new evidence, McKenzie and McGrath, along with Forrester and two local men, were taken all the way back to Roma to face fresh charges of stealing 200 head from Bowen Downs.

McGrath was tried first.

This time McKenzie confessed and gave evidence for the prosecution. He admitted he had been paid by McGrath to take part in the theft and was present when the cleanskins in the large mob of cattle were branded at Forrester's cattle yards.

Amazingly, the Roma jury found McGrath not guilty and the Crown prosecutor decided not to proceed with the trials of the other men.

Meanwhile, warrants were issued for the arrest of Harry Readford.

Harry and Elizabeth had used the ill-gotten gains from the cattle theft to buy a pub in Gulgong, near Mudgee. Even though he was wanted in three colonies, no one noticed when Harry used his real name to apply for a liquor licence and had his name published in the police gazette in order that police across the colony could check the name to see if he was an appropriate person to own a pub.

If only Harry could have stayed away from trouble, he might have lived a long and happy life as a publican with the now-pregnant Elizabeth and the daughter she was carrying.

Harry, however, was arrested in November 1871 in Gulgong for helping two men open a stolen safe. One of the men told police the robbery had been Harry's idea and he'd lent them his horse to carry the safe away.

The case against Harry wasn't very strong and he was released, but subsequent checks discovered he was wanted in three colonies and he was rearrested a week later and charged with the Bowen Downs cattle theft. Taken to Roma in late November, he was charged with 'stealing 100 bullocks, 100 cows, 100 heifers, 100 steers and 1 bull'.

Harry was in custody for a long time and the trial was finally set for February 1873, but out of 48 jurors empanelled, the prosecution accepted only seven. The frustrated judge—Queensland parliamentarian Charles Blakeney, who was born in Ireland and educated at Trinity College, Dublin—had no choice but to ask the prosecution to reconsider jurors until twelve were chosen.

The evidence, as reported by the *Sydney Morning Herald* on 1 March 1873, was overwhelming against Harry. An expert gave evidence that the handwriting on the receipt for the bull was obviously Harry's:

> Mr Lukin, the Police Magistrate at Roma, produced the recognisance of bail signed by the prisoner as 'Henry Redford,' [Henry being Harry, who was baptised Henry Arthur] in his presence. Mr. J.K. Cannan was examined as an expert, and gave it as his opinion that the signatures 'Henry Redford' to the recognisance, and 'Henry Collins' to the receipt given to Mr. Walker, were written by the same person.

The white bull was the star witness. Only a dozen or so of the other cattle had survived and been recovered; most of the rest had already been eaten by hungry South Australians. The Hon. John Baker had stalled attempts by Morehead and his agent to inspect the herd at Blanchewater while he sold off as many of the stolen cattle as he could to local butchers. Still, there was sufficient evidence to prove that the rest of the stolen herd had arrived in South Australia:

The first witness called was Edmund Butler, who proved that he was cattle overseer on the Bowen Downs Station from 1867 to the present time, that in the month of November, 1867, he was sent by his employers, Messrs Morehead and Young, to Gracemere Station, near Rockhampton, to select and purchase one or more bulls; he selected one, a very valuable imported bull, of pure white colour, branded A on the near and off rump; when he selected the bull abovementioned he placed an additional brand on him—namely, 8 on the loin, the bull outside the Court was the animal he bought at that time, he could not be mistaken as to his identity, irrespective of any brands which appeared on him, he is a very remarkable beast, he (Butler) started the bull for Bowen Downs Station, where he arrived safely, and he (Butler) saw him on the station mentioned several times during the years 1867 and 1868; during the months of March, April, mid May, 1868, a muster of the cattle was made on that part of the Bowen Downs where the bull was kept, and about 1000 head of cattle, together with the bull in question, were at that time missed from the station.

Butler then gave the damning evidence of Harry's guilt:

The next time he saw the bull was in South Australia, about 1000 miles distant from the place where he had been missed: it was at a place called Streletzski Creek; he was in the possession of a person named Allan Walke; he (Walke) told witness that he had purchased the bull with two cows from a man who gave his name as Henry Collins; there were with Collins at the time two other men whom he (Walke) knew to be named Doudney and Brooke; Walke then produced to witness a document which he said was the receipt given to him by Collins for the purchase of the cattle, and which document he (witness) then produced before the Court.

Other witnesses corroborated the evidence that the bull was stolen and disposed of by Harry Readford:

John Vernon was the next witness, and he deposed that he was stockman on the Bowen Downs run in 1867 and that he knew the bull outside the Court well, and could identify him amongst a thousand irrespective of his brands as the animal was a remarkable beast, and was in his charge from the time he came on the station up to the year 1869, when he disappeared. The next time he saw him after he was missed was in South Australia, in 1871, where he, witness, in company with Butler, found the beast in Walke's possession. The moment he saw the bull he knew him.

Allan Walke was called and said that:

He and his brother kept a general store at Streletzski Creek, and the prisoner, at the time mentioned, with his mates, came there to purchase clothes and stores, after selecting what articles they required, they proposed to sell witness two cows, branded LC: he agreed to purchase the animals provided they would also dispose of a bull they had in their mob, (the bull outside the Court was the animal he alluded to); to this the prisoner and his mates consented, before completing the purchase witness asked who the cattle belonged to, and prisoner replied that they belonged to himself, in conjunction with his brother, who owned a station in an adjoining colony, he gave his name as Henry Collins; witness's brother then drew up a receipt, which the prisoner signed, the document before the Court is the receipt mentioned; he (witness) had no doubt whatever as to the prisoner being the man who sold him the cattle and signed the receipt.

Walke also stated that, when he saw the bull at Roma, he 'identified him amongst seventy other bulls, a great many of whom were of the same colour-white'.

Ownership of the bull was incontrovertibly proven when Mr Robert Morehead's son, Boyd, the manager of Bowen Downs Station from October 1866 to June 1868, stated:

... that he knew the bull outside the Court to be the property of the owners of that station, and that he never sold the animal to any person, or authorised any other person to sell him.

James McPherson was produced as a witness for the prosecution and testified that he, Readford, McKenzie, Dowdney and Rooke:

> ... went twenty five miles up the Thomson River, and there built cattle yards, when the yards were completed he, with the others, mustered a large number of the Bowen Downs cattle and filled the yards with them, the cattle were afterwards drafted off in mobs of two or three hundred at a time to Forrester's camp, the white bull outside the court was amongst the cattle taken at that time, the object being that he would keep the cows and heifers quiet, of which there were a large number in the mob, ultimately the whole of the cattle were driven off by Readford, McKenzie, and Brooke, towards the southern colonies.

Unfortunately, McPherson, who had been unsuccessfully tried for the theft previously, proved to be a tainted witness, due to the conditions under which he gave evidence and his admitted mental illness. He did, however, prove a source of entertainment to those present, according to the *Sydney Morning Herald*, which announced that 'Mr Paul's examination of this witness occasioned some amusement' and went on:

> The witness stated that he was not a cattle-stealer, although he might have stolen some, though not to his knowledge. He admitted that he was charged with the offence of stealing these very cattle from Bowen Downs; that he was committed for trial and arraigned, pleaded not guilty, and was discharged on the ground of insanity; that he was sent to Brisbane as a lunatic, and escaped from the reception-house at that place. He also stated that he was rearrested at Armidale, in New South Wales, and was brought up to this Court to give evidence against the prisoner, under a promise of a free pardon if he gave fair evidence at the trial ...

Harry Readford's defence was almost non-existent. It consisted of a statement that he was now a married man with a young daughter and had suffered great distress since his arrest, along with bringing to the jury's notice the fact that James McPherson had recently escaped from a lunatic asylum. No witnesses were called by the defence—not one.

The case lasted a total of twelve hours; most of it consisted of hard evidence of Readford's guilt. The *Sydney Morning Herald* reported Justice Blakeney's summing up:

> The Judge observed that he trusted that the jury would not be led away by the specious although clever address of the counsel for the prisoner; and that they would dismiss from their minds the hardships said to have been endured by the prisoner, no doubt placed before them with a view to making him a martyr. They should bear in mind the train of circumstances which had been proved respecting the prisoner.
>
> He is found, at the period when this extensive robbery of cattle took place, on the Thomson, the locality from which the cattle were missed. He is shortly afterwards found in South Australia, more than 1000 miles from the scene of robbery, next in the City of Adelaide, under a false name. He is next found in the colony of New South Wales, where he is arrested and brought to Blackall, in this colony. To prove the case against him it was necessary to have the bull and the person who purchased him brought from South Australia, which unavoidably caused great delay in hearing the case. So much for the hardships endured by the prisoner.

It seemed cut and dried to Blakeney that Harry Readford had to be found guilty, even if McPherson's evidence was ignored, as the defence counsel had suggested:

> He next would submit that, supposing that the jury accepted Mr Paul's recommendation, and gave no credence to M'Pherson [sic], yet the case was plain against the prisoner.

The whole case was proven, in Blakeney's mind, by the evidence of the theft of the bull:

The bull had been identified beyond all question as the property of Messrs. Morehead and Young; it is also identified as being the one sold by the prisoner to Mr Walke, and the evidence of that gentleman could leave no doubt on any reasonable mind that the prisoner at the bar and the person who sold that animal in South Australia were one and the same person.

The judge said, therefore, that: 'He would, with these remarks, request them to consider their verdict.'

The jury took an hour to consider the verdict and jury foreman, James Nimmo, delivered it to a hushed and packed courtroom.

'Not guilty.'

There was a universal gasp of shock and surprise. Judge Blakeney sat still for several seconds and then asked the jury foreman to repeat the verdict.

'Not guilty.'

Again there were a few seconds of silence. Judge Blakeney looked at the jury and said, 'Thank God, gentlemen, that verdict is yours, not mine.'

The press of the various colonies had a field day at the expense of the Queensland judicial system. The *Sydney Morning Herald* reporter reminded the readership: 'The costs of the witnesses in this case, I am informed, were over £600.' There were scathing reports ridiculing the verdict in the *Sydney Morning Herald* and *Melbourne Argus*, and the *Brisbane Courier* bemoaned the sad state of justice in the colony of Queensland.

The squattocracy of the Darling Downs were outraged, as were the more socially respectable citizens of Roma. One landowner wrote, 'As a Magistrate of the District I beg to add my private testimony to the fact that the feeling in Roma is evidently very much against convictions for cattle stealing and the present jury list contains many names of men quite unfitted to return an honest verdict.'

Although James Nimmo, the jury foreman, had served on juries that had convicted other thieves, the rest of the twelve were suspected of accepting bribes and one had, it transpired, been found guilty of cattle stealing himself!

Judge Blakeney's explanation to the attorney-general commented that, while only the theft of the white bull could be proved beyond any reasonable doubt, he failed 'to see the possibility of obtaining a conviction for cattle stealing in any case before a Roma jury'.

The judge called for a reform of the *Queensland Jury Act*, which he said was defective in that it was framed in such a way that 'respectable people' were barred from jury duty.

The obvious miscarriage of justice caused a furore in Queensland and, in March 1873, was debated in parliament. The result was that the district court was removed from Roma for two years.

Harry Readford was arrested for stealing horses in the St George district twice in 1875, by which time the district court had returned to Roma. Once again he was found not guilty and walked free from the Roma Courthouse.

Arrested again for horse stealing in 1881, it was decided to send him for trial at Toowoomba, and there he was at last found guilty of an offence and sentenced to eighteen months in a Brisbane prison.

After his release, Harry led a relatively useful life. Over the next twenty years, he helped explore the country between North Queensland and Darwin, established overland cattle trails throughout the Barkly Tableland, and served as overseer and manager on cattle stations in the area, doing much to establish a viable cattle industry for Queensland. He established the famous Brunette Downs cattle station by overlanding a mob of 3000 head to the area and became the manager of that property.

However, it seems he took to fixing horse races at local meetings and, after a betting coup (more likely a scam) at Tennant Creek races, he had enough money to buy a small holding, which was later added to Brunette Downs. He then moved on to become manager of MacArthur River Station, near Borroloola.

As a result of the great cattle theft of 1870, several changes were made to the laws in Queensland regarding the empanelling of juries, and uniform regulations regarding cattle brands and their registration were written into law. William Landsborough, the man who founded Bowen Downs and had fallen on hard times in the years between, was made an inspector in the new Brands Office.

The most obvious result of the crime was the opening up of stock routes through the Channel Country. Harry Readford had also been the first overlander to realise that cattle fattened perfectly well on saltbush.

After the publication of the novel *Robbery Under Arms*, written by Thomas Alexander Browne under the pen name Rolf Boldrewood, Readford became somewhat of a celebrity.

Browne was an unlucky grazier who had established sheep and cattle properties but was beaten by drought at several places, including Swan Hill and Narrandera, before taking a ten-year posting as goldfields commissioner at Gulgong in the 1870s. He was then police magistrate at Dubbo, Armidale and Albury in the 1880s.

As the famous author of *Robbery Under Arms*, published in 1889, Browne retired with his family to Melbourne and became a stalwart of the exclusive Melbourne Club, where he often sat and wrote. He was author of a dozen or so successful novels.

In *Robbery Under Arms* Browne used his experiences as a police magistrate to make a credible and realistic plot. He also used his knowledge of several real people to create the character of the dashing and romantic bushranger and cattle thief 'Captain Starlight'. Browne always said the Captain Starlight character was made up from stories of different bushrangers of the era. These included Frank Pearson, who actually used the name Captain Starlight during his career as a bushranger in the late 1860s. Pearson was reputedly involved in daring deeds such as locking police in their own cells, riding his horse into a hotel bar in Barmera, South Australia, and having a shoot-out with police at a store in Engonnia, in which he mortally wounded one Constable McCabe in 1868. Sentenced to death he later had the sentence commuted to life and was released in 1884 having served fifteen years.

Another inspiration was Thomas Smith, known as 'Captain Midnight'. In May 1870, aged twenty, he was sentenced at Bathurst to five years imprisonment for cattle theft. Smith escaped with another prisoner named James in September 1872 and continued stealing cattle and horses, usually under cover of darkness, with two other escaped convicts, John Bolton and Thomas Walker.

Browne said he also drew on episodes from the lives of bushrangers Ben Hall, Dan Morgan, Frank Gardiner and Johnny Gilbert, as well as Harry Readford. From Harry's life Browne used the cattle drive and the court scene, which occurs in a town called Nomah in the novel.

For some reason Harry Readford, who was still alive and a free man when the novel appeared, was labelled as 'The Real Captain Starlight' in the last decade of his life, although he never applied the name to himself or claimed to be a hero.

Throughout his life Harry was, in fact, an habitual criminal and an incorrigible thief and liar—the type of person my mother would have said 'couldn't lay straight in bed'.

Perhaps a small fraction of the dashing Captain Starlight may be Harry Readford immortalised in fiction but, sadly, the real Harry Readford was a mere mortal and he drowned in 1901, attempting to swim the flooded Corella Creek while exploring the country beyond Brunette Downs.

He was 59 years old.

Captain Starlight would have made it across easily.

THE GUILE OF DAD McGINNIS

The scam perpetrated in this poem is so good I've often wanted to try it myself, but, sadly, I don't have a regular 'drinking hole' these days, where such a trick might be appreciated as merely light-hearted fun at the publican's expense. It might have worked at Maiden's Hotel in Menindee, on the Darling River, when I lived there all those years ago, but I don't think I'll try it anywhere in the Eastern Suburbs of Sydney any time soon. I'm too old to be beaten up by security guards and chucked out of pubs that serve gourmet food and 45 different wines by the glass!

The trick, if you're keen to try it, works like this. You order one drink and, before touching it, ask to swap it for another. You then change your mind and say you will have something else instead and you swap the exchanged drink for your third choice and drink it then refuse to pay for it because you traded it for the one before. When the bartender asks you to pay for the drink you exchanged for the one you exchanged for the one you had, you say you never actually drank that one and ... Look, why don't you just read the poem and work it out for yourself.

It's set in a mining town with two rival pubs owned by two characters with wonderful Irish names: O'Gorman and 'Kangaroobie' Riley. The hero of the story is a swagman known locally as 'Dad' McGinnis. It's by a great old *Bulletin* poet W.T. Goodge, who wrote his witty doggerel as 'The Colonel'. His poems were collected together and published in a book called *Hits, Skits and Jingles*, which is sadly long out of print.

The Guile of Dad McGinnis

W.T. Goodge ('The Colonel')

When McGinnis struck the mining camp at Jamberoora
    Creek
His behaviour was appreciated highly;
For, although he was a quiet man, in manner mild and meek,
Not like ordinary swagmen with a monumental cheek,
He became the admiration of the camp along the creek
'Cause he showed a point to Kangaroobie Riley!

Both the pubs at Jamberoora had some grog that stood the test
(Not to speak of what was manufactured slyly!)
And the hostel of O'Gorman, which was called The Diggers'
    Rest,
Was, O'Gorman said, the finest house of any in the west;
But it was a burning question if it really was the best,
Or the Miners'—kept by Kangaroobie Riley.

Dad McGinnis called at Riley's. Said he 'felt a trifle queer',
And with something like a wan and weary smile, he
Said he 'thought he'd try a whisky'. Pushed it back and said,
    'I fear
I had better take a brandy'. Passed that back and said,
    'Look here,
Take the brandy; after all, I think I'll have a pint of beer!'
And he drank the health of Kangaroobie Riley!

'Where's the money?' asked the publican; 'you'll have to
    pay, begad!'
'Gave the brandy for the beer!' said Dad the wily,
'And I handed you the whisky when I took the brandy, lad!'
'But you paid not for the whisky!' answered Riley. 'No,'
    said Dad,

'And you don't expect a man to pay for what he never had!'
'Twas the logic flattened Kangaroobie Riley!

'See,' said Kangaroobie Riley, 'you have had me, that is clear!
But I never mind a joke,' he added dryly.
'Just you work it on O'Gorman, and I'll shout another beer.'
'I'd be happy to oblige yer,' said McGinnis with a leer,
'But the fact about the matter is—O'Gorman sent me here!
So, good morning, Mr Kangaroobie Riley!'

THE TARRING AND FEATHERING OF G. MADDISON HARVEY

The Backstory

> 'Punishment is now unfashionable ... because it creates moral distinctions among men, which, to the democratic mind, are odious.'
>
> Thomas Stephen Szasz (1920–2012)

Nobody seems to know the exact origin of the phenomenon of tarring and feathering. It probably dates from some pagan practice that began way before medieval times.

The first mention of the practice in print, however, occurs in 1589, in *Principal Navigations, Voiages, Traffiques and Discoueries of the English Nation,* written by scholar and historian Richard Hakluyt. He mentions the punishment in relation to King Richard I and claims that it was a statute the king put in place to keep order in his navy during the voyage to the Holy Land at the time of the Third Crusade. The historian dates the statute at 1189 and states:

Concerning the lawes and ordinances appointed by King Richard for his navie the forme thereof was this ... item, a thiefe or felon that hath stolen, being lawfully convicted, shal have his head shorne, and boyling pitch poured upon his head, and feathers or

downe strawed upon the same whereby he may be knowen, and
so at the first landing-place they shall come to, there to be cast up.

It seems to me, if Hakluyt's transcription of the ordinance
is accurate, that it is a very odd sort of procedure for a king to
suddenly 'think up'. My assumption would be that Richard was
merely making it known that any miscreants or troublemakers
during the voyage would be subjected to a humiliating punishment that was already well known at the time.

The main purpose of the punishment throughout history has
always been public humiliation and an indication of the local
community's disapproval of the victim's behaviour or beliefs.

The most common substance we know as 'tar' today is actually
the concrete bitumen used to make roads. The tar referred to by
Hakluyt is coal pitch (technically a 'vegetable' pitch, as coal is
fossilised wood) and it boils at a much lower temperature than
water—at around 60 degrees Celsius. It might burn and injure
at that temperature, but it won't necessarily result in death. In
fact, it seems there is little, if any, historical evidence of death
occurring as a result of the actual 'tarring'. It seems that the point
of the exercise was to use a sticky material with which to make
the feathers adhere to the skin in order to make the victim look
like a chicken or strange bird—and therefore a figure of fun
and derision.

As 'pitch' derived from trees or coal was an essential ingredient
in the construction and repair of wooden ships from the earliest
days of maritime history, there would have been a ready supply of
it on the vessels that made up Richard I's navy. Indeed, sailors are
still called 'Jack Tar' to this day. However, in many reported cases,
oil, molasses, animal glue or melted pine pitch were used as handy
substitutes for 'boyling pitch'.

There was also always a plentiful supply of feathers in any village
or household in the 'old days'—all pillows and cushions were
full of them and just about every household kept chooks, geese
or ducks. Hens were also commonly kept on ships undertaking
long voyages.

The practice of tarring and feathering became extremely popular in the American colonies prior to the Revolutionary War, and remained popular into the 20th century, when laws were finally passed banning such 'cruel and malicious practices'.

The procedure was often accompanied by other practices, such as being paraded around town, tied to a lamp post, thrown into the nearest creek or river, or run out of town on a rail, where the victim was placed on a section of fence rail, carried around town to be verbally and physically abused, then finally taken to the edge of town and dumped by the roadside.

In the US there were quite a few accounts of people whose views were not appreciated by the local community being tarred and feathered on multiple occasions. There are photographs showing victims with serious skin damage.

In Australia there are very few recorded or reported cases of tarring and feathering, and those that do occur often seemed to be in the nature of a cruel prank rather than a serious vigilante action.

Banjo Paterson's poem 'Tar and Feathers' is reputedly based on an incident at Narrabri in the late 1880s, in which a circus proprietor, in an attempt to deter local delinquents from the age-old practice of 'sneaking in under the tent', caught a young lad doing so and decided to make an example of him. Evidently the local magistrate was of the opinion that the circus proprietor went a little too far in tarring and feathering the boy. The proprietor was convicted of assault and heavily fined.

I'm sure that pranks in the form of variations of tarring and feathering must have occurred in Australian shearing sheds, given that shearers' tar was always at hand and it would cause relatively little damage as it is actually formulated to melt at a much lower temperature than boiling point and heal the skin of the sheep and stop bleeding. The sheds were notorious for practical jokes, such a shearing someone's sheepdog, placing rabbit traps in beds and nailing boots to the floor, not to mention the many practical jokes played on and by shearers' cooks—as evidenced in many written anecdotes and poems.

So it does seem odd to me, therefore, that, in all my reading and research, I have never come across an account of an incident where shearers' tar is used as part of a practical joke in a shearing shed. Maybe I haven't looked hard enough and some of you reading this book will have heard of such events. Please let me know if you have.

The Story

> 'Had you not created great sins, God would not
> have sent a punishment like me upon you.'
>
> Genghis Khan

On 23 November 1921 sixteen men appeared before the Mildura Police Court charged with assault and grievous bodily harm. Twelve were later sent to trial and found guilty.

Their victim was George Henry Cochrane, alias Grant Hervey, editor and proprietor of the *Mildura and Merbein Sun* newspaper, who, on 25 October that year, had been beaten, stripped, tarred and feathered at an aerodrome on the edge of town and left for the police to find.

This incident was the culmination of a series of events over the previous two years. It was also the culmination, to a large extent, of Hervey's lifetime of misdemeanours.

While cases of tarring and feathering may be very rare in Australian history, and examples of it extremely difficult to find, there is no doubt that it happened on that spring evening in Mildura. There is plenty of evidence to prove that it occurred, and the men who perpetrated the act were more than happy to admit that they did so.

Perhaps they had chosen this particularly American form of retribution because Mr Cochrane/Hervey, who was a Victorian-born convicted criminal, fraudster and con man, had some time earlier attempted to dupe the good citizens of Mildura and steal their money by false pretences, while posing as a successful American entrepreneur and calling himself 'G. Maddison Harvey'.

According to a long feature article in the *Mildura Cultivator* on 6 August 1919, G. Maddison Harvey, a tall, imposing man who wore a full-length astrakhan coat and spoke in a broad American accent, had addressed a public meeting attended by 2000 people the previous Saturday to present his 'Greater Mildura' scheme for a new state, for which he sought financial backing.

Mr Maddison Harvey admitted he had never been to Mildura before but said that he was aware of the town's unique history and the self-reliant and pioneering spirit of its citizens, and was, therefore, proposing that the Mildura district and the Darling–Murray Valley should become an independent state, with Mildura as its capital.

During this meeting, which was the start of a series of events that led to his ultimate tarring and feathering, Harvey evidently further proposed that he was just the man to make this happen and that, if everyone present donated £5 to the cause, he would take the proposal to Prime Minister Billy Hughes and then on to Westminster and make sure it was carried through. He only required, he said, to be paid £1000 every six months to devote his life to lobbying and advocating for and negotiating with the relevant authorities until the goal of independent statehood was attained for 'Greater Mildura'.

The speech was a doozy! Reading detailed accounts of it almost 100 years later you cannot help but be impressed by G. Maddison Harvey's cunning and the way he used flattery and his knowledge of the town's history to stir the emotions of his audience. Nor can you help but be impressed by the evangelical fervour with which he presented his proposal.

To fully understand just how the tall and eloquent 'snake oil salesman' with the astrakhan coat and the fake American accent was able to manipulate the feelings and ambitions of 2000 good citizens of Mildura, we need to remind ourselves about the district's unique and fascinating origins and history.

The Mildura Irrigation Colony was the dreamchild of Alfred Deakin, Solicitor-General and Minister of Public Works in the Victorian parliament and later Prime Minister of Australia. In 1884 he visited the United States and investigated irrigation projects, especially the large-scale 'communities' based on collectives and 'company town' models. Deakin was impressed by the work of the Canadian Chaffey brothers, who had set up three 'irrigation communities' in California, and invited them to Australia. George Chaffey then visited Australia, and Deakin helped convince the brothers to sell up in California and move here.

Things did not go smoothly but Mildura was eventually set up as a Chaffey-managed company town—an alcohol-free irrigation colony, a collective and company-run community of farmers.

The project failed but, with government assistance and goodwill and perseverance, Mildura eventually prospered and the Chaffeys came to be seen as pioneers and visionaries. Those farmers who joined up to be part of the project considered themselves to be a different breed from other outback settlers and townsfolk.

Today Mildura is a thriving and prosperous city—one of the nicest towns in inland Australia—but the jury was still out in 1919, when G. Maddison Harvey and his silver tongue arrived in the town.

In his impassioned address, delivered from the town's rotunda bandstand, to 2000 of those who had survived, and quite possibly profited from, the turbulent years during which the town of Mildura had been established, Harvey was fulsome in his praise of those who established the irrigation community, knowing full well that those present were the beneficiaries of the vision and endeavours of the Chaffey brothers, and that William Chaffey, who had chosen to remain in Mildura when his brothers returned to America, was at that time the shire president.

Perhaps the fake American accent, dress and mannerisms were designed to elicit sympathy in a community that owed its existence to a family of fellow 'Americans'. The Chaffey brothers were, of course, Canadian, a distinction that was probably lost on most of the good rural folk of the district. The Chaffeys' previous irrigation communities had all been established in California, and Canadians were 'American' in any case.

The speaker reminded his audience that they had been right about the Chaffey brothers when the rest of Australia had doubted and denigrated their vision. Now, he assured them, every right-minded person in Australia was aware that the people of Mildura had been correct all along.

Having been introduced to the assembled citizenry by none other than the shire president, William Chaffey himself, the 'man with the plan' opened the meeting in prayer. Having asked the men present to remove their hats, Harvey beseeched the almighty to bless and protect the town and open the minds of those present to the soundness and wisdom of his proposal.

In his address he recalled that many had scoffed at the vision the Chaffeys had proposed, calling them 'deceivers' and 'Yankee swindlers who could not make a living in their own country'. However, he said, those who had made such criticisms had 'long ago had occasion to revise that opinion', which had been, according to the orator, merely a 'cockeyed little-minded' contemporary view of the project. He went on to say that such 'cockeyed criticism' had emanated from a despised group in society he referred to as 'the pin-minded push'. He asked those present whether they were 'lifters or leaners', and wanted to know if they were 'workers with minds and souls for a greater Mildura' or merely 'parasites on the backs of the pioneers'.

The Chaffey brothers' proposal for the irrigation community had been outlined in a brochure designed to attract investors known as 'The Red Book'. This document was, according to the speaker, 'the Magna Charta [sic] of Australia's Inland Freedom' and furthermore 'the men behind the ideas in that book were great men, who set out to do a great work'. They had, he said, been criticised but 'they had outlived such criticism' and 'built up a Mildura which would ever stand as a monument to their foresight and enterprise'.

By way of comparison he invited those present to consider other towns in the district that did not display the same enterprise, but benefited from the success of Mildura. He noted that 'for many miles on either side of Mildura the land had reaped an unearned increment' and lamented the fact that, across the river, 'the sheep still held sway'. He challenged others to learn from the example set by Mildura and stated that:

> If the Government of New South Wales had been alive to the possibility it would long ago have created another Mildura on the other side of the river.

When a loud voice from the crowd replied, 'It hasn't got the guts', Harvey was able to segue smoothly to the nub of his proposal. 'The expression,' he replied, 'if vulgar [still] summed up the situation. It hadn't got the guts.'

But there was one man in Australia, according to Harvey, who had 'the guts' and that was William Morris Hughes. He then proceeded to eulogise the prime minister, as reported in the *Mildura Cultivator*:

> Never in the history of Australia had there been another man who stood knee-high to William Morris Hughes. His suggestion was that Mr Hughes should be brought to Mildura. He appealed to every man, whether civilian or digger, to help bring Mr Hughes to Mildura. If the proposed new state was to be made the place which it should be, it was imperative that Mr Hughes should be brought face to face with the possibilities.

There was much more rhetoric and eloquence to come—along with some surprises—and the meeting lasted until 10.30 p.m.

Harvey's proposal took the form of the creation of a new state—the 'Soldiers' Memorial State' (or 'Greater Mildura'), to be settled by 100,000 returned servicemen and secede from Victoria, with Mildura as its capital. This new state was to be an outback territory, peopled by the hardy breed of farmers and rural settlers, extending up the Darling River as far as Queensland, and established on the principle of reward for hard work combined with entrepreneurial innovation.

As the speech went on, Harvey implied he was part of an

organisation that could implement the plan, and that he was the man for the job of promoting the concept. In the spirit of the Chaffey brothers, and imbued with good old Yankee know-how, he would give the region the kind of promotion and recognition it deserved.

At this point in his speech, it became obvious that Harvey was launching a daring public attack on the man who had become famous for promoting the district by using various publicity stunts and innovative methods that were funded by local cooperative organisation the Australian Dried Fruits Association, or ADFA. That man was Clement John 'Jack' De Garis, whose official title was Director of Publicity for the ADFA.

It seems that Harvey had decided that his plan to ingratiate himself with the local fruit growers and townsfolk of Mildura, in order to extract some financial gain from their gullibility, could only work if he called into question the competency and honesty of the man in whom they had previously placed their trust.

Jack De Garis was an advertising and promotional dynamo who single-mindedly and obsessively orchestrated a nationwide blitzkrieg publicity campaign in which a barrage of awareness-raising propaganda was launched at every demographic in every city, town, village and hamlet of Australia. (His story is told in the chapter 'The Prince of Ballyhoo'.)

It is not quite certain why Harvey decided that an attack on De Garis was an essential part of his plan to extract money from the citizens of Mildura, but at some point he apparently thought that it was good idea to call into question the credibility of De Garis by asking a series of questions about the corporate governance and professionalism of the ADFA. Perhaps he thought it would strengthen his position once he had the crowd on side, so he did it—at his peril.

Harvey implied that the Director of Publicity had wasted £20,000 of the people's money on second-rate and unsuccessful stunts, and announced that he had eighteen questions he would like the ADFA to answer if they could.

At that point Jack De Garis appeared from the crowd and offered to answer them.

Now, Jack De Garis was a local and there were many in Mildura who thought he was a genius, but there were also some who found his ideas and gimmicks a bit of an embarrassment and a little self-indulgent.

The general consensus was that it would be polite and fair to at least hear out this imposing American speaker.

Once De Garis was allowed onto the stage, Harvey read a series of accusations in the form of questions, including claims that other cooperative organisations gave far better service to members and other publicity companies achieved better results than De Garis and his amateur stunts. He also claimed that the ADFA had done little or nothing for returned soldiers who wished to settle as farmers in the district.

De Garis heard him out, then replied that he could answer all the accusations but wanted first to refute one claim and then ask Mr Harvey a couple of questions. This confrontation must have looked rather odd, even comical, as De Garis was 4 foot 11 inches while Harvey stood over 6 foot 2 inches.

In his one-and-a-half-hour speech, Harvey had boasted that the town was already £1 million richer when he stepped off the train that morning because of the idea he had brought to them. He also said he was motivated to come and help after despairing of the ineptitude of De Garis's campaigns, which he claimed had achieved nothing.

Jack De Garis countered by saying that, as it was his publicity that had brought his accuser to town, he had obviously succeeded as the town was, according to Harvey himself, now apparently £1 million richer!

The locals enjoyed the joke and sympathy started to swing towards their diminutive local hero.

De Garis then pointed out that the man Harvey had praised to the skies, the man who had in fact introduced him that evening, Shire President W.B. Chaffey, was the founder and life president of the ADFA.

Then came three simple questions from De Garis: 'Who are

you?', 'Who do you represent?' and 'Where have you been for the past seven years?'

Now, anyone involved in political organisations at any level knows the golden rule of public debates and meetings: never ask an opponent a question unless you know the answer.

Jack De Garis did know the answer to his questions: G. Maddison Harvey was George Henry Cochrane, alias Grant Hervey; he represented no organisation except himself; and he had—for the past four years—been in prison for fraud, attempted blackmail and forging and uttering, which, in layman's terms, means creating a scam or fraud and then perpetrating it.

The *Mildura Cultivator* reported what happened next:

> Mr Harvey, throwing off his overcoat, declared in impassioned tones that he had spent a good deal of the time mentioned in prison. He was sent to gaol on the 19th August 1915 (after eight months of trial) and he was released on the 19th June, 1919. His real name was Grant Madison Hervey. John Norton and he were in business together on the paper 'Truth' and Norton swindled him. He *had* swung the man a double-cross which broke him up but which incidentally led to his own imprisonment. It was while in prison that he evolved the scheme of a Greater Mildura. He was an Australian not an American as he had represented. Knowing Australia as he did, he felt that the people would pay more attention to 'a man from abroad' than they would to an Australian. He believed in his scheme *and had hoped to get it accepted.*

There was, as you can imagine, quite an uproar in the crowd but they quietened enough to hear Jack De Garis refute some of the claims the now-exposed con man had made. He added a statement that his 'Sunraysia' publicity campaign was now reaching its conclusion and a full report as to its success or otherwise would be published in due course by the ADFA.

Mr G. Picton, a soldier-settler, then addressed the meeting briefly and condemned Harvey for falsely criticising and denigrating organisations that had helped returned servicemen in the district.

Harvey denied he had done this and asked the chairman for permission to speak again. By this time, however, it was 10.30 at night and the president declared that he thought Mr Harvey had already said 'more than enough'. He then added that he personally resented the actions of the guest speaker and declared the meeting closed.

In spite of being exposed as a jailbird, liar and fraud, Harvey was not the victim of any 'grievous bodily harm' that evening. He did, however, harbour an even deeper grudge against Jack De Garis, which would lead him into more foolish behaviour two years later—and then he would not be so lucky!

On this occasion, however, with his proposal for a new state exposed as a pipedream at best and a scam at worst, he beat a hasty retreat.

The *Mildura Cultivator* concluded its long report of the eventful meeting held on Saturday 2 August 1919 with a short paragraph that read: 'Mr Hervey left by Monday morning's fast train.'

George Henry Cochrane (alias various versions of Grant Madison/ Maddison Hervey/Harvey) was born in 1880 at Casterton, in far western Victoria, just 25 miles from the South Australian border.

The son of a storekeeper and grandson of a convict who he claimed was a 'noble fellow' who was 'most unjustly used', young George was a tall, strong red-headed lad who became a blacksmith at a local coach-building business and then moved to Melbourne, where he worked in a foundry.

By the age of twenty he was contributing verse to the *Bulletin* and, some time in 1900, he moved to Sydney looking for work as a journalist. Before he was 23 years old, he had worked on newspapers in Melbourne, Perth and the Western Australian goldfields, and had attempted to start his own literary magazine.

He seems, in his verse writing, to have been heavily influenced by Henry Lawson's ideas and sense of nostalgia. Many of his poems contain ideas and even phrases from Lawson's verse, although young George seems to have also developed romantic, utopian notions of life in the bush. His verse is very reminiscent of Lawson's, while being nowhere near as good. Like Lawson, he began as a pro-Labor Party writer and worked on *The Worker* newspaper. Later his writings and speeches became vehemently anti-Labor Party.

Cochrane changed his name to Grant Hervey—he later claimed this was a nom de plume, but it was also the name he went by in his private life from around 1902. His collected verse, written in the decade between 1903 and 1913, reads like the efforts of a young and idealistic dreamer and he covered all the standard 'bush verse' topics of the time. Here he is talking about bush workers ending a spree in town:

From 'Leaving the Town'

So we've come to the end of our tether,
And our cheque is expended at last;
Who have lolled for the last months together
In the bars where we sit now aghast!
We have spent what we earned in the saddle,
What we made with the pick and the shears;
Now it's time for the bush-ward skedaddle,
It's farewell to the bars and the beers!
We have taken our fill of their pleasure,
Now we sit with our foreheads a-frown
For we've come to the end of our leisure,
It is time we were leaving the town!
One trip, just one more, down the harbour;
Just one noon on the sands with the girl;
'Ere we give up the beach and the barber,
'Ere our beards once more tangle and curl!
Just one night at the show to remember;

Ah! one cab-ride, dear girl, 'ere we go
Where the sun burns the plains to an ember
And the teams travel dusty and slow!

I've read a lot worse, but we've heard it all before.

It seems that whatever Hervey was writing about at the time was the most romantic and nostalgic of all topics for him. For example, he wrote about the passing of the bullock drivers, with their cursing and swearing and bullock whips being used to move the loads across the outback. The piece of silk on the end of the whip was what made the noise—it was known as the 'cracker':

From 'Silk Cracker Days'

From Portland Town, I saw them steer,
'Ere a railway line was built,
When men sinned sins with a wanton cheer
And the wayside rum was spilt!
Oh, for the days when to North and West
The waggon-ships sailed free.
And tacked and veered at the shrill behest
Of the whip-lash musketry!
Silk Cracker Days! through the steaming haze
Do I see them drive the teams,
The men whose lips and roaring whips
Make thunder in my dreams!
Silk Cracker Days! They are dead and gone!
Long crumbled into dust
Are waggon-wheels and hearts that won
The present breed its crust!
The Days are Gone! The coaly train
Has seized on all the land,
Whereon the teams in cracking days
Went cursing through the sand!

His line 'the coaly train has seized on all the land' is very similar to Henry Lawson's idea that the coming of the railway ended the golden days of the bush. As Lawson said, 'The mighty bush with iron rails is tethered to the world.'

But not long after lamenting the arrival of the railway, we find Grant Hervey writing a hymn of praise to the mighty railway and the men who work on it, in a poem called 'Rolling Her Home':

> Lashing her, crashing her; footplates a-clatter,
> Cranks swinging forward in maniac haste;
> Leaving the darkness and silence a-shatter
> The former in twain and the latter effaced!
> Gigantic and frantic, she sways in her agony.
> Her cars all a-beat like a vast metronome:
> Driving her on in her mighty protagony,
> Lo! we go gallantly—Rolling Her Home!
> Greasy old 'blues' hanging limply upon us,
> Faces embellished with coal-dust and sweat;
> With lip-curls and sneerings the swell-folk may con us,
> But we hold dominion o'er all the world yet!
> Majestic we march on the footplates in glory,
> Our sceptre the age-gripping Westinghouse brake;
> And where is the song, the romance, and the story
> To better the song that we leave in our wake?
> Flinging her, swinging her, hark! how she thunders!
> Tearing exultantly down the long grade;
> Machine-god incarnate, and chiefest of wonders
> That man with his brain and his muscle hath made.
> Lifting her, shifting her, lo! we go roaring,
> Embankment a-quiver through gravel and loam;
> Controlling her, rolling her, sending her soaring.
> Spurning space, churning space, Rolling Her Home!

Actually that's not a bad piece of rhymed verse—if you can put up with the 'agony/protagony' rhyme.

Like every other aspiring bush poet of the day, especially the younger ones, he waxed lyrical about the bush being the spiritual and restorative home of the true Australian:

> Man's work takes him forth on a Road that is lonely,
> For the heart may be lone in the mightiest throng;
> But one gathers fresh courage and strength lying pronely
> 'Mid the trees where glad winds breathe their patriot song!
> Far away the grim world fights its truceless, shrill battle,
> Lo! the hills are a refuge of silence and peace;
> Green swards and white tree-trunks, in place of Town's rattle,
> How precious and holy and healing are these!
> Aye! the Bush is a Mother who offers a chalice
> To her sons when they weary of turmoil and rush;
> Lo! she giveth them comfort—not rancour or malice
> It is good to come back to the Bush!

The Scottish-born associate editor of the *Bulletin*, James Edmond, took a liking to the aspiring young poet and began publishing Hervey's verse in the magazine.

The *Bulletin* was born the same year as George Cochrane/Grant Hervey—1880. Established by J.F. Archibald and John Haynes, the *Bulletin* introduced Banjo Paterson and Henry Lawson to the Australian public, along with Victor Daley, Mary Gilmore, C.J. Dennis, Will Ogilvie, Harry Morant, W.T. Goodge, 'John O'Brien', Charles Souter, 'Jim Grahame' and all the rest.

'The Bully' regularly published the work of more than 60 verse writers and ensured that the rhymed verse tradition was well and truly confirmed and established as part of our national heritage. The importance of the *Bulletin*, which was often called 'The Bushman's Bible', in establishing our literary tastes and authors' reputations cannot be overestimated. It was certainly *the* place to be published for any aspiring versifier.

James Edmond was the magazine's editor from 1903 to 1914, the decade in which George Cochrane, now calling himself Grant Hervey, was busy attempting to become one of Australia's great verse writers. Edmond was known for his sense of humour and love of all things irreverent. J.F. Archibald said of him that he was 'the only man I know who can get fun out of a balance-sheet'.

As the *Bulletin*'s editor, Edmond was being bombarded weekly with around 200 poems by inspiring balladists and versifiers. I find it hard to believe that Edmond would have championed Grant Hervey's verse on the basis of admiring its nationalistic sentimentality—as he probably received 100 examples of such stuff every week.

It is my guess that he was attracted to the young poet's often-clever use of rhyme and the irreverent approach he took to certain topics. Perhaps he liked poems like this one:

Kisses and Sin

Kiss now! while the girl is handy,
You can't when she's far away;
Sin now! lest your life be sandy,
Oasis-less and grey.
Kiss now! while the chance is waiting,
While it lingers at your side;
For the man who stands debating
Will gain no gladsome bride!
Sin now! 'ere gloom and fatness
And their greasy kith and kin
Have filled your years with flatness,
And you know not how to sin.
Kiss now while the girl's complacent
Kiss now! 'ere love grows cold;
Kiss now! while her mouth's adjacent
Feast now! while her hair is gold!
Sin NOW! you are growing older,
Away with your doubts and fears;
For the greyest ghosts that moulder
In the vale of our latter years

Are the haunting apparitions
Of the sins we contrived to miss,
The uncommitted transgressions—
The girls that we didn't kiss!

It would appear that the young poet was writing from personal experience when he advised his readers to 'Sin now', and 'Kiss now! 'ere love grows cold' for, a few days before his 25th birthday in November 1905, an incident occurred that gives us a clear indication of his unstable personality and criminal tendencies.

The *Melbourne Argus* reported the event in detail on Saturday 18 November:

City Sensation
Mr Walter Baker Fired At
Grant Hervey Arrested

A sensational incident occurred in Bourke Street East when Grant Hervey, well known as a writer of verse, drew a revolver and fired at Mr Walter Baker, the leading actor of Mr Bland Holt's company.

The affray occurred at about 11 o'clock. On leaving the Theatre Royal Mr Baker took the Bourke Street tram, and when near the corner of Exhibition Street saw Mrs Baker and Hervey walking towards Parliament House arm-in-arm. Mr Baker said nothing but, on reaching the White Hart Hotel he alighted, and waited under the veranda. As Hervey and Mrs Baker approached he crossed Bourke Street, and stood in front of the pair.

'What is your name?' he asked the man.

'Grant Hervey,' he replied.

'What are you doing with my wife?' continued Mister Baker and without waiting for answer struck Hervey heavily on the jaw. The man staggered back with the force of the blow, and as he steadied himself drew a revolver from his pocket. Mr Baker seized his wife, swung her around to face Hervey as a shield, and then dashed for the corner of Spring Street. As soon as Mr Baker was clear of his wife Hervey fired. The shot struck the steel pier at the side of the Imperial Hotel doorway.

Detective Howard, who had witnessed the whole occurrence, rushed from the middle of the road, and intercepted Hervey, who was in the act of following Mr Baker with the revolver in his hand. As Howard closed with Hervey, a score of people closed in on them, but as they caught sight of the revolver they scattered just as speedily in all directions. Howard held Hervey by the wrists and disarmed him. Hervey made no further resistance, and was removed to the Little Bourke Street watchhouse shouting insults after Mr Baker, who had in the meantime returned.

Hervey was charged with shooting with intent to murder, and lodged in a cell. He gave his age as 25, his occupation as a journalist, and stated that he had 'no religion'.

Hervey is a native of Casterton, but for the past five or six years has been following freelance journalism in Sydney, Perth, Kalgoorlie and latterly in Melbourne. He gained a reputation as a versatile writer, particularly in verse. During the last session of the Federal Parliament he represented the Sydney Worker in the state press gallery, and half an hour before the sensation occurred he was seated in the Senate, listening to the debate.

Mr Walter Baker was interviewed immediately after the occurrence. 'I allow my wife £200 a year,' he said. 'I bought a house which cost over £2000, and my two daughters live with her. She has everything she can desire while I toil, in spite of the doctor's express orders to the contrary. Without telling me she suddenly arrived in Melbourne the other day by the SS *Ophir*. I saw her on Monday. I remember having seen Hervey's photograph hanging in my drawing room in Sydney. When I saw him tonight I thought, "How can I stand this?" I went across to him as any man would and asked him his name and what he was doing with my wife. Then I hit him under the jaw with my left hand. I did not want to knock him down or I would have hit him on the point with the right. The blow drove him back a couple of yards. He pulled a revolver from his hip pocket. I ducked behind my wife who screamed out, "Oh, Walter!" Pushing her aside I ran towards the corner of Spring Street. He fired at me—I heard the whizz of a bullet. I dashed around the corner into Spring Street. Then, when

I heard that Hervey had been disarmed I came back. I wanted to get at him with these (holding up his fists). I had narrowly escaped being shot, for I was only five yards from him when he fired. I am old enough to be his father, if he is only 25, and when he has been in the world as long as I have he won't pull a gun on a man who hits him on the jaw. Still, I would not have preferred against him such a grave charge as "shooting with intent to murder".'

In his cell at the Little Bourke street Watchhouse last night Grant Hervey made the following statement:

'I was escorting Mrs Baker to her hotel in Brunswick Street. Baker was waiting for us at the corner of Spring Street. He came across and, after a few words, struck me. In a wave of excitement, which comes over all of us at times, I drew my revolver and fired at him. Baker—and I would like you to stress this point if you please—hid behind his wife.'

Hervey asked that a message should be sent to a member of the Federal Ministry to arrange for his defence.

Detective Howard had some difficulty in inducing Hervey to give up his revolver. Hervey fingered the trigger nervously, and exclaimed several times, 'It's alright I'm not going to shoot again. Did you see that man assault me?' He was laboring under intense excitement, but, controlling himself, he said to Howard, 'Just one moment if you please. There's a lady on the footpath I'm anxious to have escorted home. Will you ask a friend of hers to take her to the hotel in Brunswick Street—I forget the name?'

When Mr Baker came up to the detective and his prisoner he upbraided Hervey for being a coward and Hervey retorted by taunting him with hiding behind his wife.

In the watchhouse this interchange of remarks was continued.

When asked what countryman he was, Hervey replied, 'An Australian, I am proud to say.'

'That's all you have to be proud of,' said Mr Baker.

'He is under arrest,' said Detective Howard to Mr Baker. 'It's no use rubbing it in.'

Later, Mr Baker asked, 'What charge are you putting against him?'

'Shooting with intent to murder,' replied Howard.

Mr Baker looked surprised, but he dropped his eyes, and remained silent. Hervey waited a few moments and then, glaring at Baker, broke out, 'Well? Well? Haven't you got something to say? This is the psychological moment. This is where we turn the limelight on.'

'A lot you know about the psychological moment,' retorted Mr Baker.

Hervey was led quietly away to the cell, and locked up.

The revolver, when examined, proved to be a heavy Webley, of .450 calibre. It had six chambers, five of which were loaded with ball cartridges. The sixth bore traces of having been recently discharged.

When Hervey appeared in court to be remanded on the following Thursday, the *Sydney Morning Herald* reported further on what it called:

'The Baker-Hervey Affray'

At the City Court to-day, Grant Hervey appeared on remand, charged with shooting at Walter Baker, actor, with intent to murder, and was further remanded for one week. Baker asked the bench to refuse to allow bail, as there was reason to believe [the] accused might again attempt the offence with which he was charged. Mr Panton, P.M., said if Baker thought his life was in danger he should swear an information and have Hervey bound over to keep the peace.

Mr Baker stated he had been informed that last Sunday Hervey was seen in a public park with a revolver in his pocket.

Hervey gave a flat denial to this, and on being questioned by the Bench as to whether he had a revolver in his pocket at that moment turned out his pockets to show he had nothing more dangerous than a pair of nail scissors on him. The Bench allowed him bail in two sureties of £100 each.

The *Adelaide Express* and *Telegraph* gave further information that:

Detective Howard said that when Baker rushed away Hervey followed him with a revolver in his right hand. He went up to Hervey and said, 'Are you mad?' Hervey tried to return the revolver to his pocket but somebody caught him by the left shoulder. The witness was able to take the weapon away.

Mrs Baker testified that she was living apart from her husband.

On Thursday 15 December 1905, the case came to court. The *Sydney Morning Herald* reported the result the following day:

Grant Hervey Not Guilty
Melbourne, Thursday
The trial of Grant Hervey, on charges of shooting with intent to murder and shooting with intent to inflict grievous bodily harm at Walter Baker, occupied the whole of today's sitting of the Criminal Court. [The] accused in defence made a long statement. He said he made a practice of carrying a revolver, because he had received a number of anonymous letters threatening to kill him, and because his work as a journalist led him into dangerous parts of the city. Mrs Baker was an old and esteemed friend of his and he was also well acquainted with her brothers and sisters. When walking up Bourke Street with Mrs Baker he offered her his arm, as an act of courtesy due to all women from all men, and when he fired the revolver shot he merely wished to frighten Baker, and took extreme care to so fire that no damage was done.

The jury returned a verdict of not guilty, and in discharging the accused Mr Justice Hodges said, 'I may perhaps say that for your own safety and the safety of others that it is desirable you should not carry a loaded revolver. I will also make another remark with reference to your statement to the jury that besides the courtesy proper between man and woman there is also due a little fair dealing between man and man.'

So, apparently, the jury believed Hervey's side of the story and he was cleared on both charges and allowed to walk free, his only punishment being the night he spent in the watchhouse and Hodge's insult in relation to what the judge considered his ungentle-manly behaviour.

Hervey made good use of the experience by writing a poem entitled 'The Night I Spent in Quad', in which he pontificated about injustices visited upon the downtrodden and much-maligned characters who find their way into the prison system. His lifelong obsession with his convict grandfather, who he repeatedly referred to as a 'noble fellow' who was 'unjustly treated', seemed to be the spur that led to his desire to champion the cause of the downtrodden.

In this poem, which like many of his others is rather overlong and repetitive, he experiences a vision while in his cell and is visited (rather like Scrooge in Dickens' famous *Christmas Carol*) by three evil spectral figures representing men of religion, makers of the law and upright but selfish citizens.

Naturally, Hervey, speaking as the champion of the masses, destroys their arguments, defeats them and condemns them in a fierce and stirring debate:

> I spoke for them, and said: 'Behold!
> What think ye now of these
> Whom ye sent forth in days of old
> To cross uncharted seas?
> For these ye made your bitter codes,
> For these ye made the laws;
> They tramp alway the evil roads
> Of vice and crime because
> Their fathers' blood is in their veins,
> Their fathers' ways they plod.
> I called the Three the Sons of Cain,
> That night I spent in Quad.

Even at this early stage of his life, Hervey was beginning to manifest signs of irrational thinking and impetuous behaviour at best—and mental instability at worst.

In the collection of his verse, dedicated to James Edmond and published in 1913, some of the poems reinforce his proud assertion made to the police in 1905 that he had 'no religion'. Another poem in the volume, however, is a hymn of praise to the Almighty.

The volume was titled *Australians Yet, and Other Verses*, 'Ballads *of Manhood, Work, Good Cheer, Mateship, Masculine Vigour and Nationalism*', a title which perhaps gives an insight into the odd mix of philosophies that were attempting to form themselves into some sort of cogent manifesto in the mind of George Cochrane, the blacksmith who had now successfully transformed himself into Grant Hervey, poet, journalist and visionary.

The Old Testament version of the Christian God whose words he takes as inspiration in the poem called 'When a Fellow Does His Damnedest', seems to be a god specifically invented to condone the somewhat eccentric and self-serving beliefs of the author:

> I HEARD a Voice all-potent,
> Singing deep within my soul,
> 'Be a Strong Man, be a Smiter,
> Keep thy Manhood sure and whole!
> I have gathered up the splendour
> Of the earth and sea and sky,
> And to thee I give the glory
> When the proud storm pennons fly.
> Be thou worthy of the kingdom,
> Thou who sittest on this throne.
> Be a Fighter strong and valiant,
> Not a weakling slack and prone!
> Be a Captain, be a Leader, lo,
> When Wisdom's door unbars.
> Thou shalt climb with Me triumphant
> Up the staircase of the stars!'
> I heard Jehovah singing
> In a proud, exultant key,
> 'When a Fellow Does His Damnedest,

It is homage unto Me!
For I am a God of Battle,
Not a Lord of humble tears
Dear to Me the scabbard's rattle
And the thrust of stubborn spears!
Who are these that vainly murmur,
With a sad and strengthless moan?
Who are these that weep and falter,
While the Strong Man Goes Alone?
For My heart is towards the Smiters,
Towards the Leaders in the van,
Be a King, Oh! be a Master,
Be a Soldier and a Man!'

Hervey's religious beliefs could apparently move easily between vehement atheism and prophetic Old Testament Christianity, depending on his mood at the time. When arrested in 1915 he told police his religion was 'Greek' and later during his trial called on Almighty God to be his witness.

Similarly, his political views varied, from working on the Labor Party newspaper *The Worker* for several years, to a tour around western Victoria for the People's Party, speaking against Labor's referendum proposals.

He was able to swear under oath that he 'took extreme care to so fire that no damage was done' when he shot at Walter Baker in Bourke Street, and swear again under oath ten years later, that 'in a fit of insanity in Melbourne I shot at Walter Baker'.

Not everyone in the publishing world shared James Edmond's enthusiasm for the literary works of Grant Hervey. Another Scottish-Australian journalist who knew him, Wallace Nelson, said:

[Hervey] turned out poetry by the square yard with mechanical regularity. When he had done a fair morning's work he used to put his coat on and go and have a drink.

Hervey might have managed to talk his way out of a prison sentence in 1905, but he was unable to do so ten years later after managing to get himself entangled in a legal struggle with the infamous John Norton, notorious alcoholic, politician, scandal-monger, and crusading editor and proprietor of the *Truth*, Australia's only national newspaper at the time.

Once again, there was a woman at the heart of the matter.

Norton was at the time living apart from his wife, Ada, and it was common knowledge that he was very keen to attain custody of their daughter. Some time during the first week of January 1915, Hervey, who was employed by Norton as a journalist, told his employer that he had 'behaved indecently' with Ada Norton on Christmas Day, 1914, and again on Boxing Day. He suggested that he could arrange to be caught *in flagrante delicto* with Mrs Norton for the sum of £200. This would provide Norton with the evidence he needed to gain custody of his daughter.

Unfortunately for Hervey, Norton contrived to have him say all this while two police detectives and a short-hand steno-grapher were secreted in an adjoining room. At the resulting trial Mrs Norton denied the accusation, Hervey recanted the story, was found guilty of attempted blackmail and false pretences, and was sentenced to two years' hard labour. He always claimed to have been 'set up' by Norton, either because of his friendship with Mrs Ada Norton or some journalistic disagreement.

At the same time Hervey was accused of committing another crime. In October 1914 someone sent a telegram to Edward Gazzard, proprietor of the *The Casterton News* and *Merino and Sandford Record*, the local newspaper in Hervey's hometown. Gazzard and Hervey were not on good terms and the telegram, sent under a false name, asserted that the Sydney press had just announced that Mr Grant Hervey had been declared bankrupt.

Hervey was charged with 'forging and uttering', the asser-tion being that he sent the telegram hoping that Gazzard would publish the information, at which point Hervey would sue him for libel. Strong evidence was presented to show that the accused was seen to type the telegram and later imposed upon a colleague to drop parts of the typewriter he used into the harbour in order to prevent the police from linking the typed telegram-form to his typewriter. Several witnesses also testified that he attempted to get them to send the telegram at various post offices.

Hervey was found guilty of both crimes but successfully appealed the 'forging and uttering' verdict on a technicality. The judge instructed the jury to discard Hervey's evidence as it was not presented under oath, and a second trial was held. Hervey was again found guilty of the charges.

After the verdict was delivered, he made an impassioned and long-winded statement, in which he claimed to be the victim of a vicious prank that was not perpetrated by Gazzard, but by his own colleagues in Sydney. His defence was not aided by the fact that, when the Casterton and Portland newspapers published the false story, Hervey had issued writs against them in the Supreme Court and then hinted that he would settle out of court for less.

When the judge, Justice Pring, told Hervey that he simply did not believe a word he said, the 34-year-old prisoner in the dock did something out of character—he pleaded insanity:

I have tried to keep this part of my life hidden: but now I feel that I must lift the veil. When the Norton case began, the Crown Prosecutor said that the most charitable construction that could be placed upon my actions was that I was insane. Mr Norton said practically the same thing, and at one stage Judge Docker asked if I had been examined by a medical man. It is a very distressing subject to me, Your Honour, but I think it best to place certain facts before you. I think it is generally admitted that insanity is hereditary. There is a taint of insanity in my blood. My grandfather, William Cochrane, died insane; my uncle, Henry William Cochrane, is at present in an institution for the insane at Ararat Victoria; and two years ago my brother committed suicide at Broken Hill while insane. The same taint of insanity is in my blood.

Hervey then attempted to explain the effect that his 'taint of insanity' had on his relationships with women and stated that

'whenever I got into trouble before, a woman has been responsible, or rather, a woman has been at the bottom of it'.

He then told the judge:

From six to nine months of the year I can go about my business
and pleasure the same as any rational man; then there comes a
time when I have to go away from the city, and into the bush, and
hide myself from my fellow man. I must do this to keep my brain
upon its balance.

Justice Pring was unmoved by the prisoner's statement. The
judge said he had no doubt that Hervey was 'a past master in
scoundrelism' and 'a great danger to the community' and he
sentenced him to two more years of hard labour—to be added to
the two he was already serving.

For once, Hervey was telling the truth in his accounts of his
family's insanity. His grandfather died in Ararat Asylum in 1873,
having spent years there after being found guilty of attempting to
murder his wife. His younger brother shot himself through the
head in 1912 while of 'unsound mind'.

The appeal proved ineffectual, however, and the prisoner
served his four years.

———

How the 'past master in scoundrelism' spent his time in prison
is unknown, but he evidently spent some of it dreaming up the
'Greater Mildura' scam because, just six weeks after his release on
19 June 1919, having purchased an astrakhan coat and brushed up
on his fake American accent, he headed to Mildura, where he made
his speech as G. Maddison Harvey to the 2000 assembled citizens
and was exposed as a fraud and a criminal by Jack De Garis.

Hervey found it hard to get work as a journalist after his run-in
with John Norton and the law—and later claimed that he'd been
blacklisted by editors and 'boycotted in his profession'.

His reaction to this situation was to set up his own newspaper.
It seems that he harboured a stronger grudge against De Garis,
whom he had never liked in the first place, for exposing him and

this led to him establishing a very short-lived weekly newspaper called the *Mildura and Merbein Sun* in January 1921. It lasted 37 weeks.

Hervey used the paper to attack De Garis's successful newspaper, the *Sunraysia Daily*, question his integrity and belittle the success of the publicity campaign he ran to promote the district's produce.

He also published scurrilous personal attacks on the owners of local businesses who refused to advertise in his newspaper, and generally scandalised the district with his 'gutter journalism'.

During this time Jack De Garis was having financial problems in his businesses, which included orchards, processing and packing sheds in Mildura, a newspaper and a publishing business. Having successfully bought and established the Pyap farming settlement in South Australia, he was having trouble raising the capital to set up an irrigation community on 50,000 acres at Kendenup in Western Australia.

Hervey wrote long and regular articles attacking De Garis and claiming that he had defrauded the town and the ADFA. Many of Mildura's citizens took his claims to be an insult to the town.

The final straw came when Hervey printed a special edition of the *Mildura and Merbein Sun* with the headline 'De Garis Bankrupt', which was a lie. He also had posters printed and displayed in Mildura and Melbourne on Monday 24 October, which proclaimed the same brief message.

Mildura had had enough of G. Maddison Harvey, and many citizens felt the town's reputation needed to be salvaged. They decided to act.

The story was soon all over the wire service. The *Singleton Argus* reported it on Saturday 29 October:

Tarred and Feathered
GRANT HERVEY'S EXPERIENCE
A Mildura Sensation
Mildura was a centre of sensation on Tuesday last when it became known that a large number of citizens had decided to tar and

feather Mr Grant Hervey, editor of the 'Mildura and Merebein Sun', following on the publication of a statement regarding the alleged bankruptcy of Mr C.J. de Garis in a special issue of the 'Sun' on the previous Thursday. The statement was also circulated, by means of posters in Melbourne on Monday. After Mr Hervey's return from Melbourne on Tuesday morning about 100 men in some 20 motorcars assembled in front of Mr Hervey's house, but found the place barricaded.

At midday it was learned that Hervey had telephoned for a car to take him to Ouyen, and several carloads of men went to a spot on Deakin Avenue, two miles from Mildura, where there is a bridge over the main irrigation channel. When Hervey's car arrived he was seized by several men, bound, gagged, and placed in one of the cars, which immediately drove off to an aerodrome on the west side of the town. At the aerodrome Hervey was stripped naked, tarred from head to foot, including his hair, and covered with feathers. The aggressors then took away his clothes and left him to seek shelter and clothing as best he could.

Later reports state that upon the completion of the operation the bell of the local fire station was rung violently for several minutes, as a result of which over 1000 persons were soon in the vicinity, where Hervey was standing in the open with his arms stretched to the skies, calling on God to forgive his opponents, who, he said, had not realised what they had been doing. Then one man announced that Mr Hervey had been tarred and feathered. The brief speech was greeted with continuous cheers. One account states that kapok and not feathers was used.

STATEMENT BY VICTIM

Mr Grant Hervey stated on Thursday that two members of the local police force were in his car when he was assaulted, and they were also assaulted and overpowered, one being injured. He further states that sixteen informations have already been laid.

As the case proceeded through the court system, it became apparent that some of the sixteen men who were charged were local businessmen who had legitimate grievances against Hervey. He had attempted to blackmail a few of them into advertising in his newspaper in order to prevent him from revealing 'skeletons' from their past private lives, or had made accusations in the *Mildura and Merbein Sun* about their business dealings.

At first the men were charged with assault and grievous bodily harm, but then that charge was put aside and a more serious charge of conspiracy was laid against the group. If it could be proved that they planned and conspired together in order to attack Hervey, the punishment would be quite severe.

By the time the case, via the court process, had reached the Supreme Court at Ballarat, the number of accused had been reduced to twelve, there being insufficient evidence against the others.

The *Melbourne Argus* reported that Mr Maxwell, appearing for the accused, denied that the men had conspired to commit a crime as 'the mere fact of a number of people joining together did not necessarily constitute conspiracy'. He asked the jury to:

> Consider the case of a bushfire breaking out in the township without any arrangements having been made. The men of that place would flock together to put out the fire, and anyone who arrived on the scene might say, 'This is a wonderful organised enterprise.'
>
> … Hervey was a menace to Mildura, just as the bushfire was to the township. His last infamous act had set a match alight, and had had the same effect on the people of Mildura as the news of a bushfire would have. Hundreds of people have been stirred, and, by accord, had said, 'We are in it,' just as they would be in a case of fire. But that was not conspiracy. That day at Mildura, Grant Hervey was the bushfire, and the people, by impulse, had flocked out to deal with him.

The jury found the men not guilty of conspiracy.

The charge of assault and grievous bodily harm was then laid against the men and they all pleaded guilty.

The *Melbourne Argus* reported the judge's summation and sentence:

> Mr Justice McArthur said that in his long experience at the bar he had come a great deal in contact with the 'gutter press', but never had he seen anything so foul and filthy as the articles which Hervey had published ...
>
> Hervey had convicted himself of blackmail and had exhibited repulsive hypocrisy in the witness box. His Honour said that he did not believe certain things which the 'creature Hervey' had said in the box, but he wanted the whole community to understand that, despicable as Hervey was, that was no justification for men taking the law into their own hands ...

Each of the accused would be fined £25 and sentenced to three months' imprisonment, but the sentence would be suspended, upon them entering into a personal bond of £50 to be of good behaviour for twelve months.

The bonds were entered into, and a month was allowed in which to pay the fines.

Fifty quid was a lot of money in those days, but no doubt the men found guilty thought it a small price to pay for the pleasure of tarring and feathering G. Maddison Harvey.

Footnote: Grant Hervey's life became even stranger after he was tarred and feathered. In 1923 he stole a chequebook from the owner of an office he was renting in Sydney and forged signatures on two cheques. His defence was that he needed to feed his wife and child and could not afford to pay for heating or lighting, as he had been 'black banned' in his profession by John Norton. He was again convicted of forgery and sent to prison for two years. On his release he seems to have lived for a time in Melbourne, again posing as an American—this time calling himself G. Madison McGlashon. In 1929 he briefly edited a 'scandal sheet' newspaper in Sydney called *Becket's Budget*.

He became well known for his political speeches at 'speaker's corner' at the Domain in Sydney and stood as an independent labour candidate against the Labor Party in the Queensland seat of Paddington at the Queensland state elections in 1926, losing heavily to the only other candidate, the Labor Party's Alfred Jones. In 1931 he noticed an advertisement from a Mrs Mahoney in Brisbane, in the classified section of the newspaper, seeking information about her sister, a Mrs F. Hervey. At that time he was living, as man and wife, with Fiona Lockwood, who he claimed he had married in 1920. Although he knew it was not his 'wife' who was being sought in the ad, he sent a telegram asking for £20 from Mrs Mahoney. He signed the telegram form as Mrs F. Hervey and was again charged with forging and uttering.

In a bizarre speech in his own defence in court he launched a paranoid tirade against the Theodore Labor Government in Queensland, accusing Theodore of setting him up and calling himself 'the master journalist of Australia'. He concluded by telling the judge presiding, Justice Edwards, 'I regard you as the fairest judge who has ever occupied the Bench.' To which Edwards replied:

And I think you are one of the most vile criminals I have ever come across. I sentence you to two years on each charge, concurrent, and I regret I cannot make it more.

Hervey replied, politely, 'Thank you, Your Honour.'

There is no record of Hervey having married Fiona Lockwood in 1920, as he claimed, and no record of a child. That does not mean there was no child or no marriage; records are not perfect. If there was a marriage, however, it may well have been bigamous, for there *is* a record of George Henry Cochrane marrying his long-time friend, the widow Annie Crowe of Casterton, at South Melbourne on 20 October 1918—which seems odd, seeing that George Cochrane, alias Grant Hervey, was supposedly in prison in New South Wales at the time!

I find myself quoting Alice in Wonderland: 'Curiouser and curiouser!'

Having thanked His Honour, Grant Hervey went off to Bathurst Prison, where he wrote a very strange novel called *An Eden of the Good*. The story, set in the 'poisonous convict village of Sydney', featured 'real' figures from Australia's history like W.C. Wentworth, Charles Darwin and John Dunmore Lang, along with a poet hero named Randolph Cochrane and his wife, Mildura Cochrane, a convict named George Hervey, a newspaper editor named Ebenezer Weaselfidjetts, a brothel madame named Venus Colossal and a governor named Sir Dratsum Sneek, which is 'Keens Mustard' spelled backwards.

On his release from prison Hervey fled far away from the 'poisonous village' back to Melbourne, where he died from diabetes, aged 53, on 6 November 1933.

An Eden of the Good was published posthumously in 1934.

Tar and Feathers

A.B. Paterson ('The Banjo')

Oh! the circus swooped down
On the Narrabri town,
For the Narrabri populace moneyed are;
And the showman he smiled
At the folk he beguiled
To come all the distance from Gunnedah.

But a juvenile smart,
Who objected to 'part',
Went in on the nod, and to do it he
Crawled in through a crack
In the tent at the back,
For the boy had no slight ingenuity.

And says he with a grin,
'That's the way to get in;
But I reckon I'd better be quiet or
They'll spiflicate me,'
And he chuckled, for he
Had the loan of the circus proprietor.

But the showman astute
On that wily galoot
Soon dropped—you'll be thinking he leathered him—
Not he; with a grim
Sort of humorous whim,
He took him and tarred him and feathered him.

Says he, 'You can go
Round the world with a show,
And knock every Injun and Arab wry;

With your name and your trade
On the posters displayed,
"The Feathered What Is It from Narrabri!"'

Next day for his freak
By a Narrabri Beak,
He was jawed with a deal of verbosity;
For his only appeal
Was 'professional zeal'—
He wanted another monstrosity.

Said his Worship, 'Begob!
You are fined forty bob,
And six shillin's costs to the clurk!' he says.
And the Narrabri joy,
Half bird and half boy
Has a 'down' on himself and on circuses.

SECTION THREE: THE SPORT OF KINGS AND CON MEN

MELBOURNE CUPS, MACKERS AND RED-HOT TROTS

The Backstory

> 'A bookie is just a pickpocket who lets you use your own hands.'
>
> Henry Morgan

The history of Australian horseracing is also, sadly, the history of various scams, rorts, malpractices and cheating.

Australians love racing. Every few years we seem to find a new thoroughbred to admire. This tradition was established quite early in colonial times and our obsession with racing is probably due to the importance of horses in the development of the colonies in the 19th century. The horse was the main mode of transport and most men owned horses—and, when given a chance and a holiday, they enjoyed racing them.

As settlements spread out into the bush, horses became even more essential. Entertainment was limited and race meetings became the most common way to let one's hair down after a spell of hard work and to socialise after living in isolation for weeks or even months. Along with this came three other typically Aussie traits: the love of a long weekend or a holiday; the belief that handicapping the more talented performers makes things 'more interesting'; and the national love of gambling.

General public involvement in racing is far greater in Australia than anywhere else in the world and the trend was established in the mid 19th century. It is amusing to speculate that the percentage of the Australian population who actually attended Spring Carnival racing in Melbourne in the 1890s, if translated into similar figures in Britain, would have seen four million people attending the Derby meeting at Epsom!

Racing was associated with holidays and social recognition. The Autumn and Spring Carnivals in colonial Melbourne and Sydney were about social events and status as much as about horses. This gave the unscrupulous the chance to conduct their scams and cheating with a certain air of respectability.

Even the Melbourne Cup itself, the most carefully watched and monitored race of the year, has a sad history of schemes and complex machinations designed to cheat and con both the Victoria Racing Club (VRC) and the bookmakers, not to mention the poor old punters.

The obvious reason for this is, of course, the huge prize money and the enormous amount of money in the 'betting pool' just waiting to be taken by unscrupulous owners, trainers, bookmakers, punters, criminals and smart-alecs.

While some of these rorts involved violent criminal activities and distressing acts of cruelty, there are some that had a touch of genius about them and, I am sad to admit, some that bring a guilty smile of admiration to my face—although I hasten to add that one should never condone any criminal activity, no matter how benign or clever it may seem!

The Story

> 'Any money I put on a horse is a sort of insurance policy to prevent it winning.'
>
> Frank Richardson

Melbourne Cup mythology begins with the lie about Archer walking to Melbourne to win the first Cup. To suggest that Australia's most successful trainer, Etienne de Mestre, would have sent his valuable horse on such an arduous marathon walk is laughable. Newspaper accounts of the day show that Archer left Sydney on 18 September 1861 on the steamer *City of Sydney*, together with two stablemates, Exeter and Inheritor, and arrived at Port Melbourne three days later.

Archer might have walked to the nearest port of embarkation from his home on the south coast of New South Wales, or perhaps he walked from the Port Melbourne docks to the hotel stables at South Yarra, where he was trained for the Cup.

Etienne de Mestre, cunning as he was, may have enjoyed spreading the ridiculous rumour about the walk as part of his plan to empty the pockets of Melbourne's bookmakers. An injury to Archer, real or feigned, leading up to the race also helped the price get out to an appetising 8 to 1 before de Mestre pounced and reduced the odds to 6 to 1.

As well as the cunning use of misinformation, de Mestre achieved success by the more customary practice of training his horse away from prying eyes in what was then known as St Kilda Park, opposite the Botanical Hotel, where Archer was stabled, in South Yarra.

Archer defeated the favourite, and local champion, Mormon, by 6 lengths after de Mestre had backed his horse in from 8 to 1 to 6 to 1, with the result that the bookmakers of Melbourne were left reeling and inter-colonial rivalry, as it then was, became even fiercer. A further irony, which modern racegoers may not realise, is that there was no prize at all for running second.

Other Cup folklore includes the tale of the twelve-year-old 'Aboriginal' boy named Peter riding Briseis, the first female horse to win, in 1876. This is one of the best con jobs in Cup history.

The legend goes that Peter was born on the St Albans Stud property near Geelong to an Aboriginal mother; perhaps he was the son of St Albans' owner, Jim Wilson Senior, or his son, also Jim. Another version has the boy being left as a baby on the doorstep of the home of one of St Albans' grooms, Michael Bowden, to be raised by him and his wife.

As he had no 'real' surname he was, so the story goes, given the name of the property and became 'Peter St Albans', youngest jockey and first Aboriginal rider to win the Cup!

Unfortunately, this wonderful story is absolute rubbish.

Two elements of the story are true. He was known as Peter and he was very young: indeed, he was only twelve and, oddly enough, this fact explains the whole wonderful concoction. The boy had ridden Briseis, as a two-year-old, to three victories at Randwick earlier in the year, including an incredible win in the Doncaster Handicap, where he rode her at 5 stone 7 pounds (35 kilograms). However, the VRC rules did not allow jockeys to ride in the Melbourne Cup until they were aged thirteen, and Peter was a few days shy of his thirteenth birthday on Cup Day in 1876.

The regular jockey for St Albans' horses was the legendary Tom Hales, who could not make the race weight of 6 stone 4 pounds (39.5 kilograms). As Briseis won most of her big races as a two-year-old, she was given a very light weight to carry, which meant that a good lightweight jockey was required.

Few grown men could ride at that weight, but Peter was an excellent rider who knew the horse as a stableboy at St Albans and had ridden her to victory in three races in Sydney. So, cunning old Jim Wilson came up with the 'cock-and-bull' story of Peter's origins to allow him to ride Briseis in the Cup. He argued to the VRC that both the boy's birthdate and parents were unknown, but he was probably older than thirteen.

'Peter St Albans' was actually Michael Peter Bowden, born in Geelong on 15 November 1864, and there is a birth certificate to prove it. He was the son of Michael Bowden and his wife and, though christened Michael, he was known as Peter from an early age to differentiate him from his father. There is a painting at the State Library of Victoria by Frederick Woodhouse showing Michael Peter Bowden as a youth, looking very white and European, standing alongside Briseis, with Tom Hales in the saddle.

Michael Bowden was a successful jockey for several years around Geelong and also rode successfully interstate until a bad fall at nineteen saw him switch to training. He died in 1900 at the age of 35. The Geelong Thoroughbred Club awards the Peter St Albans Trophy each year to the jockey who rides the most winners at the Geelong track.

The famous St Albans Stud was the birthplace of nine Melbourne Cup winners and has a special place in the history of rorts and cons associated with the Cup.

In 1873 a protest was entered the day after the Melbourne Cup over the uncertain ownership, age and identity of winner Don Juan, who was trained by St Albans' owner Jim Wilson and ridden by his son, Jim Wilson Junior.

A South Australian gentleman named Samuel Bowler entered the protest claiming that Don Juan was a year older than he was claimed to be and that the Cup winner could possibly be, in fact, a horse called Mentor—a ring-in.

Attempts to find out who owned Don Juan ended in confusion.

Apparently the horse, which had excellent bloodlines, was bred in Adelaide by John Baker and purchased by Jim Wilson as a two-year-old for the surprisingly paltry sum of 50 guineas.

Jim Wilson intended to train the horse for the Cup and keep him away from the racetrack to get a light weight. He sold the horse to flamboyant bookmaker Joe Thompson but, in order to keep the horse's ability a secret and their involvement and intentions clandestine, they paid a man named W. Johnstone £100 to be the nominal 'owner'.

A farcical sequence of events then followed.

The horse didn't show much promise at first, so the conspirators listed him for sale at 500 guineas. When he matured, however, the horse started to show ability over a distance in secret gallops at St Albans and was entered for the Cup but not raced. Consequently he was given the featherweight of 6 stone 12 pounds (43.5 kilograms) for the Cup.

At that point Thompson started backing Don Juan to win the Cup at long odds and Melbourne's bookmaking fraternity, realising where the money was coming from, immediately slashed Don Juan's price to 3 to 1 to make him an unattractive bet for the public.

When the betting price shortened so drastically, it aroused the interest of Joe Inglis, a well-known horse owner and amateur rider over jumps. Inglis had perused the sale lists and remembered seeing the horse listed, so he checked to see if the horse was still for sale. It was, as Wilson had forgotten to remove him from the list—so Inglis bought Don Juan for the listed price!

Negotiations immediately took place and Don Juan was leased back from Inglis and raced in the ownership of W. Johnstone to win the Cup. Thompson bought the horse back for £2000 after the Cup and built a mansion called Don Juan Place with his winnings from the betting coup.

Three years later Jim Wilson Senior concocted the 'Peter St Albans' story and won the Cup with Briseis.

The following year, 1877, Wilson was again at the centre of a scandal that became known as 'the Savanaka Coup'.

This coup began when racehorse owner, pastoralist and founding member of the Victoria Amateur Turf Club (VATC), Herbert Power, traded his 1876 Melbourne Cup runner, Feu d'Artifice, for an unraced but well-bred two-year-old grey colt named Savanaka.

Feu d'Artifice had started 4 to 1 favourite for the Cup and finished fifteenth in a field of 33. Savanaka ran twice in one afternoon at the end of the carnival and won the second race over 6 furlongs easily.

Mr Power and St Albans owner Jim Wilson, who had trained Briseis to win the Cup that year, immediately hatched a plan. Savanaka was scratched from all races he'd been entered for and disappeared into a paddock at St Albans, where he was conditioned and prepared to run 2 miles, which it was later revealed he had done in 3 minutes 33 seconds in training—faster than any Melbourne Cup winner had ever run. Then he was entered for the 1877 Cup and, with no form to go on except two starts and a win over 6 furlongs a year previously, he was given the light weight of 6 stone 2 pounds (39 kilograms).

Within 24 hours of the race weights being announced, Savanaka had been backed to win £50,000, a fortune in 1877. The general public, who loved the Cup and the Spring Carnival, were bewildered—a horse that had only ever started twice and won one race over 6 furlongs was suddenly the favourite for the Cup. They could smell a rort.

The Cup was full of incidents that year. Robinson Crusoe (named because he survived a shipwreck, an amazing story which I'll get to) was facing the wrong way when the flag dropped, collided with another horse and caused many horses to lose ground. The runaway leader, Fisherman, tired quickly with about 5 furlongs to run and fell back onto Waxy, which fell in front of Savanaka.

The grey colt Savanaka managed to stay on his feet but lost many lengths. He rounded the turn in a hopeless position but flew down the straight to lose the race by half a head. The winner was the Sydney horse Chester, who had won the VRC Derby and was trained by the man who won the first two Cups, Etienne de Mestre. The winning time was a race record of 3 minutes and 33 and a half seconds.

The press were scathing in their criticism of the cynical manipulation of the rules of fair play by owners and trainers such as Power and Wilson. One reporter pontificated:

> The public gained intense satisfaction that the clever party at St Albans, whose deeds are dark and ways mysterious, got bowled over for once and that Mr de Mestre had won the Cup for the Hon. James White, a man who races for sport, not money.

Herbert Power responded by saying he could do as he liked with his own horse and mentioned the fact that Mr James White's Melbourne agent, Septimus Stephen, had collected £10,000 in £100 notes from bookmaker Joe Thompson as a result of White's bet of £400 on the Derby–Cup double. This had happened at the Exchange Hotel in Little Collins Street and Stephen was accompanied by the prizefighter Jem Mace as a bodyguard.

The obvious links between racing and betting and the shady practices of participants such as Jim Wilson did little to enhance the public reputation of horseracing in the 1870s.

After the Melbourne Cup almost-coup, Savanaka went on to win the 1879 Sydney Cup in record time.

Wilson retired in 1895 and sold St Albans and all his horses by conducting a lottery. The property remained a stud and training facility and was in the news again in the spring of 1930, when it became the secret hiding place of Phar Lap, after an attempt had been made to shoot the horse, who had been backed to win a fortune in the Cup. The property is now a housing development, with streets named after people and horses associated with the famous stud.

As well as his amazing record of victories, Phar Lap could probably have also easily won the Caulfield Cup of 1930. The fact that he was left in the field so long and scratched quite late was controversial at the time. It was, indeed, part of a 'cunning plan', a rort perhaps, rather than a con or a scam. Most racing men say it was a stroke of genius.

Nothing outside the rules of racing took place but some, mostly bookmakers, consider the actions of the participants had more than a tinge of mischief about them.

The clever coup revolved around three great horses: Amounis, Phar Lap and Nightmarch.

Nightmarch had defeated Phar Lap in the Melbourne Cup of 1929. The following spring, however, Phar Lap defeated Nightmarch four times in a row and his owner, Mr A. Louisson, had been heard to say that if Phar Lap contested the Caulfield Cup, he would take Nightmarch back to New Zealand for the New Zealand Cup—rather than run against the champion again.

The conspirators were reputed to be Dave Davis, Phar Lap's American owner, Maude Vandenberg, a widow known as 'Madame X' who was a big punter, Amounis's part-owner Bill Pearson, who was close to Mrs Vandenberg, and Eric Connolly, a big-betting punter and successful owner who was a mate of Davis.

They agreed that the great stayer Amounis, trained and part-owned by Frank McGrath, would win the Caulfield Cup if Nightmarch and Phar Lap didn't start. Mrs Vandenberg loved backing Amounis and had done so very successfully many times.

Trainer Harry Telford agreed to leave Phar Lap in the Caulfield Cup field until Louisson took Nightmarch home. That gave the syndicate time to get very lucrative odds on the Cups double, with Amounis to win the Caulfield Cup and Phar Lap to win the Melbourne Cup.

The plan worked perfectly. Over a period of time, massive amounts of money were wagered on Amounis through various agents, including Mrs Vandenberg's son, who was a bookmaker.

Seeing that Phar Lap was set to contest the Caulfield Cup, Louisson took Nightmarch home (and he duly won the New Zealand Cup).

Then, on the Monday before the race, Harry Telford scratched Phar Lap, stating that he didn't want to over-race the champion, and that a delay in Albury on the way to Melbourne had set back his preparation.

Many racing people were annoyed, especially those who had already made bets on Phar Lap based on the belief that he would run in both cups. Owners who had not entered their horses for the Caulfield Cup, thinking Phar Lap and Nightmarch would run, were also angry. In the end, only fourteen horses contested the race and Amounis started at 2 to 1 and duly won, as an eight-year-old carrying a record weight for his age. Phar Lap, of course, famously and easily won the second leg of the double, the Melbourne Cup.

Angriest of all were the bookmakers around Australia, many of whom who were sent almost bankrupt by the coup. Flamboyant bookie Andy Kerr, known as the 'Coogee Bunyip', was forced to stop trading for a time. Mrs Vandenberg was reputed to have won £200,000.

Harry Telford was not part of the scheme but was given a 'sling' for his role in the plan. I have previously mischievously reported that Frank McGrath's granddaughter, who happens to be a friend of mine, remembers hearing that her grandfather bought a very expensive imported motorcar around that time. There is no evidence, however, that Frank McGrath was part of the plan, although I am sure he was very happy with the result.

Amounis was a great champion and the only horse to beat Phar Lap twice, once when he was seven and Phar Lap was three. He ended Phar Lap's winning streak of 24 victories by beating him in the Warwick Stakes in 1930. He won 33 races, including two Epsoms and a Cox Plate, and was briefly the highest stakes-winning horse in Australian history, until Phar Lap overtook his record.

Not all racing scams, sadly, are as benign as the Amounis/Phar Lap doubles coup.

––––––––

In 1876 Briseis became the first female horse to win the Melbourne Cup after Jim Wilson concocted the 'Peter St Albans' story. That year, however, was a low point in the history of Australian racing—when the tragic loss in a storm of nine horses bound for that year's Melbourne Spring Carnival on board the steamer *City of Melbourne* was made worse by the celebrations initiated by Melbourne's bookmakers on hearing the news.

The bookies stood to lose a fortune on early betting on the horses that died. Some were Sydney horses heading to the Melbourne Carnival, and others were Melbourne horses returning from the Sydney Spring Carnival. Robin Hood (the best horse Etienne de Mestre ever trained, according to the trainer himself), Sydney Metropolitan winner Nemesis, and Melbourne horses Sovereign and Burgundy had all been heavily backed for the Melbourne Cup and died in the storm.

Racing was suffering from gambling and shady practices throughout the 1870s. The general public had lost faith in the integrity of the sport and it risked becoming a 'second-rate' sporting activity in the eyes of the media and the average Aussie.

True sportsmen and horse lovers were sickened by the blatant, disgusting behaviour of the Melbourne bookmakers in celebrating the death of the horses and their unbelievably audacious and unsporting gesture of presenting a purse to the captain of the *City of Melbourne*, as a reward for not turning back when requested to by those looking after the horses, and thus precipitating the tragic loss and painful deaths of nine valuable thoroughbreds.

The *Melbourne* Argus reported, on 13 September 1876:

> An unparalleled destruction of racing stock is one of the results of
> the terrific gale which was experienced on the New South Wales
> coast during Sunday and Monday … out of the 11 horses …
> two, Chrysolite colt and Redwood, were saved by the exertions
> of the men in charge of them, and the *City of Melbourne* having
> put back to Sydney, were landed yesterday in a very exhausted
> condition.
>
> Though no lives were lost amongst the passengers, they appear
> to have suffered considerably, as the cabins were completely
> flooded by the heavy seas by which the vessel was almost
> overwhelmed.

The 'Chrysolite colt' was the winner of the 1876 Australian
Jockey Club (AJC) Derby, a brown colt by Angler out of Chrysolite, owned by C.B. Fisher, the famous racing pioneer and business
partner of Herbert Power, who had neglected to name the horse
before he won the Derby. It was not entirely unknown for horses
to race unnamed in those days. The colt would have appeared in
the race book, or race card as it was then, as 'brown colt by Angler
from Chrysolite'.

After the storm the colt was kept alive by groom Joe Morrison,
who had ridden him to victory in the Derby. Morrison had pleaded
with the ship's captain (the hilariously named Captain Paddle) to
go back to port when the storm began, but to no avail. On the
journey back to Sydney, Morrison fed the horse beer and gin and
constantly massaged his cold body. The horse was so weak that he
had to be carried ashore at Sydney.

C.B. Fisher spared no expense in treating the horse and nursing
him back to health, and he miraculously recovered and was finally
given a name—Robinson Crusoe, although he was still often
referred to in his lifetime as 'that Chrysolite colt' or 'the shipwreck
horse'. He became a champion in his day and a great sire at stud.
He was also the horse that caused interference at the start of the
1877 Melbourne Cup!

Cheating the handicapper and nobbling horses was so rife in racing in the 1870s that many an honest trainer, owner and jockey lived in fear of his life.

An illustration of the parlous state of racing at the time can be found in the outrageous, blatant and ultimately successful, attempts made by bookmakers to stop the well-backed colt Newminster from winning the VRC Derby in 1876. Newminster had won the Maribyrnong Plate, Two Year Old Stakes, Sire's Produce Stakes and Ascot Vale Stakes, and was thus red-hot favourite to win the Derby.

It was well known that his owner, Mr A. Chirnside, and his trainer, Frank Dakin, were 'straight' racing men. This account was given in *The Australasian* newspaper:

> Mr Dakin, the trainer of Newminster, had to dismiss one of his boys found talking to a bookmaker and shortly afterwards Newminster was found lying in his stable in great agony, apparently having been poisoned.

Newminster recovered from the poisoning, so the bookmakers resorted to different tactics. They paid the entry fees for several poorly performed horses in the Derby and these also-rans caused enough interference to ensure that Newminster ran sixth.

The AJC had taken firm control of New South Wales racing by 1880, and was attempting to clean up the sport. The VRC established the 'Official Racing Calendar' in 1882 and declared that all race meetings throughout Victoria had to run in accordance with the VRC rules. Horses competing on racetracks that did not comply were banned from racing at Flemington.

More importantly, the VRC decided to register and license bookmakers in 1882 and the AJC quickly followed suit. Racing was slowly building a better public image, although unlicensed bookmakers still operated off course, and heinous deeds would never be completely wiped out.

In 1885 another of Frank Dakin's horses, the Melbourne Cup favourite and well-performed stayer Commotion, who had run third in the 1883 Cup and second in 1884, was found to be 'suffer-ing from injury to the sinews of his off fore leg' according to *The Herald*, which went on to report that:

> Treatment was resorted to without avail, and the horse was scratched for all engagements. To-night's Police Gazette contains a notice offering £1000 reward for information that would lead to the conviction of the persons implicated in laming him. It is stated that a stable boy had received £200 to lame the horse by striking him with a heavy blunt instrument, probably a hammer, on the fore leg. The horse is lamed for life. The reward will not be paid for the conviction of the stable boy alone.

Some of the shonky practices of the 1860s and 1870s were slowly eliminated from thoroughbred racing by the AJC and the VRC, but unregistered or 'pony racing' was growing in popular-ity in Sydney and Melbourne by 1890 and that form of racing, along with harness racing under lights at night, provided an outlet for the rorts and scams of the 'less savoury' elements of the racing industry.

Pony racing is a forgotten part of our racing history. Many people today assume that thoroughbred racing is the only form of horseracing we've ever had, but 'unregistered' or 'pony' racing was huge in Sydney and Melbourne.

Old photos show massive crowds at pony tracks from the 1890s to the 1930s, and many horses were trained in suburban backyards for these races, although several pony trainers had huge stables.

Prior to World War II there were six racetracks between the CBD and Botany Bay in Sydney alone. Apart from Randwick, there was Kensington, Rosebery, Ascot, Victoria Park and Moorfields. These were exclusively designed as 'non-thoroughbred' or 'pony' tracks. They are all gone now. The Kensington pony track was where part of the University of New South Wales now stands, Ascot was taken over as part of the airport and the rest went to housing developments.

There were also other tracks for unregistered horses at Glebe, Menangle, Parramatta, Hornsby and other suburbs.

Wayne Peake's definitive book, *Sydney's Pony Racecourses—An Alternative Racing History,* has documented, and thus preserved, the history of this fascinating and forgotten form of racing.

A brief look at just one of the characters associated with 'the ponies' will give some idea of the way racing rorts and scams were embedded in our society before WWII.

Writing in his book about 'Baron' Bob Skelton, Wayne Peake refers to him as 'the embodiment of the phrase "colourful racing identity" before it became merely a euphemism used by the press to identify a mobster'. Skelton was reported to have started at least three brawls and a minor riot at racetracks, and once convinced a leading jockey to change his name by deed poll so he could ride Skelton's horses as an 'unknown' rider. According to Wayne Peake:

> Among his more straightforward devices was the bogus sale of horses that had been racing in poor form to a close associate, such as Barney Goldstein. The horses often won at their next starts in new colours after being heavily commissioned. Later the horse would return to Skelton's ownership.

During a bitter dispute between the Pony Owners and Trainers Association (POTA) and the Australian Racing Club, which was the governing body of the sport, the trainers called a strike and boycotted meetings, including the Rosebery Cup. Skelton and a handful of other non-POTA trainers provided sufficient entries for the meeting to go ahead and Skelton won every race except the Cup!

The McKell Labor Government managed to wipe out pony racing in WWII by taking over the tracks for military camps and then creating the Sydney Turf Club (STC), which used the tracks that re-opened after the war and raced under AJC rules, with thoroughbred horses only.

Someone asked me recently why the 'ponies' were also often called 'the mackers'. Since Wayne Peake is a mate of mine, I was able to tell them the answer. It is simple rhyming slang: 'pony' = 'macaroni' = 'mackers'.

The first harness meeting conducted under electric lights was held on 6 February 1890 at the Harold Park Paceway, which closed in 2010. After the demise of the pony tracks, 'the trots' became incredibly popular. It was generally acknowledged that it was easy to 'rig' trotting races by placing horses in winning or impossible positions during races, or causing them to 'break' out of a trotting or pacing gait and gallop, which meant they fell back and lost all hope.

It has been noted that Australians at times have a relaxed attitude to bending the rules and seem content to accept that life is full of scams and schemes. Perhaps it's our convict heritage. The working men who happily went regularly to 'the trots' to bet their weekly wages commonly referred to them as 'the red hots', because they knew, or suspected, the races were shonky!

As a child I was taken to Harold Park on Friday nights and remember there were three enclosures for the public—the 'paddock' along the finishing straight, the 'leger' on the opposite side of the track, and the 'flat' at the home turn—and the crowds were massive.

Even as a kid I knew that a driver could easily put his horse in two unfavourable positions in a race—the 'death' or 'death seat' or 'facing the breeze' was outside the leading horse with no cover, and 'one back on the fence' was behind the leader, where you could not get out to win.

Likewise there were two winning positions—the 'pole', which was in front on the inside, from where you could control the tempo of the race, and 'one out one back', which was racing behind the 'death seat' horse with cover, from where you could pull out and win in the straight.

It is claimed that the demise of harness racing in Sydney, and its rapid decline in popularity in the 1970s and 1980s, was caused by master criminal George Freeman. The claim is that Freeman took the 'red hots' to a new level of cheating and race fixing by telling drivers which horse would win each race and giving all the losing drivers a $50 bet on the winner.

While the 'mackers' and the 'red hots' might have often been shonky, there is no doubt that thoroughbred racing—the so-called 'Sport of Kings' and realm of 'gentlemen'—was not immune from scams and rorts, long after the bad old days of the 1870s … and right up to the present day!

BOTTLE QUEEN

Here is a yarn about a 'pony' that was trained by a couple of 'bottle-ohs' for her first race at the Kensington track in an attempt to hopefully win at long odds by deception. It's a classic tale that I heard decades ago and put to verse. My version is based in Botany or Mascot, but I have seen versions of this yarn from as far afield as New Zealand.

These blokes are attempting to cheat the handicapper by training the horse away from the track and conning race officials into believing she's nothing more than a cart horse used to collect bottles. Obviously the joke is that the horse was also trained to stop to collect bottles!

Bottle Queen

Traditional/Jim Haynes

> We bred her in the suburbs and we trained her after dark,
> Sometimes down the Botany Road and sometimes in the park,
> And the way we used to feed her, it often led to rows,
> We pinched the chaff from stables and the green stuff from
> the Chows.
>
> Now her sire was imported but we never knew from where
> And her mother, Black Moria, was a bottle dealer's mare.

We bought a set of colours; they were second-hand and
    green,
And we had to call her something, so we called her Bottle
    Queen.

In the evenings when we galloped her I usually took the
    mount,
We didn't have a stop-watch, so me mate, he used to count.
She showed us four in forty-nine, one-forty for the mile,
But she coulda done much better, she was pulling all
    the while.

Now that's something like a gallop, on the sand with ten
    stone up,
It'd win the English Derby! Or the Wagga Wagga Cup!
And when we thought we had her just as fit as she could be,
Me mate, he bit his sheila for the nomination fee.

We bunged her in a maiden and they dobbed her seven
    stone,
Talk about a 'jacky', she was in it on her own!
So we worked her on the bottles when the cart was good
    and light,
It was bottles every morning and training every night.

We walked her down to Kenso on the morning of the race,
The books had never heard of her, we backed her win and
    place,
Then we rubbed her down and saddled her and led her to
    the track,
And told that hoop his fee was good ... if he brought a
    winner back!

Well, they jumped away together but The Queen was soon
    in front,
As for all the others, they were never in the hunt!

She was romping past the leger; she was fighting for her head,
When some bastard waved a bottle ... and our certainty
stopped dead!

Now when folks who know hear, 'Bottle-Oh', they say,
'There's poor old Jim,
He mighta made a fortune, but the bottle did him in.'
Yes we shoulda made a motza, my bloody oath we should,
Except I guess you might say that The Queen was trained
too good!

So, don't talk to me of racing, you can see I've had enough.
It's a game for men with money and for blokes who know
their stuff.
And if someone tries to tell you that the racing game is
clean ...
Just remember what I told you, my tale of Bottle Queen.

THE WHISPERER
[EXCERPTS FROM 'RACING AND RACEHORSES' BY A.B. PATERSON ('THE BANJO')]

The Backstory

> 'He who fights and runs away will live to fight
> another day.'
>
> Proverb

The most vivid memory that abides with me of south-coast racing is of a meeting held many years ago in the Shoalhaven District.

The attendance consisted mostly of the local agriculturalists, horny-handed sons of the soil quite formidable in appearance and character. The foreign element was provided by a group of welshers, side-show artists, prize-fighters and acrobats who followed the southern meetings as hawks follow a plague of mice.

The centre of the course consisted of a field of maize fully ten feet high and when one bookmaker decided to 'take a sherry with the dook and guy-a-whack' (a slang expression meaning to abscond without paying), he melted into the maize and took cover like a wounded black duck.

The hefty agriculturalists went in after him like South African natives after a lion in the jungle. For a time nothing could be seen but the waving of the maize and nothing could be heard but the shouts of the 'beaters' when they thought they caught sound or scent of their prey.

After a time all and sundry took a hand in the hunt; so the 'wanted man' simply slipped off his coat and joined in the search for himself, shouting and waving his arms just as vigorously as anybody else.

When the searchers got tired of the business and started to straggle out of the maize he straggled out too, on the far side, and kept putting one foot in front of the other till he struck the coach road to Sydney.

The Story

> 'I know a trick worth two of that.'
>
> Shakespeare—*Henry IV*, part 1, act 2, scene 1

A whisperer is a man who makes a living, often a very good living, by giving tips for races.

The well-dressed stranger or countryman who goes to a race meeting, as he leans over the rails and studies the horses, will find an affable stranger alongside him and they drift into conversation. The affable stranger says, 'That's a good sort of a horse,' and the ice is broken and before long the countryman is 'told the tale'.

Now, the tale has many versions, and it all depends on the listener which version is brought forward. The crudest plot that finds patrons is the old, old friend-of-the-owner story. In this drama the whisperer represents himself as a great friend of the owner of a certain horse, and if necessary he produces a confederate to represent the owner. The whisperer and confederate talk in a light-hearted way of putting a hundred each on, and they agree that they will do it if the price is good enough, but if they cannot get a fair price they will wait for another day.

The stranger thinks he ought not to miss such a chance as this, and carelessly suggests that he would like to be allowed to put a tenner on with their money. They demur and say that they have a good deal of other money to put on for friends and if they tried to put too much on, it might spoil the price. However, as being entreated to do so, they take the stranger's tenner as a great favour and that is the last he sees it.

This is a simple way to get money, but it has its drawbacks. If the stranger is an absolute novice, he may be persuaded to back a horse with no possible chance, and then the gang never lose sight of him and they try to get another tenner out of him for the next race.

If he looks like a man who knows anything at all, they have to suggest backing a horse with some sort of a chance, and if that horse happens to win, they have to leave the course hurriedly, because it is a very awkward thing to have an infuriated country-man looking for you with a racecourse detective when you depend on your wits for a living.

So the friend-of-the-owner story is only tried on novices and as a last resource, for it can only be worked on a very raw fool and raw fools as a rule have not enough money to be worth robbing. Also it is a breach of the law, and the true artist in whispering can 'find 'em' with that.

The higher-grade class of narrative depends for its success not on the tale but on the way it is told. The artistic practitioner goes to the races and picks out by some unerring instinct the right 'mark'. He may select a countryman or a sailor or a stuck-up-anyone who looks as if he has money and is ready for a gamble. The whisperer tells a tale suited to his more educated client.

This time the tale is that he has a friend in a racing stable (which is quite true), that White Cockade is the favourite but has not been backed by its stable and will not try to win, and that he knows a horse that is on the whole 'an absolute cert if they spur it'. He can find out all about it from his friend in the racing stable. Will the client have £20 on it if he can find out that it is all right? The client, anxious to be up to date, says he will.

Off goes the whisperer and comes back very mysterious. 'Good thing! Paleface second favourite at 6 to 1. Better have twenty on it. The favourite is as dead as mutton!'

He hypnotises the client, who soon gets the suggestion that he must back Paleface; it would be absolutely chucking a chance away not to have a good punt on Paleface, 6 to 1 is a real gift about Paleface; after they have conversed for a while the client would eat a tallow candle and swear it was milk chocolate if the whisperer offered it to him.

It was once said of a really great whisperer that he could talk a punter off a battleship into a canvas dinghy in mid-ocean.

Like horse taming, it is all done with the eye and the voice. Having hooked his fish, the whisperer now pilots him up to a bookmaker and sees the money put on, and they go off to watch the race.

The favourite runs wide at the turn and loses his position and never quite gets into the fighting line, but Paleface hugs the rails and comes away in the straight and wins easily. The whisperer and his client go off together to draw £120 of the best and the whisperer, if he handles his client properly, should get at least £20 for himself out of it. More than that, the client will be good for more betting, certainly until the hundred is gone, and probably a bit more on the top of that.

Some of these whisperers do really well when money is plentiful and sportsmen generous, and they build up quite a connection with country punters. Some of them keep the same clients for years. No one has ever actually heard of a whisperer selling his business or floating it into a company, but that may come later on. They deserve all they make, too. Do you think, oh most astute reader, that you could make a living by going to the racecourse and finding out winners and then inducing perfect strangers to back them and give you a share of the proceeds?

Like most other professions, whispering tends to be overcrowded. Practically every ex-jockey or stable hand with the necessary brains has his little circle of punters, and some of the boys in the stables learn to 'whisper' winners before they can see over the half-door of the stable. It takes a really good judge of racing and of human nature to keep his clientele together for long; and sometimes even the masters of the art make mistakes, as the following absolutely true tale of the trainer and the whisperer will illustrate.

It was when things were dull in Melbourne but booming in Sydney that a crowd of Melbourne followers of racing came up to Sydney on the track of the money. One of the Melbourne visitors was an expert whisperer and he had not long been on the Sydney course before he saw a genuine bushman, bearded, cabbage-tree-hatted, sunburnt and silent.

Bearing down on the bushy, he told him the old tale, and said that he had a friend in Layton's stable and that one of Layton's horses was 'a certainty if they backed it'. Layton, it may be mentioned, was a leading Sydney trainer.

After the usual spellbinding oratory on the part of the whisperer, the bushie agreed to put £10 on the horse and went away to see some friends, arranging to meet the whisperer after the race. The horse won all right and the whisperer was at the meeting place bright and early.

He had not long to wait. Up came the bushman, smiling all over, and the whisperer expected a very substantial 'cut' out of the winnings. 'Did you back it?' he said. 'What price did you get?'

'I got fives—fifty pounds to ten.'

'You won fifty, eh? Well, what about a tenner for me, for putting you on to it?'

'Oh, I don't know. Why should I give you a tenner? I'd have backed the horse whether I saw you or not.'

The whisperer tried persuasion and even pathetic appeal: he reduced his claim to 'two quid', but even at that the pastoral individual was adamant. At last the whisperer lost his temper.

'You'd have backed it without me telling you! You, you great yokel! What do you know about racehorses?'

'Well, I ought to know something. My name is Layton. I train that horse. I've just been away for a holiday in the bush. But I'll tell you what I'll do. I'll give you two pounds if you can point me out any man in my stable who told you to back it.'

As he finished speaking, as the novelist says, 'he looked up and found himself alone'.

HOW THE FAVOURITE BEAT US

Throughout history, horseracing has inspired some of Australia's favourite poets, including Lawson, Paterson, Ogilvie, Morant, C.J. Dennis and the man who inspired them all, Adam Lindsay Gordon. With his knowledge of literary forms and old ballads, Gordon was a master of rhythm and rhyme. In one of his most famous galloping ballads, 'How We Beat the Favourite', he used a variation of a metrical form called 'amphibrachic', where three syllables are used and the middle syllable is accented. It really doesn't matter how he did it; what matters is that the rhythm and rhyme sweep the story along at such a galloping pace the reader can't help but get excited and swept along at the same time.

The poem begins with a trainer telling a jockey that their horse has trained well, is fit and ready, and might win; although another horse called The Clown is a favourite to beat her. Here is the start of Gordon's poem, just to give you a feel for the style:

> 'Aye, squire,' said Stevens, 'they back him at evens;
> The race is all over, bar shouting, they say;
> The Clown ought to beat her; Dick Neville is sweeter
> Than ever—he swears he can win all the way.

> 'But none can outlast her, and few travel faster,
> She strides in her work clean away from The Drag;
> You hold her and sit her, she couldn't be fitter,
> Whenever you hit her she'll spring like a stag.

'And p'rhaps the green jacket, at odds though they back it,
May fall, or there's no telling what may turn up.
The mare is quite ready, sit still and ride steady,
Keep cool; and I think you may just win the Cup.'

Of course, after many ups and downs and much excitement, the favourite is beaten.

Now, Banjo Paterson admired, and was inspired by, Adam Lindsay Gordon and, in 1894, Paterson wrote a parody of Gordon's famous galloping verse, using the same rhyme and metre. The poem is called 'How the Favourite Beat Us', and it humorously reverses the roles and adds the double twist of a betting coup gone terribly wrong. It tells the story of an owner who tries to back his horse, fails to get a good price, attempts to get the jockey to pull the horse and is ironically defeated in his trickery by a mosquito ... and his own horse.

The poem appeared in the racebook for the Rosehill meeting on 9 November 1894, the Saturday following the Melbourne Cup. Banjo uses the same rhyme scheme and scansion as Gordon's original, and the story appears to be set in Newcastle as the mosquito in question is one of the famous 'Hexham greys' from the mangrove swamps near the Hunter River. A 'brown' is obsolete slang for a penny.

How the Favourite Beat Us

A.B. Paterson ('The Banjo')

'Aye,' said the boozer, 'I tell you it's true, sir,
I once was a punter with plenty of pelf,
But gone is my glory, I'll tell you the story
How I stiffened my horse and got stiffened myself.

''Twas a mare called the Cracker, I came down to back her,
But found she was favourite all of a rush,

The folk just did pour on to lay six to four on,
And several bookies were killed in the crush.

'It seems old Tomato was stiff, though a starter;
They reckoned him fit for the Caulfield to keep.
The Bloke and the Donah were scratched by their owner,
He only was offered three-fourths of the sweep.

'We knew Salamander was slow as a gander,
The mare could have beat him the length of the straight,
And old Manumission was out of condition,
And most of the others were running off weight.

'No doubt someone "blew it", for everyone knew it,
The bets were all gone, and I muttered in spite,
"If I can't get a copper, by Jingo, I'll stop her,
Let the public fall in, it will serve the brutes right."

'I said to the jockey, "Now, listen, my cocky,
You watch as you're cantering down by the stand,
I'll wait where that toff is and give you the office,
You're only to win if I lift up my hand."

'I then tried to back her—"What price is the Cracker?"
"Our books are all full, sir," each bookie did swear;
My mind, then, I made up, my fortune I played up
I bet every shilling against my own mare.

'I strolled to the gateway, the mare in the straight way
Was shifting and dancing, and pawing the ground,
The boy saw me enter and wheeled for his canter,
When a darned great mosquito came buzzing around.

'They breed 'em et Hexham, it's risky to vex 'em,
They suck a man dry at a sitting, no doubt,
But just as the mare passed, he fluttered my hair past,
I lifted my hand, and I flattened him out.

'I was stunned when they started, the mare simply darted
Away to the front when the flag was let fall,
For none there could match her, and none tried to catch
    her—
She finished a furlong in front of them all.

'You bet that I went for the boy, whom I sent for
The moment he weighed and came out of the stand—
"Who paid you to win it? Come, own up this minute."
"Lord love yer," said he, "why, you lifted your hand."

''Twas true, by St Peter, that cursed "muskeeter"
Had broke me so broke that I hadn't a brown,
And you'll find the best course is when dealing with horses
To win when you're able, and *keep your hands down*.'

RINGING THE CHANGES

The Backstory

> 'The Stewards demand explanations,
> But listen with cynical looks.
> It's obvious in their estimations
> The trainers are all licensed crooks.'
>
> Anonymous

'Ringing the changes' is a term derived from campanology, which is the art of bell ringing, where all possible combinations of a set of bells are rung. The phrase derives from the fact that each time the bells are 'rung' the order is 'changed'.

In horseracing, when one horse is changed for another illegally, it is called a 'ring-in' and the act is known as 'ringing-in'. So perhaps this collection of stories should be called 'Ringing-in the Changes'.

This practice of ringing-in is probably as old as the Sport of Kings itself. In Australian racing history there are many examples of the scam being carried out and, as the only examples we know about are the ones where the scammers got caught, there have probably been many more that we will never know about.

It would seem that the practice was well entrenched in the racing industry by the time Australia became a nation in 1901. A bestselling paperback racing thriller of the period was *Rung In* by Arthur Wright, one of the popular *Australian Bookstall* series (just 1 shilling—or 1 shilling and 1 penny posted!).

In 1915 at Albion Park in Brisbane, a Sydney couple, Vera Cleary and Arthur Arnold, pulled off a ring-in that proved very profitable but ended with them being banned for life and facing fraud charges in court.

The racing writer 'Magpie' told the basic elements of the story in a nostalgia piece in Brisbane's *Sunday Mail* in January 1941:

Xylite Turned Out to Be Blacklock
'Magpie's' Turf Budget

REPLYING to several readers, the horse Blacklock was disqualified for life for having been entered and run as Xylite, at Albion Park, on Saturday, October 9, 1915. Similar disqualifications were imposed on Vera Cleary and Arthur Arnold for being concerned in the affair.

Entered for that Albion Park meeting as a horse with a poor racing record, Xylite was allocated to the Fourth Division Handicap, five and a half furlongs, with 8.2.

W.H. Playford rode him, and after the horse had been literally backed off the cards by a fashionably dressed lady in black, he won the race with his ears pricked ... there were 21 starters.

When Xylite's quote in the betting eased to 12 to 1, the 'mysterious lady in black' moved swiftly into the ring and caused a sensation by the manner in which she backed the horse. Then leisurely she walked towards and into the grandstand and shouted to all and sundry:

'Xylite won't be beaten, he's a racecourse certainty.'

After the correct weight flag had been hoisted the 'Lady in Black' calmly collected the winning bets and departed from the course.

What happened next does not reflect too well on the manner in which racing officials carried out their duties at the Albion Park track in 1915.

Xylite was entered as an unraced four-year-old horse but chief stipendiary steward on the day, Mr John White, was very suspicious about the horse's age and the experienced way it galloped to win the race.

Consequently he followed the horse and its owner-trainer back to the horse's stall, examined the horse's mouth and asked to see the registration papers. John White concluded that the horse was a six-year-old and was shown a receipt for the lease of the horse—to Arthur Arnold from Vera Cleary.

The receipt showed the horse's age as four and Arnold said that this must have been a mistake copied from the advertisement he had answered for the lease of the horse.

Raceday steward John White later swore in court that he then said, 'Nonsense! There is something wrong about you and the horse too.'

White then asked Arnold to sign a statement regarding the horse's *bona fides*. Arnold refused and the steward then asked Arnold, 'Where is Vera Cleary? Now, wasn't that Vera Cleary who went around the ring backing the horse?'

When Arnold denied any knowledge of the horse being backed, John White called the racecourse detective and a policeman, Sergeant Farrell, who stated that although he 'thought there was something wrong' he didn't have 'sufficient particulars to go on'.

At that time horses owned and raced in Queensland needed full registration papers to race. Horses owned out of state and merely leased, however, required only proof of ownership. So, amazingly, the correct-weight flag was hoisted and Arnold was allowed to leave the course. The prize money was not collected and the horse was abandoned in its stall at a nearby stable.

When the horse was found and impounded by the police days later, it proved to be a well-performed Sydney horse named Blacklock that had won many races on unregistered or 'pony' tracks around Sydney.

The Story

'If your ship doesn't come in, swim out to meet it!'

Jonathan Winters—Comedian (1925–2013)

In the modern era of Australian racing, and that inevitably means 'since Phar Lap', there have been some wonderfully clever scams and schemes concocted by various 'colourful racing identities' and 'racetrack characters' to make large amounts of money by substituting a faster racehorse for a slower one.

The horse known as 'The Ring-in King' or 'The Prince of the Ring-ins' was a well-performed conveyance with the delightfully plebeian name of Erbie that began his racing career around the same time as the mighty Phar Lap and managed to win 24 races on metropolitan and provincial tracks around Sydney.

Erbie was eventually banned for life from Australian racetracks, which seems a little unfair as Erbie, being simply a very speedy herbivore, had no idea what class of race he was competing in, or what name he'd been given in the race book.

The real 'Prince of the Ring-ins' was, of course, his owner-trainer, who went by the very appropriate name of Charlie Prince.

Erbie disappeared from the racetracks of Sydney and environs sometime in 1933 and never won again, well, not legitimately.

During 1934, however, a horse called Duke Bombita easily won a race at Holbrook, 300 miles south of Sydney. Not long afterwards a horse called Chrybean won a race at Kilmore, in rural Victoria. In July and early August, a horse known as Redlock won races at Murray Bridge and Kadina in South Australia.

While all the horses named above were legitimately registered and active on racetracks at the time, not one of them was active on the days they were recorded as the winners at the tracks mentioned.

Yes, you guessed it. Erbie had stood in for them as a proxy, while they had a rest in a paddock somewhere, or were hidden away in a stable.

There had been some level of suspicion about Redlock's win at Murray Bridge, especially as he was backed to win a lot of money in a massive betting plunge that day and won by 12 lengths. The stewards did question Charlie Prince about the horse's identity, but they were satisfied when he produced a receipt showing his ownership of Redlock, who was registered in Victoria and had raced in his correct grade according to his form.

It took the keen eye, good memory and suspicious mind of Bert Wolfe, a racing journalist who wrote under the name of 'Cardigan' for the *Melbourne Herald*, to expose the scam and reveal the truth about the exploits of 'Erbie alias Redlock alias Chrybean alias Duke Bombita' ... and alias who knows how many others.

Cardigan's scoop went out on the wire service and was picked up as far away as Rockhampton in North Queensland, where the *Morning Bulletin* reported:

'RING-IN' ALLEGED
RACEHORSE REDLOCK IDENTICAL WITH ERBIE
Melbourne, August 12

Allegations have been made that Redlock, the gelding whose easy win in the Trial Handicap at Murray Bridge on July 28th first aroused suspicion, and who registered another striking win at Kadina, South Australia, is a 'ring-in'.

According to the Melbourne 'Herald's' turf writer, who went to Kadina to see the gelding, the so-called Redlock is actually Erbie, while the real Redlock has been located in a paddock near Malmsbury. It is alleged that Erbie, who had been disqualified for life, appeared under many names last year. He raced at Holbrook, New South Wales, as Duke Bombita. On November last, he won in a sensational manner at Kilmore as Chrybean. Now he has reappeared as Redlock.

'I have no hesitation in asserting that the gelding which raced at Kadina on Saturday is our old friend, Erbie, in a new guise,' declares 'Cardigan,' the 'Herald' turf writer, wiring from Adelaide. 'I know Erbie well. I have watched him race and win on numerous occasions in Sydney and on provincial tracks within the metropolitan radius. I know his markings and characteristics. After seeing Redlock win the Trial Handicap at Kadina, and at the Wallaroo meeting the previous Saturday, I say definitely that Redlock is Erbie. The blaze down his face is missing, and the brands are different.'

The blaze down his face was indeed missing. Oddly enough, however, it reappeared when Dr Wakeham, a veterinary surgeon, used solvent to rub the horse's face and remove the hair dye. Even more amazing was the revelation that awaited another vet, Dr Miller, and a 'brands expert', Mr Dow, when they shaved the horse's rump, for there were the brands that identified ... guess who? Yes, it was Erbie!

But where was Redlock while Erbie was doing all the dirty work of winning his races for him?

To find out, we need to go back to the story as reported by the *Morning Bulletin*, or back to a town 100 miles north of Melbourne:

> The secretary of the V.R.C., Mr. A. Kewney, and the V.R.C. stewards, and the stipendiary steward of the Northern District Racing Association, Mr. D. Reid, yesterday went to Malmsbury to see the gelding, declared to be the real Redlock, which was running loose in a paddock there. It is stated that the animal's brands were undoubtedly the brands and markings of Redlock.
>
> Corresponding with this the officially registered markings and characteristics of the animal were duly noted by the stewards and photographs taken for future reference. A report will be made to the V.R.C. committee.

Inhabitants of the farm obviously knew nothing of the horse's connections. They explained that a relative had requested that a horse belonging to a friend might be allowed to run in the paddock for a while. They understood the horse was to be kept for about a month.

POSSESSION OF HORSE.
> Following receipt of advice that the V.R.C. stewards had discovered a horse at Malmsbury bearing similar brands and markings to Redlock, the South Australian Jockey Club officials to-day took action under Rule 7 of the Australian Rules of Racing. With the consent of Redlock's owner trainer, C. Prince, they took possession of the gelding now at Morphettville and placed him under guard at E. R. Shadrick's stables ... The police are also making inquiries, and they questioned Prince today.

The report goes on to say that 'an inquiry would be held and … the first prize of £25, won by Redlock at Kadina on Saturday' would be 'withheld pending the result of such inquiry'.

Now, this was 1934, the time of the Great Depression, and twenty-five quid was a lot of money.

Charlie Prince was probably not too upset at losing the £25, however, as he had won huge amounts of money every time Erbie was victorious when racing as some other horse, including around £1000 at Murray Bridge.

Besides, he had other things to worry about now.

Prince was subsequently banned for life from racing and served two years in prison for fraud. He eventually admitted to winning 'about twelve' races with Erbie when he was racing under another name.

Erbie's days of winning races for other, less-talented equine conveyances were now over. He, too, was banned for life and became such a celebrity that his sale at auction, after being 'confiscated' from the now-jailed Prince, was reported in the *Queenslander* on 10 January 1935:

RACEHORSE 'RING IN' SOLD AT AUCTION
Erbie Realises 48 Guineas
The disqualified racehorse Erbie, who had been 'rung in' at Murray Bridge and Kadina as Redlock, was sold at public auction in Adelaide to Mrs W. G. Watt, of Strathalbyn, for 48 guineas. She intends to use him in the hunting field.

Whether Erbie enjoyed hunting with Mrs Watt in the saddle we don't know, but there is a photo of him in his old age with Mr Watt, in a paddock on their property at Strathalbyn. He looks happy enough.

When you come across examples of the relentless pursuit of truth, as demonstrated by people like Bert Wolfe, alias 'Cardigan', in tracking down and exposing the nefarious activities of scoundrels like Charlie Prince, it goes some way towards restoring your faith in the Sport of Kings and the integrity of the majority of those involved in the industry.

Now and then the eagle eye of a stipendiary steward can bring about the downfall of the less-than-honest trainers and owners who are willing to risk their livelihoods and reputations on illegal practices such as ringing-in.

On 4 January 1941 Steve Bowen, a steward who officiated in the country areas of Southeast Queensland, was enjoying an off-duty day at the Saturday races at Eagle Farm in Brisbane when he noticed something odd.

The winner of the trial handicap that day was a horse called Daylate, owned by a certain J. Jackson and trained by J.H. McIlrick. The winner had been heavily backed in the betting ring, with punters taking more than £1000 from the bookmakers. This was an unusual amount of money to be won on a trial handicap and, oddly enough, it was reported that a 'mysterious lady in black' placed most of the bets. (Members of the Queensland press writing for the racing section seem to have a predilection for mysterious ladies in black.)

Steve Bowen was a man who took his job seriously and, although he was having a day off, he was as alert as ever. What Bowen noticed, and thought peculiar, was that Daylate's mane hung in an unusual pattern—in three separate sections across his neck—whenever the horse tossed his head.

Race stewards need to be observant and have good memories and Bowen recalled that the only other horse he had ever seen with this peculiarity was a horse named Brulad, which was owned by Fred Bach, a farmer from Oakey, on the Darling Downs.

Brulad was a promising horse as a two-year-old. He had finished third in the Queensland Turf Club (QTC) Champagne Stakes in 1938, had been heavily backed when he won a Juvenile Handicap, and had run the fastest registered time for a two-year-old that season.

Bach had been offered £1000 for the horse but refused it.

On the horse's return to racing as a three-year-old, he showed no form in six starts and his trainer, Clive Morgan, suggested to Fred Bach that the horse needed a long spell.

On closer inspection Steve Bowen became convinced that Daylate was, in fact, Brulad and told the racecourse detective, Charles Prentice, of his suspicions. The detective was at first unconvinced but when Clive Morgan, who happened to be at the track that day, said that he thought the same way, the game was up.

Daylate's trainer, J.H. McIlwrick, was asked to produce the horse and said it was no longer in his stable. Detective Prentice then drove to Oakey to interview Fred Bach, but he was not at home. Family members told Prentice that Brulad had become sick and died and the carcass had been burned by Bach's two sons, Jack and Frank. One son, Jack Bach, said that he saw the body burned.

Thirty kilometres away from Oakey was the cattle station that was the address for Daylate's registered owner, J. Jackson. When he enquired there for J. Jackson, Prentice was told that all his mail was given to Mrs Bacon, whose husband worked on the property.

Mrs Bacon was Fred Bach's married daughter.

Prentice smelled a rat and rushed back to McIlwrick's stable and staked it out. At 10 p.m. that night he saw Fred Bach enter the stable and fifteen minutes later he emerged, leading the horse.

When Prentice approached him and asked his name, Bach shook his hand and, according to the detective, replied, 'Oh, you are Mr Prentice. How are you? Now you've got me. There's nobody else in this. There is only me. I am Jackson. I suppose I'll get life. I'll take full responsibility for everything.'

Fred and Jack Bach were banned by the QTC for life—from all Australian racetracks.

This story had a very important footnote.

Just before the ban was imposed, Jack Bach and his brother Frank had purchased an old mare named Bern Maid with a foal at foot. On 22 June 1940 the foal was sold to a neighbour, Mr E.A. Hadwen, who later raced him twice, for one win on protest at Toowoomba, and then leased him to a trainer named Roberts, who won with him three times locally and then nominated him for a race in Brisbane.

The Brisbane stewards refused the nomination without explanation (which they were entitled to do by the rules) and, when Roberts' lease expired at the end of the horse's three-year-old season, Mr Hadwen decided to race him again and sent him to Sydney. Again the QTC ban was applied and the horse could not race.

Only the local track at Toowoomba recognised the horse's *bona fides*, and that is where he raced, as a stallion, until he was six, for eleven wins.

In an attempt to clear the horse to race at other tracks unhindered by the QTC ban, he was put up to public auction and subsequently purchased for £2000 by flamboyant restauranteur Azzalin 'The Dazzling' Romano.

The horse was, of course, Bernborough, the greatest champion of his era. There were always rumours that the champion's 'real' ownership included men other than Romano.

The next example of ringing-in skulduggery on our list was also hatched on the Darling Downs. It also involves a great example of 'sleuthing' to uncover the ring-in, but this time by a racing official sitting in his office and meticulously doing his job.

This ring-in was exposed by a man doing a very thorough and systematic check of results and statistics. It was a part of a job that most of us would consider rather mundane and boring—but he apparently did it remarkably well, without any lapse of concentration.

In early 1949 a Sydney horse, a six-year-old bay gelding named Halmahera, was bought by Darling Downs trainer John Conway and taken to Queensland, where he won several races at Toowoomba before being sold to 'a man from Mareeba', according to Conway. The trainer later said, at the subsequent Australian Jockey Club (AJC) enquiry, he had no interest in the horse after he sold him.

Apparently the 'scam' was that Conway passed the horse on to a mate of his friend Everard Crane, who then registered him as a different horse, Denilinger.

It was not unheard of for horses to go unregistered until they were six years old—but it was not usual.

While waiting for the official registration to go through, Crane and trainer Maurice Mulcahy took the horse to Narrabri. On 19 August 1949, the *Sydney Morning Herald* reported:

COONAMBLE, Wednesday.—Registration particulars for the bay racehorse Denilinger are being questioned because both sire and dam were stated to be chestnuts.

It is an axiom that the mating of chestnuts can produce only chestnuts. It has never happened any other way, according to official view.

Crane comes from Warwick (Qld.), where he breeds horses. When he was at Narrabri with Denilinger he told race officials that, although he had not bred the horse himself, he had had the horse running at the property for some time. He had noticed that he could gallop and started to race him. The stewards want the opportunity to check all these statements and therefore cited the party to appear.

Meanwhile, the eagle-eyed Mr Noblet, AJC Registrar of Horses, noted the breeding of the horse and queried the registration. As is mentioned in the *Herald* article, the mating of two chestnuts could not produce a bay horse.

In the meantime, Denilinger had won two races at Narrabri, a maiden handicap and an improvers handicap. Massive bets had been placed and a lot of money won.

As well as querying the horse's origin, officials at Narrabri had been alerted to the fact that the horse had been recently branded, but it was not until the supposed genetic impossibility of the horse's colour was noticed by Mr Noblet that the penny dropped. An enquiry was held and the *Sydney Morning Herald* gave details:

Former Sydney galloper Halmahera
Breeding Theory as Origin of Denilinger Doubts
From THE TURF EDITOR
Denilinger was the centre of an inquiry listed for hearing here to-day before the stewards, of whom A.J.C. stipendiary steward,

Mr. H. Stokes, was chairman. The parties cited did not appear and were disqualified until such time as they do ...

Entry Queried

When Denilinger was registered his sire was stated to be Red Dennis (chestnut) and his dam a Deerborough mare (chestnut). The registrar of racehorses in Sydney, Mr. F. Noblet, queried the correctness of the details and the registration was sent back to the Q.T.C., where it originally had been lodged. In the meantime, Denilinger was taken to Narrabri, where he won two races in easy style. Two girls backed him and collected £1,500, bookmakers say. Denilinger was nominated for Walgett. Mr. Stokes wants to interview the party because of an allegation that Denilinger is identical with Halmahera.

Halmahera has won many races and, therefore, would not have been eligible for the Maiden Handicap and the Improvers' Handicap which Denilinger won at Narrabri.

Colonel Roberts and his assistant, Messrs. Fairhall and MacFarlane, were in charge of the Narrabri meeting.

Mr. Gray is secretary of the Walgett Diggers' Race Club. Trainer Gallagher was at Narrabri races and noticed that Denilinger's brand seemed to be of recent origin. He was called to-day to give evidence on that issue. In a recent interview Conway had said he had sold Halmahera, which he had bought in Sydney, to a man in Mareeba (Qld.) district. Q.T.C. officials have not been able to trace the new buyer.

The men, not surprisingly, failed to appear at the hearing at Coonamble. The *Brisbane Worker* reported on 22 August that:

A Coonamble solicitor acting on their behalf sought an adjournment, which was refused by the stewards. Conway had also been ordered to produce the well-known performer, Halmahera, for inspection by the stewards. Some time ago it was reported that Conway sold Halmahera to a man at Mareeba (N.Q.). Denilinger was registered by Crane as being by Crimson Dennis from a Deerborough mare. He is a six-year-old bay gelding. Halmahera is a six-year-old bay gelding by Wee Warrah–Happy Mail.

Although there seemed to be some doubt in the newspapers as to whether Denilinger's sire was 'Red' or 'Crimson' Dennis, it was of no real consequence, as it was agreed that his colour was said to be 'chestnut' by Crane, while Denilinger was bay.

What's more, it was fairly obvious that 'Denilinger' didn't actually exist and, therefore, it was really irrelevant which stallion, real or imaginary, red or crimson, Crane claimed had sired him. What did matter was that the sire and dam were on the registration application as chestnut—and the horse in question was bay.

On 19 November, the *Sydney Morning Herald* reported:

Four Racing Men Disqualified

After investigating an alleged 'ringing in'—at Narrabri races on July 1 and 2 this year; an Australian Jockey Club steward, Mr. H.H. Stokes, yesterday disqualified four men for life. Mr. Stokes began his investigations soon after a gelding named Denilinger won the Maiden Handicap at Narrabri on July 1 and the Improvers' Handicap at the same course next day.

His finding yesterday was that Denilinger was identical with Halmahera, who had won many races in the country before Denilinger won at the Narrabri meeting.

Neither Denilinger nor Halmahera were produced for the stewards' inspection. The men disqualified, all Queenslanders, were: G.E. Crane, owner of the gelding Denilinger. Maurice Andrew Mulcahy, trainer of Denilinger. Leslie Clyde Wrigley, jockey, who rode Denilinger in his races at Narrabri on July 1 and 2. John Conway, who owned, and trained the gelding Halmahera when he last raced ...

Mr. Stokes found that Denilinger and Halmahera were the same horse.

The irony of this case did not become apparent until a year later, when the AJC's set of qualifications for registration based on colour inheritance was questioned by geneticists.

Less than a year after the Halmahera/Denilinger case, on 1 June 1950, the racing paper *Sydney Sportsman* reported on three yearlings being refused registration by the new AJC registrar, Mr Lilley. The bans were based on colour:

EXPERTS AGREE COLOR THEORY HAS FLAWS
Club's Action Causes Stir

Nothing less explosive than the atom bomb could parallel the furious controversy raging in racing circles following the shock announcement this week by the A.J.C. Registrar of Racehorses (Mr. G.W. Lilley) that he had rejected registration of three yearlings because of alleged breeding irregularities ...

In each case the A.J.C. banned registration of the yearlings because both the sire and dam were described as chestnuts and the yearlings were not of the same color.

The respective owners were rocked to their foundations when the A.J.C. informed them by letter of the imposition of the ban.

But *Sportsman* has it on the authority of Dr. R.B. Kelly, a Doctor of Veterinary Science, Animal Geneticist, and Council of Scientific and Industrial Research Officer in charge of the F.D. McMaster field station at Badgery's Creek, that there are obvious flaws in the theory that chestnuts must always necessarily reproduce chestnuts.

'Practically all hypotheses with respect to the inheritance of coat color in horses have been developed from studies of the Stud Book regulations—that parents of stated colors give progeny having a certain color,' Dr. Kelly said. 'But color is ill-defined. For instance:—

(a) Any color has a range of, say, from this to that,

(b) The ranges overlap, e.g., chestnuts and washy bays,

(c) Possibly two men describing the color of a borderline animal (as in b) could describe the animal differently.'

EXCEPTIONS TO RULE

Dr. Kelly pointed out that Messrs. F.A.E. Crew and A.O. Buchanan Smith, of the Breeding Research Department, University of Edinburgh, in their work 'The Genetics of the Horse,' display a ·

table which shows that a chestnut mated with a chestnut produced a chestnut. But, in an appendix to their work, they include a further tabulation which collates the investigations of veterinarians of world repute into color inheritance, and this shows that, from 7797 stud book recordings of dual chestnut matings, there were 88 progeny whose color ranged from black to roan.

'So, obviously, there must be a flaw in the hard and fast rule that chestnuts get only chestnuts when one observes that the percentage of their investigations revealed that more than one in 100 differed in color from chestnut.'

'The genetics of the subject are not wrong, but the interpretation of a situation must be governed by the knowledge that genetics is a study of variation and as such does not present hard and fast rules for particular results.

'But,' Dr. Kelly concluded, 'it deals with variants as they occur.'

In view of Dr. Kelly's remarks, and the conflicting opinions of other less qualified persons who appear to be paddling in the stream of confusion, it is strongly suggested that the A.J.C. review the whole question of registration of these yearlings before any finality is reached regarding a permanent disbarment from the Stud Book.

So, it would seem that the 'scientific basis' on which the identity of Denilinger was called into question was soon after thought to be false and unfounded; the evidence upon which the participants were banned could have been called into question a year later, although there is little doubt that justice was done.

In a further twist to the story, geneticists have since agreed, and proven, that a mating of two pure chestnut horses *can* only produce a chestnut horse. So Mr Noblet was right all along!

As a personal observation, *a propos* the racing journalist's enthusiastic sense of the importance his 'scoop', I'm sure the rest of the population—outside of the racing world—did not find the *Sportsman*'s revelations about horse colour genetics to be 'nothing less explosive than the atom bomb', which was obviously dominating world news in 1950.

In May 1972 another infamous ring-in occurred. This time in the town of Casterton, in far western Victoria (which was oddly enough, the hometown of John Henry Cochrane, alias Grant Hervey, whose story is also told in this collection).

On 12 May 1972 there was a Friday TAB meeting at Casterton and trainer Jack Barling had taken his runner, Apex Star, across from Hamilton, 65 kilometres east, to run in the Muntham Handicap. Apex Star finished second to a horse running as Royal School, trained by Ross Afflick and ridden by Stephen Wood. Royal School won easily, ears pricked under a tight hold.

As Jack walked back to unsaddle Apex Star, he met up with old friend Jim Cerchi, who trained at Coleraine, a small town on the Calder Highway halfway between Hamilton and Casterton.

Jack was surprised when Jim said, 'The winner's a ring-in! I've seen the horse before—it's not the same horse.'

As a result of Jim's comment, Jack made a note of the winner's brand—it was 'T 1 over 5'. He then informed the stewards that he'd been told Royal School was a ring-in.

The horse's brand had been checked and matched the brand on the registration papers handed to stewards presiding at the Casterton meeting. It wasn't until the VRC checked its official records on the following Monday and noticed that Royal School's brand was 'LD 1 over 4', that it was realised that a ring-in, as reported at the time, had really occurred.

It was too late to prevent the horse's owner Rick Renzella from collecting $33,570 from the Balaclava TAB, and that was just the daily double winnings!

The horse that had been 'rung-in' was the well-performed Regal Vista, which Renzella had purchased for $6000. Regal Vista had previously won the Group Two Liston Stakes over 1400 metres at Sandown. Royal School had been bought for $350 at the town of Rylstone, in country New South Wales, and had raced at picnic meetings.

The horses did look alike. They were of similar size and colouring with similar markings, except that Regal Vista had a small white star on one side of his face and a large scar across his rump from a paddock mishap.

The stewards at Casterton were criticised during the enquiry for missing the obvious differences and not heeding the warning that the horse was a ring-in.

The betting plunge was rather obvious. The horse was backed from 33 to 1, to 7 to 2 on course, and opened on the tote, where all the early money had gone, at 4 to 1. It paid $3.80 on the TAB.

The stewards had allowed the horse to leave the course, in spite of the racetrack rumours and the betting plunge.

At the enquiry, the steward in charge on the day, Bill Brewer, stated that the papers presented identified the horse as Royal School. In hindsight, Brewer admitted, they were obviously forged.

The VRC asked Renzella and Afflick for the registration papers. Each man said the other had them and then, later, that they had not been returned by the stewards on the day.

Assistant steward Frank Beattie said he put the papers into Afflick's hand. They were, of course, never found.

Afflick and Renzella had cunningly raced the real Royal School on the other side of the state, making sure it ran badly every time. In its previous four starts the horse had run last, third-last and second-last twice. They knew the stewards at Casterton would not be familiar with the horse—and would, therefore, trust the registration papers.

With Stephen Wood aboard, the horse easily won the Casterton race, which was the second leg of the daily double, by 3 lengths.

Renzella claimed he won $100,000, all from TAB off-course betting. At the enquiry Mr Peter Murphy QC, appearing for the Casterton Racing Club stewards, produced evidence of huge payouts at the Flinders Lane, Village Belle, Frankston and Seaford TAB agencies, as well as the massive payout at Balaclava, where a $33,000 cheque was issued, made payable to R. Renzella.

The daily double that day, on which much of the money was won, paid $119 dollars for 50 cents.

Renzella told Afflick not to show the VRC investigators the real Royal School, as they would realise it wasn't the horse that won at Casterton. As a result of this, the VRC officials actually inspected

Royal School at Afflick's stable, but were told it was another horse with the same brand, called Royal Manor.

Royal School was finally located in Afflick's Cranbourne stables and impounded by the VRC, but Regal Vista couldn't be located and Renzella, hilariously, offered a $2000 reward for anyone who could produce the horse.

First witness to give evidence at the VRC inquiry was Mr Eric Jeffrey, deputy registrar of racing for Victoria. He testified that only six other horses besides Regal Vista had the brand 'T 1 over 5', and Royal School was certainly not one of them.

On 4 July 1972, Renzella and Afflick were disqualified from racing for life, jockey Stephen Wood for twenty years, and float driver on the day, a Mr G. Canavan, for ten years.

As the resulting court case for fraud developed, accusations were made that Rick Renzella had killed and disposed of Regal Vista. Renzella finally produced the horse in an attempt to aid his cause and prove he was no horse killer.

Renzella's defence counsel, Mr Phillip Opas QC, later described his client as 'cunning but not clever', adding that it was 'not clever' to produce Regal Vista.

Opas, who developed a certain affection for Renzella during the trial and later wrote a book about the case, said he thought Renzella did not 'destroy the evidence' by killing Regal Vista because he genuinely loved horses.

The judge, Justice Rapke, did not seem to share defence counsel's sympathy for Renzella. He was, the judge said, guilty of a fraud that was 'born in a mind that was primed by greed and nurtured in cunning' and 'executed with boldness'.

He then sentenced Renzella to two years jail.

Regal Vista and Royal School were also banned for life. With their owner in prison they needed a good home, and they found one. Phillip Opas QC took both horses to his farm at Mount Macedon, where they lived out the rest of their lives together.

It would be nice to report that Rick Renzella reformed and came out of prison and ran a home for retired racehorses. Sadly, however, that would be far from the truth. He became, instead, a used-car salesman and, in 1985, was named in the Victorian state parliament as one of a group of dishonest car traders who forged roadworthy certificates and wound back speedometers.

In 1992 Rick Renzella was arrested as part of a gang that stole more than 50 Toyota Land Cruisers and 'rebirthed' them. He avoided conviction that time but, towards the end of 1993, police observed him stealing a Land Cruiser and followed him back to a property in the southeast Melbourne suburb of Highett, where they found two dozen Land Cruisers being dismantled. This, and the discovery of a rather large hydroponic marijuana crop, took him back to prison.

Rick Renzella was almost a comical character—the kind you sometimes find in the racing world. He was accurately and amusingly labelled by *Herald-Sun* editor Andrew Rule, as 'a man of many parts—most of them stolen'.

But at least Rick Renzella did have, according to Mr Justice Rapke, the ability to carry out a cunning plan with boldness. Which is more than can be said for the most comical of all racecourse ring-in gangs—the five-man mob who planned and bumbled their way through what became known as the 'Fine Cotton Affair'. But that is another story.

Footnote: Phillip Opas OBE QC passed away in 2008. He was famous for his spirited defence in 1967 of Ronald Ryan, the last man hanged in Victoria. Opas always thought Ryan was innocent and felt he let him down. He campaigned vigorously for the death penalty to be abolished in Victoria, and it was in 1975.

BUCKED OFF ITS BRAND

This is one of the old *Bulletin* poems about a horse thief who comes up with a simple bushman's explanation for the disappearance of a horse's brand. I know there are already enough stories in this collection about horses' identities being changed and disguised, but I love the combination here of tall story and attempted con.

I wish I knew who 'R.A.F.' was but I don't. Many of the regular *Bulletin* poets used several noms de plume, probably to get their poems published more regularly. Some of the poets had different pen names depending on whether they wanted the poems to be credited to them or not.

Bucked Off Its Brand

'R.A.F.'

Take my word, he could buck, could Brown Baron;
And to ride, who could ride like Long Jack?
There was never a thing born with hair on
Could throw him when once on its back.

In the crush went on saddle and bridle
And he set Jack a go pretty hard;
But his previous efforts seemed idle
When he flung down the rails of the yard.

A few bucks, and the gear was all lying,
Busted girths, broken bit, on the sand;
And away through the trees he went flying,
Nothing on him but Jack, and the brand.

Through the paddock the Baron went sailing
Jack keeping him straight with his hat,
We saw him jump over the railing
At the creek on the Kurrajong Flat.

And then, where on earth were they hidden?
Though the boss swore he'd soon have 'em back,
And rode as he never had ridden,
The traps had to start on their track.

But Jack was not beaten by trifles,
When he and the Baron were found,
It took four police, ditto rifles,
'Ere Jack would set foot on the ground.

When we came to examine the Baron,
All the brand mark had disappeared clean;
'Twas the horse, we could swear, with a scar on
The place where the 'Z9' had been.

Jack explained, in the dock at his trial,
That the horse slung his brand on the track;
To the charge gave indignant denial,
Said, when caught, he was bringing him back!

For a saddle, Jack sits now on stone
And for reins has a hammer in hand,
'Cause an ignorant judge would not own,
That horses could buck off their brand!

THE BIGGEST FARCE OF ALL TIME

Part One: The Lighter Side—The Beagle Boys Go to the Races

> 'Our crime against criminals lies in the fact
> that we treat them like rascals.'
>
> Friedrich Nietzsche

This is the story of a gang of five hilariously incompetent villains who resembled a cross between the Beagle Boys and the Three Stooges—plus two. They perpetrated what one of them later called 'the biggest farce of all time' on Saturday 18 August 1984—the most incompetent racing scam in Australian history, known as the 'Fine Cotton Affair'.

The *dramatis personae* of the gang were:

- **Hayden Haitana**—a likeable rogue and 'battling' racehorse trainer from New Zealand, who had trained in South Australia for more than a decade. According to an anonymous local racing identity, quoted in a *Coffs Coast Advocate* article by Greg White in 2009, Hayden was 'notorious for being a bullshit artist, particularly when he'd been drinking, which was pretty frequent'.
- **John Gillespie**—a 'company director from the Gold Coast' and an inveterate petty criminal with more than 350 convictions for crimes such as false pretences, stealing and armed robbery. He had shared a cell in Boggo Road Prison with Haitana's brother

Pat, a well-travelled jockey lately residing at Coffs Harbour. Gillespie and Pat Haitana had discussed a ring-in plot in prison, and Pat suggested his brother as the trainer to carry out the scam. Later, in Bathurst Gaol, he talked to a trainer named Doyle about a scheme to look at horses for sale and buy two similar horses. Soon after he bought a poorly performed horse from Central New South Wales for $2000 and a much better performed Sydney horse for $10,000.

- **Mick Sayers**—a Sydney heroin dealer, gambler and 'SP' bookie who helped finance the scam and was owed money by Gillespie and the gang.
- **Robert North**—a real estate agent and 'Brisbane socialite' who knew Gillespie and later referred to him as 'a compulsive liar'. North said they had discussed the ring-in idea many times and called himself 'the greatest fool' for getting involved and believing Gillespie, as he had 'never met a man who told lies' like him. North's home was used as the Brisbane headquarters for the gang.
- **John Dixon**—a video salesman and ex–Victorian police officer who provided transport, and took one horse from the Gold Coast to Robert North's home on the day of the race, then made sure Hayden Haitana was taken to the racetrack.
- **Tom DiLuzio**—a Brisbane electronics engineer and small-time racehorse owner who arranged the sale of the horse that gave the whole debacle its name. He gave his girlfriend a half share, sold the other half to a Brisbane businessman and drove to Ballina to buy the ring-in horse, with a dud cheque.

The supporting cast included:
- **Pauline Pearse**—a nurse and DiLuzio's live-in girlfriend, who nominally owned a racehorse in partnership with elderly Brisbane businessman Mr McGregor-Lowndes.
- **Gus Philpot**—a naive young apprentice jockey, who was clueless about what was going on.
- **Mr McGregor-Lowndes**—a retired carnival operator who had made his money in fairground and sideshow attractions

(including, according to some, the legendary 'dancing ducks' scam, where ducks 'danced' because the 'stage' they were on was a hotplate). He was also reputed to have a conviction for selling sparrows painted yellow as canaries. He nominally part-owned a racehorse he had never seen, and never did (unless he visited the horse long after the affair had played out).

- **Bill Naoum**—a successful milk vendor from Ballina, on the New South Wales North Coast, who retired early in life and went into training horses. He was the owner-trainer who innocently 'sold' the gang the ring-in horse, and was paid with a dud cheque.

It is also the story of three completely innocent and, sadly, mistreated equine 'fall guys'.

One of the horses was a poorly performed eight-year-old who had won two races on registered tracks in 70 starts. He was made to race three times in eight days, then not trained at all. Finally, he was left all day in a horse float in the Eagle Farm Racecourse car park before being dumped in a paddock close by and left there.

The second was kept in a poorly fenced paddock, where he managed to rip a large gash in his hindquarter on the barbed-wire fencing.

The third horse was bought with a dud cheque and then subjected to a six-hour road trip from Ballina to Brisbane, covered by a thick horse blanket, in the middle of a warm August, in a horse float pulled by a Toyota Corolla, driven by a man who knew nothing about horses apart from the fact that he'd part-owned a few.

When the third horse arrived in Brisbane, in the yard of a suburban home, he was 'flushed' in order to be rehydrated. This involved having several metres of garden hose shoved up his nose and into his stomach, which was then filled with water. In the process he had a blood vessel in his nose ruptured as the hose was clumsily extracted. So he then had his head tied to the rafters until the bleeding stopped. The next day Clairol henna hair dye was applied to his coat, turning it bright red. The dye was hosed off the following day and he was fitted with the wrong racing shoes, had his legs painted with Taubman's high-gloss white paint and was taken to Eagle Farm to run in a race piloted by a jockey who had never seen him until he was legged aboard.

The miracle is that he won the race—well, actually he didn't, though he was first past the post—just!

Who were these three equine participants in the drama?

Well, the first was a horse called Fine Cotton, foaled in rural New South Wales on 29 November 1976, by Aureo from a mare called Cottonpicker, whose father was the Melbourne Cup winner Delta. He had won a dozen races at picnic meetings and two races at registered meetings at Wellington in the Central West of New South Wales.

Fine Cotton was a brown horse who had two white socks on his back legs, just above his hooves, and a few white hairs on one side of his face. He was branded with a 'K'. He was bought by John Gillespie in July 1984 then sold again on 30 July for $1200 to Pauline Pearse and Mr McGregor-Lowndes. He was kept at Hayden Haitana's stable at Coffs Harbour and raced at Bundamba on 1 August and again on 4 August, after being galloped hard on the morning of each race day to ensure he would not run well later in the day. He was then raced again at Doomben on 8 August and transferred to John Thompson's racing stables on the Gold Coast.

Thompson's wife, Marie, later said the horse was not trained at all in the days leading up to the race at Eagle Farm on 18 August, and looked 'in poor condition and dehydrated' when he was picked up on the race-day morning.

The second horse was a faster, better-performed horse named Dashing Soltaire, by the sire Boucher from a mare called Ideal Image. He was also brown and was part-owned by the famous actor James Mason, Sydney racing identities Jack Ingham and J.B. Foyster, and the wife of another well-known owner and punter Don Storey (about whom more later). He had been trained in Sydney by noted trainer Vic Thompson Junior.

As a two-year-old, Dashing Soltaire had been one of the early favourites for the Golden Slipper after winning one of the lead-up races. The horse was bought by Gillespie in mid 1984 and was sent to Coffs Harbour to be trained by Wendy Smith, a girlfriend of Gillespie's. He was transferred to Haitana's yard on 4 August and met with an accident and injured his hindquarter badly on barbed wire on 7 August.

The third horse was Bold Personality, a bay foaled on 13 August 1977, by the American stallion Bold Aussie from a mare called Miss Personality. He had a white star on his forehead and no white markings on his legs. Being a classic 'bay' in colour, his lower legs were black, as were his mane and tail. Bold Personality was a good class sprinter who had been trained by Tommy Smith, Sydney's leading trainer, and then sold to race in the Northern Rivers area of New South Wales.

Here is how the whole farcical scam went down ... and out!

———

In Boggo Road prison John Gillespie chatted to Pat Haitana and a criminal named 'Kid', who was associated with Sydney gangster Mick Sayers, about a scheme for a ring-in. Pat suggested that his brother, Hayden, might be interested.

After his release from Boggo Road, Gillespie worked for Sayers running an 'SP' shop, then did time in Bathurst Gaol and met Doyle, and the plot was hatched. Mick Sayers funded the exercise and two horses were found that would pass for one another at a glance. One was a poorly performed picnic galloper, Fine Cotton, and the other a horse that had performed well at a much higher level, the Sydney sprinter Dashing Soltaire.

Hayden Haitana moved from South Australia to Coffs Harbour and applied for a training licence with the local racing club. Although his licence had lapsed in South Australia, there was no objection to him being granted a licence to train at Coffs Harbour. He then proceeded to over-train and over-race Fine Cotton in southern Queensland. Although Haitana drank a lot and talked a lot, it seemed there was no notion around the Coffs Harbour racing fraternity that anything surreptitious was afoot when he arrived in the town and started training a horse that ran very poorly north of the border.

Asked why no one in the district had prior knowledge of the scam, one local racing identity who appeared as a witness in the resulting court case told the *Coffs Harbour Advocate*, anonymously, that Haitana was such a 'bullshit artist' that he 'could have sat around the bar and described the plan down to the tiniest detail and not a single person would have believed a word'.

Meanwhile, Gang member Tom DiLuzio, a small-time racehorse owner, found two relatively disinterested parties to nominally own Fine Cotton. One of them was his live-in girlfriend, Pauline Pearse.

All went well and the ringing-in was planned for the Wednesday meeting at Eagle Farm on 15 August. Mick Sayers, who had bankrolled the venture, was arranging the money to finance the plunge with some of his Sydney underworld connections.

Implicated by rumour and association as the backers of the plunge were noted figures such as Kerry Packer, who was said to have declined to get involved, and Sydney financier Ian Murray and commission agent Gary Clarke, both of whom were known associates of Sydney bookmaker Robbie Waterhouse.

Ten days before the plan was to be activated, however, disaster struck. On 5 August Dashing Soltaire was injured and required stitches after running his hindquarters onto barbed wire.

When John Gillespie heard the news, he rang Sayers and said the scam would have to be postponed. What Sayers told Gillespie sent him ashen-faced back to DiLuzio and Dixon, with whom he was drinking at his Gold Coast residence.

The ring-in had to go ahead—they had a few days' grace but that was all. They needed another horse.

Gillespie and his team hurriedly began looking for any horses for sale that might, just might, pass for Fine Cotton at a pinch. There were very few to choose from, but there was a horse roughly the same age and height which was for sale at Ballina, near Lismore, on the New South Wales North Coast.

This horse was Bold Personality, owned and trained by Bill Naoum. Bold Personality's colour was bay, not brown and he had different markings to Fine Cotton, but he would have to do.

By this time, however, the gang had exhausted their budget and did not have the $20,000 required for the purchase.

Undeterred by such trivial matters, Gillespie wrote out a dud cheque and Tom DiLuzio set off in his Toyota Corolla, pulling a borrowed horse float. The transaction was completed, and the horse suffered a six-hour trip in a closed-in trailer wearing a thick rug and arrived severely dehydrated at North's home at Wellers Hill in Brisbane.

Hayden Haitana then rather clumsily 'flushed' the horse, a process normally performed by a vet, with a garden hose and ruptured a blood vessel in its nose. Any horse known to have bled is automatically disqualified from racing for three months, so they obviously couldn't call a vet. Instead, they then tied the horse's head to the rafters to stop the bleeding.

After his ordeal was over and the bleeding stopped, poor old Bold Personality was subjected to something even more humiliating. The gang decided to make him look like Fine Cotton and, apparently without consulting Hayden Haitana, John Gillespie did a tour of the district's chemist shops and bought up as many packets of Clairol henna hair dye as he could find.

Years later Haitana recalled:

> They thought that if they got enough hair colouring to fill up a couple of buckets, you could cover the horse with it to make it look like Fine Cotton. But, as it turns out, it doesn't take to horse's hair; there must be a chemical disbalance there ... The horse came out red like a Hereford bull. I couldn't believe it.

At that point Haitana had had enough. He just wanted out of the whole thing, so he drove back to Coffs Harbour. He was, however, ordered to come back (or maybe 'brought back') and was again at Robert North's house early the next day.

On the morning of the race the whole gang met at North's suburban home in Brisbane and decided to wash the horse to remove the dye. At this point they also realised they hadn't fitted racing shoes, so they called a farrier, who arrived without realising he was to shoe a racehorse. The farrier only had trotting shoes, so the horse was fitted out to win a trotting race, and then they started washing the red dye off as best they could. Haitana remembered:

> I was in the shower and you would hear the horse out in the backyard being very agitated jumping around. I looked out the window and here's these guys trying to paint its legs and the farrier trying to shoe it.
>
> I said to them, 'Why are you doing this? You don't change the horse's colouring; you change the papers to fit the horse.'
>
> Of course I shouldn't have done that because the papers disappeared immediately.

Haitana bandaged the back legs so the paint would not show, but the paint would not dry on the wet horse and was running off slowly for the rest of the day.

The gang decided to take both horses to the races. This move was based on the ridiculous notion that they might be able to swap them after the race had been run and won. Dixon brought Fine Cotton to the house in a horse trailer, so the horse went along for the drive and spent the day in the horse float in the car park at Eagle Farm.

It was a nervous time for the racing game's version of the Beagle Boys' Gang. The first scare of the day came when Hayden Haitana, who had been 'taken' to the races by Dixon, was called over the public address system to report to the steward's room. A terrified Haitana was relieved when he was only fined $2 for the late announcement of the jockey.

The jockey was young Gus Philpot, a promising apprentice who was hoping to win race 5, the Apprentices' Cup (which he did, on Goleen, at 4 to 1, after the fiasco of race 4 had unfolded). Philpot was apprenticed to trainer Bill Wehlow, the man who had trained the great Gunsynd before the horse was sent to Tommy Smith. Wehlow's daughter had taken a booking over the phone late the previous day for Philpot to ride Fine Cotton in race 4.

The second problem to be dealt with was that, just before the race, they bumped into Bill Naoum, the man from whom they had purchased the horse that was about to run in the next race disguised as another horse! Naoum doesn't appear to have been suspicious that anything untoward was happening—perhaps he had not presented that dud cheque as yet, or the bank had not yet bounced it back.

One version of the story says that Gillespie took Naoum to the grandstand bar and kept talking to him while race 4 was run and won by a horse Naoum still technically and legally owned. Gillespie supposedly kept his head between the television screen and Naoum's line of vision and talked non-stop while the race was run!

Other versions of the day's activities have Gillespie watching the race with members of the Queensland police force.

Meanwhile, Haitana was nervously legging Gus Philpot into the saddle on the back of a horse that was sweating rather odd-coloured perspiration, while white paint ran out from under the bandages on his leg.

Philpot later said his association with the affair made him unpopular with trainers and cost him a successful career in Brisbane. He eventually became a trainer in Victoria and years later recalled that he thought Haitana was nervous that day as he legged him up, but put it down to the fact that he was just a country trainer unused to the 'big time' of Eagle Farm.

There was a huge pre-post betting plunge on Fine Cotton that took his price from 33 to 1, to 7 to 2. There also seemed to be more people on course than normal that day, and they all wanted to back number 5 in race number 4, although the form guide read:

Hard to recommend after 8len 10th La Teppo Dbn Inter 1200m Aug 8. Earlier form not encouraging.

Which meant that Fine Cotton had run tenth, 8 lengths behind the winner, in a restricted 'intermediate' handicap ten days earlier—and was a 'donkey' or 'hairy goat' in racing parlance.

Gus Philpot was unaware of the fuss in the betting ring.

He simply got on board a horse he thought was the poorly performed 'hopeless case' called Fine Cotton. Not long after, he also thought he'd won the race.

Poor old Bold Personality, pathetically disguised as Fine Cotton and skilfully ridden by Gus Philpot, battled head to head down the straight with Harbour Gold, the horse who would otherwise have been a short-priced favourite for the race but was actually 11 to 2 and 6 to 1 with some bookies. Philpot's mount won by a short head.

No sooner had he done so than a large section of the crowd—led by a man (or 'a few men') near the winning post, yelling, 'Ring-in!'—began booing and hooting. Within 30 minutes Harbour Gold was declared the winner and Fine Cotton was disqualified, although he was not declared a non-starter—which meant that no one who had backed him was entitled to a refund. The bookies kept the lot.

In his *Sun Herald* column the next day, racing journalist Max Presnell commented that it hardly seemed fair that 'innocent' punters who had simply 'followed the money' in the betting avalanche had lost the lot. He said that, 'General feeling at Warwick Farm was that Fine Cotton should have been declared a non-runner.'

In an interview with Patrick Bartley for the *Sydney Morning Herald* in 2014, Gus Philpot said he was so naive at the time that he didn't even know the horse's odds. He recalled that when the crowd started booing and yelling, 'I thought they were booing me because my ride was a roughie and I must've beaten the favourite.'

Luckily for Philpot, the stewards were either not very good at their job or genuinely realised how naive young Gus was. He said himself in the *Sydney Morning Herald* interview years later:

> It was refreshing actually now I think back, the stewards immediately exonerated me and I was still a bit dazed when I got back to the jockeys' room and some of the older blokes were pointing out the window, saying you've just ridden a ring-in.
>
> And I pulled one of them aside and said 'What's a ring-in?'

The affair had a big effect on Philpot's life, as his ambition to be a top rider in Brisbane was never likely to succeed due to his association, albeit innocent, with the 'Fine Cotton Affair'. But Philpot's life certainly wouldn't be the only one adversely affected by the failed scam.

Underneath the headline 'Police Guard Plunge Horse', the *Sun Herald* the next day carried a photo captioned 'Jockey Gus Philpot brings Fine Cotton back to scale'. The photo quite clearly shows Bold Personality, complete with a small white star on his forehead (which Fine Cotton didn't have), being led back by the clerk of the course to weigh-in.

According to the *Sun Herald*:

Officials became suspicious of Fine Cotton's identity when he showed a glaring form improvement to win.

He had finished 10th in a field of 12 at the Brisbane Doomben track at his previous start.

Soon after the race stewards had asked trainer Haitana to produce Fine Cotton's registration papers.

He was escorted to the horse's stall but a search of the gear failed to produce the papers.

Haitana then told stewards he was certain he had brought the papers to the track but someone must have removed them from his race day gear bag.

The papers, of course, had never been in the bag. Haitana, as he said years later, had actually precipitated the 'disappearance' of the registration papers when he chastised the gang members for trying to alter the horse instead of the papers.

If the stewards had been doing their job more diligently that day, they might have noticed a horse parading before the race with the wrong brand, the wrong colouring and the wrong markings. The betting ring was going crazy as the horse's price tumbled from 33 to 1, to 7 to 2, and he had been backed all day all over Australia.

It would not have been hard to notice the horse was Bold Personality, as he was actually in the race book—as a starter in race six. He had been entered for the Open Flying Handicap and scratched quite late. His name still appeared as a starter in the morning newspapers. That probably explains why Bill Naoum was at the races that day.

Commenting on the quality of the Queensland Turf Club (QTC) stewards' 'due diligence' on that day, Gus Philpot said later in life, 'I reckon you could have put a rhinoceros in the race and no one would have noticed.'

Not long after the failed search for the registration papers, a public address announcement was broadcast asking trainer Hayden Haitana to visit the stewards' room for the second time that day. The announcement, like the search of Haitana's gear bag, failed to produce what was being sought—it failed to produce Hayden Haitana!

The whole fiasco had become too much for Haitana's nervous system. As soon as he was out of sight of the stewards, he had a beer to settle his nerves and realised that, for once in his life, it was no good just getting drunk and letting things run their course. Haitana high-tailed it to the car park, jumped into the horse float with his old friend Fine Cotton, and drove off into the sunset.

I mean this quite literally, for, having made a slight detour to leave Fine Cotton happily munching grass with a bunch of other horses in a paddock he had often noticed not far from the Eagle Farm Racecourse, Haitana headed west, towards the sunset and the state of South Australia.

Also called to the stewards room were Fine Cotton's registered owners, one of whom, 75-year-old retired businessman Mr McGregor-Lowndes, duly appeared and told the stewards he was as surprised as they were at the horse's form reversal and 'didn't think he could win' and 'didn't have a penny on him'.

At the QTC enquiry ten days later, Mr McGregor-Lowndes said that Hayden Haitana talked him into buying the horse. He also said that he believed he was the sole owner of Fine Cotton until he met Miss Pearse on the day of the race, and that he had never seen the horse or Miss Pearse until that day (of course, he never actually saw the horse that day, either—he saw Bold Personality!).

There were three gang members missing from the QTC enquiry, although all three had been 'required to attend'.

Tom DiLuzio did not attend, according to Miss Pearse, because of a 'family commitment'. So the hearing was adjourned. DiLuzio did attend on the Friday and read a prepared statement in which he said he could only answer questions about a horse he did own, Zardulu. According to him, he didn't own Fine Cotton and refused to answer questions about the affair. He asked for proof of the QTC's legal right to question him and would not answer questions without legal advice.

Unfortunately for DiLuzio, Pauline Pearse had given evidence on the Monday that she had never signed anything to acknowledge she owned Fine Cotton, and she had also identified DiLuzio's signature on three entry forms for the horse in various races. She said DiLuzio had been paying all the horse's expenses and she had 'little knowledge of racing' and had 'not really known what was going on'.

All five members of the gang were banned for life. They were then all charged by the police with the criminal offence of 'conspiracy to defraud'.

Hayden Haitana, John Gillespie and John Dixon were also charged with falsely pretending that Bold Personality was Fine Cotton in order to defraud the QTC.

Warrants were issued and Dixon, DiLuzio and Robert North were arrested.

Meanwhile, Haitana had given an interview to *60 Minutes* while on the run, which really embarrassed the police, who couldn't find him or Gillespie. In the interview he precipitated a string of far-reaching events by mentioning bookmaker 'Bob' Waterhouse as a 'possible' connection to the scam.

After being spotted wearing dark glasses and shopping in Woolworths at Renmark, in the Riverland, Haitana was finally arrested by South Australian police while having a beer in the pub at Truro, just east of the Barossa Valley, on 21 February 1985.

After being interviewed, he refused to sign any statements and said:

It's got nothing to do with you. It all happened in Queensland and there are plenty of heavies in this. I only want to talk to the Queensland police.

The trial lasted six weeks and concluded in early November 1985.

Surprisingly, the judge, Mr Justice Loewenthal, discharged Dixon as not having a case to answer. He accepted that Gillespie, who had skipped bail and was still on the run, had conceived the idea and was 'instrumental in organising and arranging substantial betting on the race in question'.

Tom DiLuzio was found not guilty. Haitana and North were found guilty and sentenced to twelve months hard labour.

Two weeks later, the *Sydney Morning Herald* announced:

The alleged mastermind of Queensland's Fine Cotton ring-in conspiracy, John Patrick Gillespie, 45, formally of Benowa on the Gold Coast, was flown out of Melbourne yesterday under police custody ...

Gillespie was arrested by detectives on Tuesday during a dawn raid on a house in the Victorian town of Cobram.

Police alleged Gillespie had been found hiding in a cupboard in his sister's home.

Gillespie was found guilty and given four years in prison.

Fine Cotton was finally discovered grazing peacefully where Haitana had left him near Eagle Farm, in a spelling paddock used by the Queensland Mounted Police.

Television producer John Stainton, who created the Steve Irwin television series, bought Fine Cotton. Stainton also bought the rights to the story and planned to use the horse to make a documentary mini-series about the affair, but eventually gave up because 'it was a legal minefield'.

Hayden Haitana served six months, returned to South Australia and somehow eked out a living outside of racing for 25 years. In an interview in 2010 with Simon White of the *Adelaide Advertiser,* he said he kept a few cows and chickens, grew his own vegetables, fixed bicycles for backpackers, bought and sold old cars, and sneaked into racecourses when he could. He spent his spare time with his grandkids, helping men in prison and looking after those just out of jail, making sure they met parole requirements while looking after their money for them so they didn't gamble it or have to steal. He was finally allowed back on racetracks in 2013, almost 30 years after the event and fifteen years after the others involved.

John Gillespie served most of his sentence and was soon in trouble again. In 1992, he became a founding director of the International Millionaire's Club and the International Horse-owners' Club; both companies were incorporated in the British Virgin Islands, and struck off the companies register in 1995.

In 1996 Gillespie was involved in a scheme buying horses from a stud in Shropshire in the UK to be imported into Thailand. All that eventuated was that the stud's owner, Peter Hume, ended up with £50,000 less in his bank account.

In November 1998 three 'officials' from the imaginary nation of Melchizedek were arrested in the Philippines for selling 'internationally recognised Melchizedek passports' to hundreds of local Filipinos, Chinese and Bangladeshis for $US3500 each. Others paid large amounts of money to be guaranteed 'government work' on a Pacific territory known as the 'Dominion of Melchizedek'.

Two men, an Australian named Dennis Oakley, who was Melchizedek's 'minister of the navy and the coast guard', and a Malaysian national, Chew Chin Yee, whose business card identified him as Melchizedek's 'honorary consul in Hong Kong' and 'minister of public works and gaming', were arrested. According to Philippines police, the ringleader, a brother-in-law of Chew Chin Yee, had managed to get away. No prizes for guessing—yes, it was John Gillespie.

In 2008 Gillespie 'ripped off' ex–rugby league player Greg Mullane, who he managed to con into being the front man for a property scam that left a Forbes farmer $150,000 poorer over a non-existent $10 million feedlot development to be financed by a non-existent multi-million-dollar collection of famous artworks, which was also used to attract investors into a $250,000 anti-wrinkle cream marketing scheme and another similar scheme for anti-arthritis cream for horses. All the projects—surprise, surprise—left investors broke.

As late as 2016 Gillespie was involved in an offshore tax scam known as 'The Panama Papers Affair'.

But 30 years earlier, at the time of the Fine Cotton Affair, Gillespie had already been labelled, quite rightly, 'The King of Cons' by *Sydney Morning Herald* journalist Roger Crofts. Clearly, he had form.

Ten years before Fine Cotton, Gillespie had defrauded flood victims of the 1974 Queensland floods by scamming the official relief scheme. In 1977 he held up a TAB with a plastic pistol. Just before the ring-in in 1984, he had bought $100,000 worth of opals from eight different dealers at Lightning Ridge just as the banks closed one Friday. Three dealers compared the cheques and discovered they all had the same serial numbers. Gillespie served two years for the fraud, concurrent with his sentence for the Fine Cotton Affair.

Before 1990, when he turned 50, Gillespie had accumulated more than 350 convictions, and he has been adding to the total ever since.

There was, however, a happy ending for the innocent horse at the centre of it all. Fine Cotton was ridden recreationally until he was twenty and then retired to a paddock where he died in 2009, aged 32.

Part Two: The Dark Side—Person or Persons Unknown

> 'When the prison doors are opened, the real dragon will fly out.'
>
> Ho Chi Minh

This is where the story steps out of the category of slapstick French farce and enters the grim world of crime thriller. There were more characters involved in the Fine Cotton scandal than those we have already met.

Who were the puppet-masters pulling the strings that made the 'Beagle Boys Gang' dance to their tune? Well, the truth is we still don't know, for sure but we have some prime candidates and plenty of theories.

Let's look at the cast of Part Two:

- **Robbie Waterhouse**—a dashing 30-year-old bookmaker who described himself as 'aggressive' in his approach to his profession. He was the son of 'leviathan' bookie Bill Waterhouse, was educated at the exclusive Shore School in Sydney, and was married to Gai Smith, daughter of legendary trainer Tommy Smith.
- **Bill Waterhouse**—Robbie's father and legendary rails bookmaker, barrister and supposed descendant of Henry Waterhouse, a colonial pioneer and naval officer who arrived in Australia with the First Fleet. His records showed he had taken one substantial bet on Fine Cotton and then closed the book on the horse.
- **Father Edward O'Dwyer**—a Catholic priest, punter and friend of Robbie Waterhouse who drove from Warwick Farm races to the Appin Greyhound meeting to place a bet of $1000 on Fine Cotton for Robbie Waterhouse.
- **Ian Murray**—a Sydney financier and professional punter, and associate of Robbie Waterhouse, who bet $57,000 on Fine Cotton.

- **Bobby Hines**—a bookmaker's clerk who worked for Robbie Waterhouse and flew to Kempsey on the day of the race to bet $3000 on Fine Cotton for his boss.
- **Mark Read**—a big Sydney bookmaker and rival of the Waterhouses who took huge bets on Fine Cotton, including one of $9000 to $6000 at very short odds, and stood to lose a fortune. He declared loudly when the money kept coming at short odds, 'If this isn't a ring-in, I'm not here!'
- **George Freeman**—an extremely clever master criminal who may have used his knowledge of the ring-in to pull off the greatest 'double-cross' scam in Australian gambling history, but was not implicated in the affair at the time and didn't suffer from any of the repercussions. Freeman was a sworn enemy of the Waterhouses.
- **George Brown**—a likeable, quiet Sydney horse trainer who was brutally murdered on 2 April 1984, four months before the Fine Cotton ring-in.
- **Mr Digby**—a horse trained by Harry Clarke that won a maiden handicap over a mile at Canterbury Park Racetrack in Sydney on 5 August 1981.

Let's start with George Freeman. His name is rarely, if ever, mentioned when the famous events that led to Australia's best-known and most farcical racing fraud are discussed, but one theory says he was almost certainly at the centre of the entire affair—like a spider in the middle of the web of intrigue, which involved huge gambling debts and death threats.

George Freeman's career as a clever and ruthless master criminal was the direct result of his experiences in juvenile detention facilities at Gosford and Tamworth as a youth. Like many other career criminals, including his friend Lenny McPherson, he was physically and sexually abused in juvenile prison and came out determined that he would never be the victim again—others would.

He was released in 1953, aged eighteen, and after a stretch in Parramatta Prison for stealing in 1954, and other stints in prison over the following decade, he served his last sentence in Fremantle Gaol in 1968.

After that, Freeman never did time again but was named as a 'crime boss' in a royal commission, was detained in the USA as an 'excluded person', banned from entering Britain, and formed a friendship with alleged American crime-syndicate boss Joe Testa. He was said to have killed at least two men, ruined harness racing in Sydney by fixing almost every race, and run the city's SP's, illegal casinos and prostitution rackets. He lived in a heavily guarded mansion at Yowie Bay, south of Sydney.

A friend of his once said, 'George was blamed for everything but the Newcastle earthquake.'

The important factors that link Freeman to the racing industry in general, and to the Fine Cotton Affair in particular, are his association with racing through the Mr Digby enquiry and the fact that Mick Sayers owed Freeman a lot of money and told him about the Fine Cotton ring-in as means of pacifying him and reassuring him that he would soon be paid.

Freeman's involvement in the Mr Digby race-fixing scandal shocked a lot of decent racing people. The reluctance of the Sydney Turf Club (STC) and Australian Jockey Club (AJC) to take action also gave many grave fears about the industry's future credibility.

What had happened was that Mr Digby, a maiden galloper, started in a 1600-metre race at Randwick on Bank Holiday, Monday 3 August 1981, and finished ninth. Two days later he stormed home, winning by 7 lengths over 1900 metres in a higher-class race at Canterbury.

Form reversal was one thing: Mr Digby had shown some moderate ability as a stayer, but had never run a place before in his life. What scared racegoers more was the fact that he was backed in to 11 to 8 favouritism to win more than $400,000 in the betting ring. This was an insult to the dignity of the Sport of Kings. It seemed like a return to the 'bad old days', when blatantly obvious rorts were tolerated and officials turned a blind eye.

When investigations came up with evidence that George Freeman was involved, many racing club members were worried that thoroughbred racing was descending to the inglorious level of the 'red hots', i.e. the trots or harness racing. Bookmakers and punters complained, but the AJC decided not to open an enquiry.

On 6 August 1981 Freeman, divorced and aged 46, married 24-year-old Georgina McLoughlin, a former model. At the slap-up reception, held at the Hilton Hotel, Freeman openly boasted that the money he'd won on Mr Digby was paying for the 'do'. Mr Digby's trainer, Harry Clark, was a guest at the wedding.

The very week of the Mr Digby win at Canterbury, the *Sun Herald* began a series of exposé articles about 'the world of Sydney gambling', which included an interview with George Freeman, described as a 'colourful identity' who had been named under parliamentary privilege as a leading figure in organised crime, and who described himself as 'a professional punter and commission agent'.

When the AJC finally opened an enquiry into the 'Mr Digby Affair' on 12 August, it was noted that Sydney solicitor, horse owner, punter and STC board member Don Storey was also present at Freeman's wedding.

There were calls for Storey to be dismissed from the board after he was also named in parliament by crusading MP John Hatton, who wanted to know if it was true that he had backed Mr Digby and two other horses (one of them the hilariously named Wilpado) to win $1.3 million.

Storey said he had been following Mr Digby and had backed it not just that day but every time it ran, as the horse had shown some ability to stay, which it had. The STC overwhelming supported Storey at an extraordinary general meeting.

Don Storey said he had met Freeman at the races a few times, was surprised to be invited to the wedding but saw no harm in it, as it was a big gathering and at least one member of the AJC board was also attending.

The AJC stewards report concluded: 'Despite our careful scrutiny not only at the time of the race and then through the subsequent inquiry, we were unable to discover the cogent evidence we believe is required to take action.'

The enquiry did raise some concern that Peter Black, Mr Digby's registered owner, was not actually paying the training fees. As a result the horse's ownership was transferred to Jean Clark, the wife of trainer Harry Clark.

At his second run back from a spell, Mr Digby won again, over 1600 metres at Randwick, landing one bet of $80,000 to $20,000. This seemed to justify the AJC decision.

The press scrutiny, however, continued. Time form analyst Don Scott, founder of the famous Legal Eagles betting syndicate, challenged the AJC's conclusions about how much the horse had improved in sectional times in two days, from 3 August to 5 August. There was also cynicism about the AJC conclusion that the betting on the race was 'normal'—with Scott and others pointing out that it was not 'normal' for a midweek race to take half a million dollars out of the betting ring.

Then the AJC opened another enquiry, on 13 November 1981. Trainer Harry Clark and jockey Keith Banks faced the common charge of 'not allowing a horse to run on its merits' at the 3 August Randwick meeting and were found guilty and disqualified for a year, which all but ruined their careers.

As was usual at that time, whoever planned the 'skulduggery', if there was any, remained unpunished.

Mick Sayers owed George Freeman a 'substantial' amount of money. Like most things in this complex saga, accounts differ— the amount owed is often said to be more than $500,000 and at other times as low as $8000, which was still 'substantial' to most people in 1984.

One theory about the ring-in having to go ahead when it did is that Mick Sayers had told Freeman about it in order to save his skin and ingratiate himself with Freeman to buy time to repay the debt.

Armed with this knowledge, Freeman made plans of his own and, when Sayers called him to say the ring-in was postponed, he saw a chance to make even better plans and told Sayers that, if it didn't go ahead, he would be killed.

When John Gillespie returned ashen-faced to his fellow gang members that day at the Gold Coast, having phoned Sayers to tell him Dashing Soltaire was injured, Gillespie had said that they had to find another horse within days and go ahead with the ring-in. What he also told the gang was 'or someone is going to die'.

Whether Gillespie thought *he* was going to die or Mick Sayers was going to die, I don't know—maybe both. Gillespie certainly claimed he was marked down to die after the race, but that's another story altogether.

The 'George Freeman pulling the strings' theory, developed by some who have studied the events closely, is that Freeman forced the ridiculous ring-in to go ahead by threatening to kill Sayers if it didn't. He then spread the word about it and cunningly tricked Robbie Waterhouse into believing it and betting on it. Freeman then made sure it was exposed. According to this theory, Freeman then backed Harbour Gold, whose price had drifted out to around 6 to 1, knowing the pathetic ring-in attempt would fail.

It is claimed, in this theory, that the man, or men, yelling 'Ring-in!' at the track that day were sent there by Freeman to ensure the scam was exposed.

There are a few factors that make this theory plausible.

Firstly, George Freeman was far more intelligent and ruthless than Sayers, or Gillespie, or the rest of the 'Beagle Boys'. Knowing that the plan was bound to fail one way or another, it's just the kind of thing he would have thought up.

Secondly, there was long-held enmity between the Waterhouses and Freeman, and he could have seen this as a chance to not only make money but to 'get the Waterhouses'.

In his memoirs Bill Waterhouse admitted that he once bought a gun because he feared Freeman would have attempts made on his life. He always claimed George Freeman set Robbie up over the Fine Cotton Affair and the implication is that Freeman had enough influence within the AJC, where there was a certain amount of dislike for the brash young bookie, to make sure the Waterhouses 'took the fall'.

All that was ever proven against Robbie Waterhouse was 'prior knowledge' of a rort at Eagle Farm, yet he was banned for life and served a prison sentence for perjury.

Bill Waterhouse's only 'alleged' crime was the accusation, never substantiated, that he put a false bet from Ian Murray in his book so it appeared he had at least taken some money on Fine Cotton. Bill claimed he took one large bet and then shortened the price so he took no more. The bookie fielding next to him, Bruce McHugh, testified that Bill did not appear to have prior knowledge or act in any way to indicate he did. The court, however, believed Bill must have had prior knowledge, based on the fact that he was Robbie's father.

Ian Murray admitted to having prior knowledge and betting with different bookies on Fine Cotton; he never appealed his life ban.

No one had ever heard of the racing crime 'prior knowledge' before, and the concept had certainly never been used to ban people for life. The AJC enquiry, held separately from the QTC one, seemed to 'go after' Robbie Waterhouse with a certain degree of obsession.

This could simply be attributed to the fact that the AJC was annoyed that the industry's reputation had been dragged through the mud by the incompetence of the Queensland racing management and a scapegoat was needed. Robbie was thought to have been involved in a few suspect racing results and it was time to clean up the image of the sport.

Up in sunny Queensland, Racing Minister Russ Hinze blamed unsavoury elements 'from down south' and the QTC were rather miffed when the AJC started up a separate enquiry.

One thing that doesn't quite gel with the theory that Freeman pulled off a cunning double-cross and backed Harbour Gold is the fact that the horse's price drifted out but never firmed back in. If Freeman did win the reputed $1.5 million on the horse, it certainly wasn't on the TAB or an Australian racetrack, where the amount of money needed to be invested to win that much (around $300,000) would have affected the betting to at least some degree (actually a large degree) and shortened the odds.

So the theory seems flawed.

On the other hand, John Gillespie, after his release from prison for his part in the ring-in, claimed that it was exactly what he and Sayers had done—not Freeman.

In 2010 Gillespie claimed the whole scheme was designed by Sayers as payback on Freeman. The money Sayers owed Freeman, according to Gillespie, was lost in a race where Freeman paid off every jockey to get the result. Sayers then planned the entire Fine Cotton Affair to scam the money back from Freeman by getting him to 'fall in' to Fine Cotton while they backed Harbour Gold.

One suspects that perhaps Gillespie knew Freeman did something of the sort to him and Sayers, and decided to claim it was the other way around to save face.

In a Queensland *Sunday Mail* article by reporter Adam Shand in May 2010, Gillespie is reported to have said he 'found it amusing that people regarded him as a bumbling failure of a race fixer'.

'I don't mind if people think it was a joke, or whatever,' Gillespie added, 'because I walked away with $1.8 million.'

Naturally, no one believed Gillespie for a minute. AJC Chief Steward John Shreck, the man who pursued Robbie Waterhouse so doggedly through the enquiry, said, 'Dick Francis [famous author of racing novels] could not think up something like that ... With great respect to Mr Gillespie, anything he says you would have to take with a great big pinch of salt.'

Gillespie certainly claimed he was marked down to die after the race. In the *Sunday Mail* interview in 2010, he claimed that Freeman called him at Robert North's home after the race:

> Bob handed the telephone to me and Freeman said to me: 'We know what you have done and I am sending two men to Brisbane to fix you up'. I replied that they had better be your best blokes otherwise they wouldn't be coming back. Then I hung up on Freeman ...
>
> I looked around and Bob, who had the heart of a split pea, had fainted and fallen to the ground.

Gillespie went on to claim that he deposited his $1.8 million in an offshore account and Sayers had hidden up to $12 million in winnings in a Swiss bank account.

He also claimed, in the 2010 interview, that he fled to the USA in 1985 after Russ Hinze, famed 'big man' of Queensland politics and Minister for Racing in the Bjelke-Petersen Government, told him the police had information that he, Gillespie, would be killed if he attended court on the fraud charges. The 'hitman', according to Gillespie, was to be Chris Flannery, who had murdered other people for Freeman.

Given that it was hard for Russ Hinze, who passed away in 1991, or Mick Sayers, who was gunned down and killed in the driveway of his Bronte home in February 1985, to corroborate the story in 2010, and given that taking $14 million dollars out of a betting pool in Australia in 1984 without affecting a horse's odds is a bit hard to imagine, and given that John Gillespie has more than 300 convictions for lying about things—one is tempted to agree with John Shreck's assessment of Gillespie. Maybe a big tonne of salt might be required, rather than a big pinch.

Gillespie also claimed Mick Sayers was murdered for his role in the Fine Cotton Affair, while it is generally accepted that Sayers was killed for stealing heroin from big-time drug dealer Barry McCann. Sayers picked up the heroin from McCann, went to get the cash, then came back dishevelled and claimed he'd been robbed. McCann gave him a few days to produce either the drugs or the dough.

When he pulled into his driveway a few days later, having been to the races, Sayers was gunned down in front of his girlfriend by two of McCann's men, who'd been waiting in a van. McCann himself was murdered in 1989.

———

In all the theories about the Fine Cotton Affair, there always seems to be one or two annoying pieces of information that don't fit each theory and make you wonder.

One such odd piece of information that clouds the water and makes you pause for a moment before you dismiss the double-cross theories is that Hayden Haitana, after he accompanied the stewards to the horse stall after the race and told them the papers were missing, didn't leave the course at once. He said later he went to have a beer after the race and waited until Harbour Gold was declared the winner before leaving the course. He was, perhaps, still making for the car park as the public address system was asking him to report to the stewards' room.

This puzzled me until I realised that he also admitted, or claimed, later that he had $50 on Harbour Gold to win, and picked up the money before he scarpered.

Who knows? The case gets murkier and more complicated the more you research it. In writing this story I have come to feel, like the White Queen in *Alice Through the Looking Glass*, that I have 'believed as many as six impossible things', though not necessarily before breakfast.

Another, less popular, theory is that George Freeman did back the ring-in horse, not Harbour Gold, then blamed Robbie for a failed scam and dumped on him.

Mark Read, who sensed a scam and drew everyone's attention to it on the day, seems to have immediately suspected Robbie Waterhouse. As well as having a lot to lose, as he had freely taken bets on the horse once he had looked at the form and decided the real Fine Cotton could not possibly win the race, it was rumoured Read also had a score to settle, as he had previously lost heavily on a race which he believed was 'fixed' by Robbie Waterhouse.

At the hearing in December 1984, Robbie Waterhouse told Judge Goran that he believed Mark Read had attempted to link his name with the ring-in. He also said it was suspicious that Haitana, in the *60 Minutes* interview (for which Robbie claimed the trainer was paid $20,000), referred to 'Bob' Waterhouse as a bookmaker he suspected of being involved. Robbie pointed out that he had never been known as 'Bob'.

Yet another theory is that Bold Personality wasn't supposed to win, just divert the money away from Harbour Gold. This theory has some legs if you consider what the horse had been through in the previous 48 hours, the fact that a naive apprentice was chosen to ride it, and that the 1500 metre race was the wrong distance for Bold Personality, who normally stopped like a shot duck after 1200 metres.

Maybe Freeman simply wanted to 'get' Robbie Waterhouse.

———

The 1980s was not a decade in which New South Wales could be very proud of its record of fighting organised crime or achieving justice for the victims of organised crime.

To understand how hard it was for people like jockeys and trainers to resist the machinations of people such as Sayers and Freeman in the 1980s (or for any 'normal person with a frailty' to resist crooks like Neddy Smith, Barry McCann, Chris Flannery, Robert Trimbole or Stan 'The Man' Smith), we need only look at the still unsolved murder of trainer George Brown.

Brown was a quiet, well-liked Randwick trainer whose body was found in his burning car at the top of Bulli Pass, south of Sydney, on 2 April 1984.

Brown hated spirits and rarely drank, but he had a blood alcohol reading of .365 (which implied forced alcohol consumption), his arms and legs had been twisted and broken, and his head smashed by a heavy, blunt instrument. The inquest into his death was being held as the Fine Cotton scandal unfolded in August 1984.

Brown was born in Queensland and worked with horses all his life, as a strapper in stables in the UK, where he also rode over jumps, and later at Brian Courtney's Melbourne stables where, ironically enough, he had once been the strapper of a horse called Regal Vista, which was later involved in the famous ring-in at Casterton in Victoria in 1972.

During 1983 George Brown's stable brought off a number of successful plunges, but he was not known as a big gambler outside of his own horses.

One of Brown's successful 'plonks' occurred late in 1982 at Canterbury on a horse, Rocky Vale, which had only arrived in the stable a few days before. Ever generous, Brown gave jockey Kevin Moses a 'sling' of $1000 and all his stable workers $50 each. He also gave the horse's previous trainer $250.

His friend Geoff Newcombe, a horse owner and school principal, remembers Brown as a nice bloke, a good trainer, but 'a lousy businessman'. In spite of the successful betting coups in 1983, his training business was heavily in debt. His new partner, de facto wife Pat Goodwin, had taken out two personal loans totalling $10,000 and a second mortgage on her house for $15,000.

Both George Brown and Pat Goodwin were previously married and her separation had been particularly acrimonious, with her husband accusing her of an ongoing secret affair with Brown.

Brown had let his sister in on an anonymous phone call in which he was told to make sure that his stable star, McGlinchy, did not win a certain race—and he told her he had done so.

He was also alleged to have taken his poorly performed filly Risley to Brisbane to be part of a 'form reversal' plunge, or ring-in, earlier on 31 March 1984. The horse was backed heavily, from 14 to 1, to 4 to 1, but ran poorly and Brown returned home very agitated. According to Pat Goodwin, he was worried that 'it had gone wrong' and told her he was unhappy with the jockey and 'disgusted by the whole thing'.

The horse's jockey, Maurice Logue, always maintained that the horse he rode was Risley and it ran badly, but true to form.

Journalist John Ellicot, who has thoroughly investigated the case for years, makes the point that, if Brown reneged on a ring-in or a doping scheme in which big criminals were involved, he was 'a dead man walking' after the Risley failure.

Others have commented that a shooting, beating or being forced into some new rort or extortion plan would seem to be a more likely punishment for failing to pull off a planned ring-in or doping—not torture, mutilation and savage murder.

One popular theory is that the murder was a beating gone wrong, possibly committed by men paid to do the deed who got high on drugs before the job. Many believe that the cruelty and vindictiveness of the crime indicate a personal vendetta and are not the usual features of a gangland retribution killing.

One odd fact rarely mentioned in the case is that Brown's car had been firebombed outside Pat Goodwin's house in February 1984, weeks before the Risley race on 31 March, and the couple never reported it to police.

Nevertheless, the murder of George Brown was linked, perhaps inadvertently, to the Fine Cotton scandal in two ways.

Hayden Haitana claimed, in the *60 Minutes* interview, that he went into hiding because 'a man with a gun' said to him when he wanted 'out' of the whole thing, 'Do you want to end up like trainer Brown?'

During the bitter Waterhouse family feud, Bill's younger son, former bookie, art dealer and options trader, David, who was best man at his brother's wedding to Gai Smith, claimed that Robbie set up the Fine Cotton ring-in. He also said that Robbie had expressed some level of worry over the idea that he might in some way be linked to events surrounding the death of George Brown. David also claimed that Robbie had admitted to having involvement in ring-ins. Arthur Harris, who had worked for Robbie as a form analyst, claimed he had 'heard a story' that two men were sent to teach Brown a lesson but were 'high on drugs and went too far'.

This story is dismissed by the rest of the Waterhouse family as mere spite and vexatious innuendo in a family feud, an attempted smear to prevent Robbie from getting his licence back in 1997. The 'lies and false allegations' caused Robbie to sue a newspaper for printing the story, but he lost the case when the court ruled the story was written in such a way that he was not defamed.

Claim and counter-claim ensued, with one side and then the other making allegations as to who paid for what and gave money to whom. It was pointed out that a Supreme Court Judge, Justice Bill Ormiston, in an unrelated case involving art dealing, had called David Waterhouse 'a devious and unreliable witness ... whose commercial morality was of the lowest order'.

The Waterhouses excluded David from the family trust and 'ex-communicated' him completely from the family.

In all the investigations into Brown's murder, and the Fine Cotton Affair, no link was found between the two events. John Ellicot concluded that the truth about the murder either 'lies in the murky side of racing—or in the heart of a person with a terrible vendetta'.

Although police re-opened the George Brown case in 2007, nothing came of it. There is still no real evidence about who was responsible, and certainly no evidence that Robbie Waterhouse was in any way involved. The coroner's verdict was 'murder by person or persons unknown'.

————

It is certain, however, that Robbie Waterhouse sent his clerk Bob Hines to Kempsey and Father O'Dwyer to Appin to back Fine Cotton, and that he lied in court, ostensibly to protect a good mate and client in Ian Murray. So, it can be concluded that he obviously had prior knowledge that 'something' was happening.

Then again, so too, apparently, did hundreds of others around Australia.

Robbie Waterhouse, Father O'Dwyer and professional punter Gary Clarke had criminal charges against them arising from the Fine Cotton scandal quashed in 1988.

Robbie Waterhouse was found guilty of lying to the Racing Appeals Tribunal in 1992, and appealed the decision, had his appeal dismissed and served eight months in periodic detention in 1993. He applied to have the 'warning off' lifted by the AJC in 1993, 1994 and 1996. It was finally lifted in 1998 with the proviso that he could not own horses or hold a bookmaker's licence.

In 1999 Robbie applied to the Thoroughbred Racing Board to hold a licence, but withdrew the application during the family feud and accusations. In 2000 he applied again and was refused. In 2001 his application was finally accepted and he recommenced bookmaking in August 2001.

Bill Waterhouse returned to betting on course after being reinstated in 2002.

Hayden Haitana was finally allowed back on racetracks in 2013.

John Gillespie is still banned, as far as I know, for his part in what Haitana once called 'the biggest farce of all time'.

George Freeman died from an asthma attack in 1990; apparently it was exacerbated by his addiction to the synthetic pain medication pethidine.

The police still don't know who murdered George Brown.

After weeks of reading and researching, I certainly don't know who the real mastermind was behind the plunges on Bold Personality, aka Fine Cotton.

I don't even know if the various parties wanted the horse to win, lose, win-and-get-away-with-winning, or win-and-be-found-out-and-get-disqualified.

Actually, come to think of it, I *do* know who was responsible—it was 'person or persons unknown'.

FATHER RILEY'S HORSE

This is the best racing rort story Banjo Paterson ever wrote, and he wrote a few! It has everything—a bushranger faking his own death, a Catholic priest ringing-in a horse to win money for the poor box, and a ghost riding a winner and somehow making the weight!

Now, as I have pointed out previously, the poems in this collection, unlike the stories in prose, are not necessarily factual—they are just entertaining examples of Aussie humour and our obsession with tricks and rorts. So, of course, the events in this poem could not possibly happen.

But, hang on a minute. It occurs to me that faking your own death is a feature of at least one other story in this collection—and Catholic priests being involved in ring-ins? Well, I seem to recall a certain Father Edward O'Dwyer being warned off racetracks for life for his part in the Fine Cotton scandal.

Perhaps Banjo wasn't writing fiction after all! Maybe he knew that old dog trapper named Hogan, who seems to have the 'good oil' on what was really going on.

I find this poem very amusing if recited in an Irish accent. It is the only poem I know of Paterson's, apart from 'A Bush Christening', where he uses zany 'Irish humour' with jokes like 'a banshee (which is Spanish for an elf)' and 'He had called him Faugh-a-ballagh (which is French for "Clear the course")'. Faugh-a-ballagh is an ancient Irish battle cry which means, in Gaelic, 'Get out of the way' or 'Clear the way'. It is the motto of the Royal Irish Regiment.

Father Riley's Horse

A.B. Paterson ('The Banjo')

'Twas the horse thief, Andy Regan, that was hunted like a dog
By the troopers of the upper Murray side,
They had searched in every gully—they had looked in
    every log,
But never sight or track of him they spied,
Till the priest at Kiley's Crossing heard a knocking very late
And a whisper 'Father Riley—come across!'
So his Rev'rence in pyjamas trotted softly to the gate
And admitted Andy Regan—and a horse!

'Now, it's listen, Father Riley, to the words I've got to say,
For it's close upon my death I am tonight.
With the troopers hard behind me I've been hiding all the day
In the gullies keeping close and out of sight.
But they're watching all the ranges till there's not a bird
    could fly,
And I'm fairly worn to pieces with the strife,
So I'm taking no more trouble, but I'm going home to die,
'Tis the only way I see to save my life.

'Yes, I'm making home to mother's, and I'll die o' Tuesday
    next
An' be buried on the Thursday—and, of course,
I'm prepared to meet my penance, but with one thing I'm
    perplexed
And it's—Father, it's this jewel of a horse!
He was never bought nor paid for, and there's not a man
    can swear
To his owner or his breeder, but I know,
That his sire was by Pedantic from the Old Pretender mare
And his dam was close related to The Roe.

'And there's nothing in the district that can race him for
    a step,
He could canter while they're going at their top:
He's the king of all the leppers that was ever seen to lep,
A five-foot fence—he'd clear it in a hop!
So I'll leave him with you, Father, till the dead shall rise again,
'Tis yourself that knows a good 'un; and, of course,
You can say he's got by Moonlight out of Paddy Murphy's
    plain
If you're ever asked the breeding of the horse!

'But it's getting on to daylight and it's time to say goodbye,
For the stars above the east are growing pale.
And I'm making home to mother—and it's hard for me
    to die!
But it's harder still, is keeping out of gaol!
You can ride the old horse over to my grave across the dip
Where the wattle bloom is waving overhead.
Sure he'll jump them fences easy—you must never raise
    the whip
Or he'll rush 'em!—now, goodbye!' and he had fled!

So they buried Andy Regan, and they buried him to rights,
In the graveyard at the back of Kiley's Hill;
There were five-and-twenty mourners who had five-and-
    twenty fights
Till the very boldest fighters had their fill.
There were fifty horses racing from the graveyard to the pub,
And their riders flogged each other all the while.
And the lashin's of the liquor! And the lavin's of the grub!
Oh, poor Andy went to rest in proper style.

Then the races came to Kiley's—with a steeplechase and all,
For the folk were mostly Irish round about,
And it takes an Irish rider to be fearless of a fall,
They were training morning in and morning out.

But they never started training till the sun was on the course
For a superstitious story kept 'em back,
That the ghost of Andy Regan on a slashing chestnut horse,
Had been training by the starlight on the track.

And they read the nominations for the races with surprise
And amusement at the Father's little joke,
For a novice had been entered for the steeplechasing prize,
And they found it was Father Riley's moke!
He was neat enough to gallop, he was strong enough to stay!
But his owner's views of training were immense,
For the Reverend Father Riley used to ride him every day,
And he never saw a hurdle nor a fence.

And the priest would join the laughter: 'Oh,' said he, 'I put
      him in,
For there's five-and-twenty sovereigns to be won.
And the poor would find it useful, if the chestnut chanced
      to win,
And he'll maybe win when all is said and done!'
He had called him Faugh-a-ballagh, which is French for
      'Clear the course',
And his colours were a vivid shade of green:
All the Dooleys and O'Donnells were on Father Riley's horse,
While the Orangemen were backing Mandarin!

It was Hogan, the dog poisoner—aged man and very wise,
Who was camping in the racecourse with his swag,
And who ventured the opinion, to the township's great
      surprise,
That the race would go to Father Riley's nag.
'You can talk about your riders—and the horse has not been
      schooled,
And the fences is terrific, and the rest!

When the field is fairly going, then ye'll see ye've all been
    fooled,
And the chestnut horse will battle with the best.

'For there's some has got condition, and they think the race
    is sure,
And the chestnut horse will fall beneath the weight,
But the hopes of all the helpless, and the prayers of all the
    poor,
Will be running by his side to keep him straight.
And it's what's the need of schoolin' or of workin' on the
    track,
When the saints are there to guide him round the course!
I've prayed him over every fence—I've prayed him out
    and back!
And I'll bet my cash on Father Riley's horse!'

Oh, the steeple was a caution! They went tearin' round and
    round,
And the fences rang and rattled where they struck.
There was some that cleared the water—there was more fell
    in and drowned,
Some blamed the men and others blamed the luck!
But the whips were flying freely when the field came into
    view,
For the finish down the long green stretch of course,
And in front of all the flyers—jumpin' like a kangaroo,
Came the rank outsider—Father Riley's horse!

Oh, the shouting and the cheering as he rattled past the post!
For he left the others standing, in the straight;
And the rider—well they reckoned it was Andy Regan's
    ghost,
And it beat 'em how a ghost would draw the weight!
But he weighed in, nine stone seven, then he laughed and
    disappeared,

Like a banshee (which is Spanish for an elf),
And old Hogan muttered sagely, 'If it wasn't for the beard
They'd be thinking it was Andy Regan's self!'

And the poor of Kiley's Crossing drank the health at
    Christmastide
Of the chestnut and his rider dressed in green.
There was never such a rider, not since Andy Regan died,
And they wondered who on earth he could have been.
But they settled it among 'em, for the story got about,
'Mongst the bushmen and the people on the course,
That the Devil had been ordered to let Andy Regan out
For the steeplechase on Father Riley's horse!

ACKNOWLEDGEMENTS

I need to thank:

The wonderful team at Allen & Unwin
- Rebecca Kaiser for her continued support, patience and good humour.
- Susin Chow for her remarkable skill in proof reading, improving and correcting my prose and her insightful suggestions.
- Genevieve Buzo for calmly and professionally guiding the project to fruition.

Also . . .
- My sister Jillian Dellit for her many hours of research, suggestions, proof reading drafts and lifelong support.
- My old mate Grahame Watt for permission to use his poem 'The Mongrel'.
- Dr Wayne Peake, University of Western Sydney for sharing his encyclopedic knowledge of 'Pony' racing. Wayne's definitive book, *Sydney's Pony Racecourses: An Alternative Racing History,* is available from Ascot Press.
- My good friends Ellen and Bruce Montgomerie for all their help with racing stories and research. Bruce's book on legendary trainer Frank McGrath is being written as this book goes to print.
- George and Paul on *Talking Lifestyle 954.*
- All those responsible for Trove.
- My wife Robyn for putting up with me in writing mode.

I wish to acknowledge two great Aussie books about the Tichborne Affair:

- *The Claimant* by Paul Terry, Echo Books, 2016, and
- *The Man Who Lost Himself* by Robyn Annear, Text Publishing, 2002.

The definitive book on Ern Malley is:

- The *Ern Malley Affair*, Michael Heyward, UQP 1993.

I have extensively used Trove and Newspapers.com, a subscription service, to research this book.